The 390th Bomb Group Anthology includes 83 stories written by 45 members of the 390th Bomb Group relating their personal adventures during the World War II years of 1943, 1944 and 1945. The stories include combat briefs, mission stories, humor in the midst of war, evasion and imprisonment after being shot down.

Some of the stories were written as they happened during the war years while others are recollections of those events so prominent in the minds of those who lived them. The reader will be provided new insight into the war in the air by these personal accounts.

The 390th Bomb Group was one of the most famous units in the Eighth Air Force. This unit flew 301 missions against Hitler's "Fortress Europe." This effort had a profound affect on the outcome of World War II in Europe.

The
390th Bomb Group
Anthology

VOLUME 1

The

390 th

BOMB

GROUP

ANTHOLOGY

by Members of the
390th Bomb Group (H)
1943 - 1945

Compliled and Edited by

Wilbert H. Richarz
Richard H. Perry
William J. Robinson

Published by

390th Memorial Museum
Foundation, Inc.
6000 East Valencia Rd.
Tucson, Azriona 85706

Dedication

THIS BOOK IS DEDICATED TO
THOSE MEMBERS OF THE 390th BOMB GROUP,
BOTH LIVING AND DEAD, WHO CONTRIBUTED
TO THE SUCCESS OF
THE EUROPEAN AIR CAMPAIGN
DURING WORLD WAR II

AND ALSO TO

COLONEL JOSEPH A. MOLLER
FORMER COMMANDER OF THE 390th BOMB GROUP

Insignia of the 390th Bombardment Group (H), and of its component squadrons: The 568th Squadron, the 569th Squadron, the 570th Squadron, and the 571st Squadron.

Preface

When the stories and accounts in the following collection were first received and the idea for a book of this type was envisioned, it was thought that the contributions would be screened and edited. However, it was soon apparent that any changes that might be deemed necessary by a second party, such as an editor, could only alter, and perhaps even destroy, the context, flavor, mood and/or intent of the original text. It was clear that the stories would convey their special meanings only if the integrity of the authors was protected and their work generally unaltered. With the exception of the correcting of typographical errors or the rearrangement of sentences which were unclear because of inadvertent word placement, the following contributions are just as they were originally written.

The reminiscences collected in this volume were written by the individual contributors and the Foundation and the editors, while grateful, cannot, and do not, accept responsibility for the content of, or opinions expressed, in the individual stories. They are the creations of their authors. The sole purpose of this volume is to preserve those memorable experiences which typify the courage and comradeship of the men of the 390th Bomb Group during the greatest air assault in history.

Table of Contents

ix

Photograph Sources

390th BOMB GROUP

THE SQUARE **J** GROUP

PARHAM, ENGLAND — STATION 153
JULY 1943 - AUGUST 1945

Aircraft: Boeing B-17 *The Flying Fortress*

Missions: 301 Operational Missions

Bomb Load: Dropped over 19,000 tons of bombs

Losses: 176 aircraft lost

        144 missing in action

        32 other causes

Wins: Officially credited with:

        Destruction of 377 enemy aircraft

        57 probably destroyed

        77 damaged

In this unusual shot, a Fortress of the 390th Bomb Group is shown winging steadily over a small German town, en route to Brunswick. The target for the day was the Waggum main assembly plant of the Luftwaffe's ME 110 twin-engined fighters. 11 January 1944.

Prologue

It was Colonel Moller's, idea that the stories from members of the 390th about their wartime experiences should be published in book form. The former Commander of the Group felt that such a book should begin where the "Blue Book", *The Story of the 390th Bombardment Group, (H)*, ended and that it should be a less official, closer-to-the-heart, record that would not so much tell all about the 390th in terms of facts and figures, but rather would tell the story of what the 390th was all about in terms of emotions, attitudes, and character.

The guiding philosophy was suggested by Col. Moller in his closing remarks at the Hangar Party of the Fifth Reunion at Tucson. It was there that he alluded to the fact that what the 390th is now and what it was then is inextricably interwoven when he said that the members of the 390th looked upon each other with admiration, respect, and even affection. With classic finesse he left the question of how this came to be and what had sustained it for all to reminisce upon, ponder about, and perhaps draw conclusions concerning the how and the why of the 390th. He obviously felt that a book that attempted to offer some answers to this question would not only be a continuing memorial to the organization, but would also assist its members in their search for explanations and understandings of what the 390th was and is all about.

It is magnificently obvious that what the 390th was and is depends in turn on what its members were then and what they are now. To determine what they were requires but a bit of speculative reminiscing to return to the pre-390th days of 1941-43.

1

While it is true that at that time not every man was motivated to the same degree for exactly the same reasons, it is safe to say that the future member of the 390th came from modest circumstances and that he volunteered to serve his country because he was unequivocally patriotic. He believed that he had been fortunate to have enjoyed the freedoms of living in the United States of America. No matter how troubled his upbringing he knew that the life that he had enjoyed was far better than anything promised by Hitler, or Mussolini, et al. He went to war because he wanted to go and because he felt that he should go.

He also saw the war as the great adventure. The opportunity to see the world, wear a uniform, and go off to war was heady stuff. He carefully cultivated a "50 Mission Crush" in his service cap, wore his leather A-2 jacket at every opportunity, and gloried in his new-found role as a "combat" man. Sure the risks were great, but he was ever the optimist and he "knew" that if anyone would come back it would be he.

Our 390th man was one of the best trained fighting men

Crew of *Skippy* in interrogation after their last mission, 26 November 1943.

in history. Whether air crew, ground crew, or support he was ready to do his job the day he reported to the Group and he stayed ready throughout his tour. The concepts of close formation flying, Norden Sight bombing, Zone Firing, and Gee Box navigation were a part of everyday life. And he employed his skills in a type of warfare that was and is unique in history. Primitive it was, a step above World War I, and almost ludicrous when compared to modern-day weapons delivery systems. It was early, before dawn take-offs loaded with 5,000 pounds of bombs and 2,700 gallons of gasoline. It was Fighters, the cold, anoxia, four to six hours of wearing an oxygen mask, cumbersome clothing and heavy flak suits, and long periods of boredom and over-lapping wing close formation flying punctuated by split seconds of high tension fear. It was the ethereal tautness of high altitude, boring through dark flak from the IP to the target and bombs away no matter the consequence. Primitive and unique — it was a type of activity that never happened before and will never happen again. It was a time

Men of the 390th Bomb Group parade during memorial services at their Eighth Air Force base in England, 9 May 1945.

in which history was indelibly written.

The men of the 390th were brave men. Few individuals ever quit, and the Group was never stopped. When a wounded Bird was forced to drop out of formation its place was immediately taken by its designated replacement. Aborts were few. Ernie Pyle said it for all B-17s when he described the raid on St. Lo in these words, "And it seemed that if God himself had stood forth with outstretched arms and beseeched them to turn back they could not have done so," As one pilot said it, "Our job was to put the bombs on the target and that's what we did."

Throughout it all perhaps the greatest weapon of the men of the 390th was their sense of humor. In the direst of circumstances, the darkest of moments, there was always the quick retort, the scathing observation, the penetrating comment — sometimes macabre, sometimes irreverent — but always humorous at the critical time when it was needed most. And it follows that with this kind of sense of humor in the face of everyday war, the men of the 390th played hard whenever the opportunity presented itself. Some of their extracurricular exploits are legendary in themselves.

The best evidence that these observations about the 390th are indeed true are the stories that are included in the following collection. As one reads them the character of what the 390th is all about comes through with vividness and poignancy. In their totality they also bring us back to the original thought that what the 390th is now in the 1980's is a product of what they were then. Harry Truman said it very well when he said, "People don't change. They just get older and we get to know them better." It seems that this is precisely the point Col. Moller made at the Fifth Reunion. The members of the 390th look upon each other with admiration, respect, and affection because of what they were in their youth and they have just gotten older — aged and mellowed like fine wine perhaps, but basically the same — good men.

Joseph A. Moller in pilot's seat of B-17.

The Sights and Sounds

by Joseph A. Moller

Commanding Officer, 390th Bombardment Group (H)

LET us take a minute or two to think back to some of the sights and sounds we once knew so well.

Do you remember your thoughts as you took off on your first mission?

Can you remember what the first burst of flak you ever saw looked like; and how, on priority targets, the flak seemed so thick you could almost walk on it?

Recall watching the enemy fighters — the bandits — as they came in with their guns blinking?

Of course you remember that some of the enemy fighter Gruppes were so good that we even nick-named them — the

5

Augsburg Bluebellies or the Abbeville Kids?

Recall some of the earlier missions before our fighters went all the way with us; and how, as soon as our fighters had to turn back, the bandits seemed to come up in swarms?

And then we would have to fight all the way to the target.

Remember the intercom chatter?

The yell of a gunner as he got a fighter?

The news that a B-17 was going down?

The boys counting the chutes as some of the crew got out?

Recall the turn at the I.P.?

The bomb run; flak in the target area; "Bomb-bay doors coming open";

Remember the relief you felt when you heard "Bombs away", and then the turn off the target?

And then all you had to do was to fight your way towards home until our fighters could come in?

And when our fighters did come in, can you remember watching one of the greatest sights ever seen by man?

Often a hundred or more fighters climbing, diving, twisting turning with one going down every now and then in smoke or flames?

And all of this taking place some four or more miles above the earth.

For these were the sights and sounds mere mortals never saw nor heard.

But we did;

We were a part of it,

We made it happen.

Combat Life

Square J Flying Fortresses flying through one of Germany's heaviest anti-aircraft defenses, Bremen, 16 December 1943.

An Airman's Prayer

by Wilbert H. Richarz

Now I lay me down to sleep,
And pray the Lord my soul to keep;
And should I die upon the morrow,
Let no one grieve in useless sorrow;
For when I go into the blue,
I but take the chance — as others do;
But should I return to live and tell,
Of the thirty-fifth time I cheated hell,
I'll thank you Lord for being kind,
And putting at rest an uneasy mind.
In any event I hope you know,
That no matter how, or where, or when I go,
That when I go into yonder blue,
I'm climbing the steps that lead to you,
And because I'm not an angel yet,
It's as close to heaven as I can get!

(Framlingham, 1945,
written the night before No. 35)

Front:
Angelo Martin, BTG;
"Hap" Hallek, WG;
"Snake" Myers, TTG;
Will Richarz, RO-G;
"Dixie" Anderson, TG.
Back:
Bob Ennis, N; Leroy
Zotter, B; Jack Bouton,
Pilot; Tex Deffenbach, CP.

Mission 23

by Wilbert H. Richarz

Radio Operator-Gunner, 570th Squadron, Cocaine Bill

IT WAS a beautiful day for flying — a clear clean day — the sun shining bright and the clouds fleecy white. Through my window in the radio room I could see peaceful little villages almost five miles below, set among the green of the valleys and the white glare of occasional patches of snow. It was about an hour before target time and the ground station was in one of its infrequent silent periods. In the background noise of my headphones I could hear the faint familiar sound of far-away stations communicating with each other — my mind drifted and soon I had enough air castles built to set myself up in the real estate business.

I came to, with the proverbial start as Jack, our pilot's

9

voice broke in on the interphone with a casual "You'd better man the waist gun Rich — we're under fighter attack" He might as well have asked me down to the corner drugstore for a Coke for all the excitement reflected in his voice. Well, I rolled up the sidewalks, shut the blinds, and hung up the "to let" sign on my air castles and despite the tangling tentacles of all the cords I had to disconnect and reconnect I made it back to the waist gun in little short of record time.

I must have connected those self-same cords a dozen times or more — all wrong — as I feverishly scanned the sky outside the right waist window for the attacking planes. I tried to plug the oxygen hose on the electric suit plug, the microphone cord on the oxygen hose, my head phone plug on the mike connection — and probably would have succeeded, too, if the connections weren't made differently. At that moment I had the intellectual inspiration that maybe the guy who designed those cords had foreseen such a situation and acted accordingly.

I finally connected the last cord and by that time the ship was already vibrating with the chatter of Hap and Dixie's guns. The interphone was having a busy time of it as each crew member called out everything he could see. The main force of enemy fighters seemed to be hitting the squadron below us and by looking as straight down as I could I saw the fighters attacking in waves of thirty or more with orange flashes of flame spouting from the twenty millimeter cannons in the leading edges of their wings. With each pass they made, bombers would tumble out as many as three at a time, and go spinning end over end belching flame and black smoke. Some few turned out of the formation streaming flame out behind to die a slower death. A fortress pilot once wrote a story about his ship called *Queens Die Proudly* and I thought of this as I watched those ships go down. No Queen ever went to her death more majestically or with more dignity than those Queens of the sky — for even in bitter defeat they went down proudly.

In three or four passes the low squadron of ten ships had

been completely wiped out (we later found out that one ship made its way back) and then the fighters began to queue up to attack our squadron in force. I searched the sky for our fighter escort, but couldn't see a friendly fighter anywhere. Occasionally someone on the interphone — after searching the sky vainly for our escort — would voice our collective opinion with "Where in the hell is Eddie?" We didn't know then that Eddie and the entire fighter escort had troubles of their own up in front of the formation.

With no fighter escort to help us and after viewing the comparative ease with which the attacking force had eliminated the low squadron, we were hardly capable of overconfidence concerning the immediate future. I stood staunchly up to the gun, my finger on the trigger, determined to do or die — and then I had to laugh in spite of myself at how very dramatic I was being — how much better it would be to consider this as casually as a camera gunnery mission — how much better chance I would have of hitting something — how much better would be our chance of survival — my survival. I can't say I completely convinced myself of these facts, but it helped and though I still felt rather pessimistic as to the mathematical possibility of our surviving the coming onslaught unscathed, I did feel less like something out of Metro Goldwyn Mayer and more like settling down to do the job for which I had been trained.

The fighters came in on us like so many angry bees — diving at our formation from the rear and breaking away to circle and try again. Dixie (tail), Hap (ball) and Snake (upper turret) were all talking on the interphone at once — calling out attacking ships and remarking about the ships they could see going down. Then Dixie would break in with "Get off the damn interphone — here they come" — and then, since Dixie was in the best position to call out the tail attacks, there would be a momentary silence while Dixie gave us the poop. Suddenly he called out, "Here come three at four o'clock high" — that being my side I strained against the plexiglass — much like a kid at the front window on a rainy day — to see if I could pick them up. I saw this one joker at three o'clock, about 400 yards out — a sleek-looking dull-colored F.W. 190, his blunt nose swinging in toward us fast. I picked up my lead and opened fire at about 300 yards just as his ship swung into position to fire on us. I was vaguely conscious of the fact that everybody seemed to be firing at once and when my gun joined in the chattering chorus the whole ship was vibrating. I fired in long bursts and I could see flashes of flame on the wings and engine cowling where strikes were being scored, and though I kept firing and seemed to be hitting him he kept boring in. His ship wavered — the gap of distance between us closed rapidly and before I realized it he was practically flying formation with us. He came in high — between our ship and Pepper's ship which was flying off our right wing. the nose of his ship was no longer pointed at us, therefore he was not in position to fire on us and I found myself looking at a gunner's dream, a no-deflection shot, the legendary sitting duck — and that a mere 50 yards or so away. After a brief moment in which I made sure I wasn't having hallucinations I centered my sight on him and cut loose with everything but the kitchen sink. The 190, now clearly defined against the sky, wobbled and wavered, smoke streaming out from around the engine in a dense cloud and over the sight of my bucking gun I could see the pilot fumbling desperately to unfasten his canopy cover. The next thing I knew the canopy flew off and the pilot tumbled out over the side. In the instant that he seemed to hang there in mid-air I could see clearly the details of his flying suit — then he was whisked away below our tail. I stopped firing and yelled into the interphone, "I got him, I got him," only to find to my surprise that Snake was doing the same thing from the top turret. We had both tracked the same ship in and fired on it — each not knowing that the other had been shooting at it.

Hap was calling out from the lower ball that he had just shot another one down and the bombardier was saying something about the bomb bay doors coming open. Dixie's guns were still hammering away at "Bombs away" and just before I made my way back to the radio room to check the bomb bays — those cords again — I remember I could still

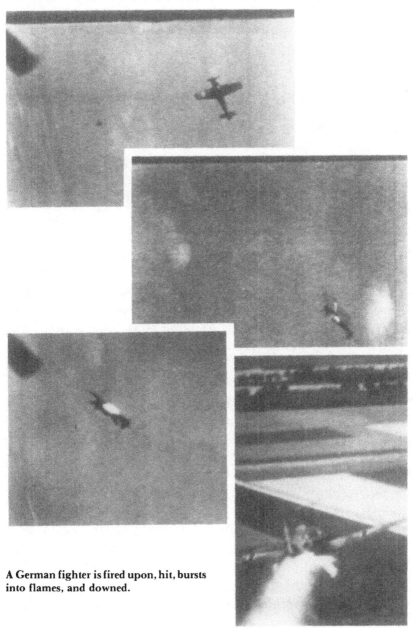

A German fighter is fired upon, hit, bursts into flames, and downed.

see the fighters queuing up. Right after bombs away Dixie got his "kill" — a twin engine job — and the co-pilot confirmed it, with Hap's able assistance.

The attacks gradually dwindled in number and intensity, and shortly after bombs away I was back at the radio, disinterestedly copying code and wondering vaguely if it had all been a dozing dream.

—England, 1945

Mission 23 —
The Rest of the Story

By Wilbert H. Richarz

WHILE flying with the 570th Squadron of the 390th Bomb Group as a radio operator I wrote a story about Mission 23 in which I told of being under fighter attack and of my shooting down an FW 190. I called it "Mission 23." Now 38 years later I'd like to tell the rest of the story. In doing this I'll be the first to admit that I am totally dependent upon my memory and the events I remember may well not be precisely the same as those remembered by other observers of the same events. This obvious phenomenon was greatly in evidence at the Fifth Reunion of the 390th in Tucson. People do have a way of exercising selective memory, especially concerning War Stories, and I am sure I am as guilty as anyone else. With this in mind plus the fact that I do not intend or imply any retroactive criticism and/or credit, I will just relate the events as I remember them.

The events are related in two parts. The first pertains to the crew that flew off our right wing that day and how what happened to them led to my shooting down the FW 190. Much of this information was told to me by the waist gunner of the aircraft off our right wing (our enlisted crews were housed in the same Quonset Hut). The second part refers to the unspoken communication that took place between myself and the pilot of the FW 190.

Mission 23 began well before dawn with a full load take-off. The aircraft that was to fly our right wing was between 200 and 300 feet of altitude when somehow the bailout bell was accidentally triggered. Apparently the people in the front of the aircraft could not hear it because of the engine noise of full throttle, but the crew members in the back heard it loud and clear. One of the waist gunners hooked on his chest pack and ran back and jettisoned the waist door. The other waist gunner was right behind him. When the first gunner looked out he saw immediately that even in the dim light the houses and trees of a village were plainly visible. Recognizing that they were quite possibly too low for a safe jump he naturally hesitated. The other gunner thought that his own life was now in mortal danger because the first man was "too chicken" to jump so he took immediate corrective action. In his own words, "I planted my number twelve boondocker in his back and booted him out — and when I saw what I had done I knew I had to jump too!" Luckily, both chutes opened at tree top level and the boys made an early morning visit to the village. Their only comment was that they came mighty close to getting to try returning their chutes to the factory for new ones under the guarantee that "the chute is guaranteed to 200 feet and if it does not open send it back to the manufacturer and they will issue you a new one."

Meanwhile the aircraft continued on the mission minus the waist door and the two gunners. Later, when the fighters hit the formation the lower ball gunner shot all the ammunition out of the lower ball guns and both waist guns and shot down three fighters in the process. Naturally there were a few minutes here and there while he was in transit between gun positions when his aircraft was vulnerable. It apparently was during one of these times that the 190 that I fired on made an unopposed pass at that aircraft.

As I told in "Mission 23," I picked up the FW 190 as it was making a pass at the other aircraft off our right wing. As a result my first bursts were over the top of the other B-17. I hit the 190 right away and apparently out of control he drifted over the other aircraft and wobbled into a position high at three o'clock. He was so high in fact that I had to put the Bell Adaptor practically on the floor in order to shoot. Then the aircraft pulled a little further away and I swung the gun for the kill. It was then that I saw the pilot was not flying the plane but was struggling to release his ejection canopy. As I aligned the sights on him he looked down at me and our eyes locked. His look was one of fear and pleading — he was begging me not to shoot — imploring me to let him go. From a practical viewpoint I knew I should shoot. The Germans had few pilots but plenty of airplanes. If I let him go he could come back tomorrow and shoot down who knows how many B-17s. Besides, how many B-17s had he accounted for already? Then there was the fact that the German fighter pilots had allegedly shot our airmen in their chutes many times and committed other less than chivalrous acts. I had always thought that we were too chivalrous with our code of honor — bomb in the daytime, don't shoot men in chutes, bomb only military targets, ad infinitum. War was war. But I could not pull the trigger — I held off. The code was too strong. The next split second the canopy blew and out he went. Then for an instant he was held motionless in space — vulnerable — and again I instinctively swung the gun on him and again he pleaded with his eyes and again I held off. Then he was whipped away by the slipstream.

In the days and years that have followed I have thought of that German pilot many, many times and I have pondered, "What if I had shot?" What became of him? How were both our lives affected by the staying of the trigger? How would things have been different had I pulled the trigger? I wonder if he survived the war. I wonder what he is doing now. I wonder how often he thinks of me. And how?

Crew of *Cabin in the Sky.*

Stories from the
Cabin in the Sky Crew

by *R. D. Brown*

Pilot, 571st Squadron, Cabin in the Sky

THE following anecdotes cover interesting experiences of the *Cabin in the Sky* crew members. This was one of the original crews in the 571st Bomb Squadron.

REGENSBURG MISSION — 17 AUGUST 1943

No effort will be made to cover the trials and tribulations of this mission, i.e., early take off, fighters, headwinds, ditchings, etc. Plenty has been written on these items. This story covers two phases — the bomb run and the arrival in Africa.

The *Cabin* crew was leading the 390th Bomb Group which was flying in the high group in the wing formation

17

behind the 95th Group. Col. (later General) Le May was the Command Pilot in the lead aircraft.

The *Cabin in the Sky* had Major Von Arb (571st Squadron Commander) in the Copilot seat. Lt. Col. Wittan (390th Bomb Group C.O.) stood between the pilot and copilot's seats. Bob Brown, the pilot, had good supervision.

Everything went pretty smooth through the IP and bomb run. Finally, there were those wonderful words on the intercom "Bombs Away". Brown was making the turn off the target to the rally point when the ball-turret gunner (Davidoff) yelled, "Man, Lt. Forbes you hit the 'h---' out of the target, right in the middle. Wahoo!!"

The mission continued across the Alps, the Mediterranean and finally to a landing at Telergma in Africa. A command jeep arrived to pick up Col. Wittan. His only comment to anyone was to Doug. Without any outward emotion, he said, "Forbes, the next time you brief your gunner to report on bombing results, remind him that it takes at least twelve seconds for the bombs to hit the ground." Sure enough, Doug admitted he had told Duke to yell "bulls-eye", no matter where the bombs hit.

Doug's comment later on was that he didn't want Big Ed (Col. Wittan) chewing his butt all the way to Africa.

This is the way it went on the *Cabin*. Needless to say, Doug did hit the target dead center that day; as he did most of the time — as long as our navigator, Brumfiel, could point out the target to him. *A great team!*

That night the crew bedded down on PSP (Pierced Steel Planking) laid down on the desert floor to act as the runway, taxi-way and hardstand for the B-17s. The crew woke up in the morning looking like human waffles.

FLYING THROUGH A BALLOON BARRAGE

Lt. Brown, pilot of the *Cabin in the Sky*, was rousted out of his Nissen Hut one morning when he was not scheduled to fly a combat mission. He was told to round up his crew and lead a search mission. Take off was to be ASAP.

The RAF had had a bad night and many of their crews were missing after ditching in the English Channel.

Brown led a six ship formation that actually flew quite close to the French Coast. No German fighters approached this small formation, but each of the planes was fully manned with gunners always alert for possible attack by the enemy. The search mission was over six hours. It concluded at sundown.

The crews were briefed to make landfall off the North Sea at Norwich. The British Ground Defense Force (GDF) was instructed to turn on the squeakers and searchlights on the balloons since the group would be returning after dark.

The Ground Defense Force goofed. Nothing was on, not even the buncher (radio beacon). The navigator was briefed to make the landfall at a minimum of altitude and to avoid the balloons which would be visible over Norwich. Unfortunately the squeakers were not on and there were no lights on the balloons, SNAFU—Yes. Before a correction could be made, Gordon-Forbes, the bombardier, called out excitedly, "Skipper, hard right, balloons dead ahead." That's the way

Pilot R. D. Brown points out German fighter "kills" painted on nose of *Cabin in the Sky* to Doug Gordon-Forbes, Johnny Clark and "Lucky"Dolan.

it went for the next five to six minutes—an eternity. Gordon-Forbes kept his head in the front bubble calling hard right, hard left, level out; steering the pilot around the balloons so the miserable cables hanging down could be missed.

Brownie gave the formation the word to go in trail at maximum power climb with all external lights on.

Post-mortem revealed that all crews involved responded similarly. In the *Cabin* it was Brumfiel putting on Doug's chest chute, clearing the way to the escape hatch and standing by to help if need be. Tate went forward to help anyone that might need it in getting out the front hatch. Hart put the pilot's chute on and cleared the passage way. Everyone agreed they felt it would be only seconds before a cable would cut through the plane someplace. The lead pilot cussed the GDF. The guys in trail cussed him. (The only pilot in the trailing aircraft that can now be identified was Dick Perry with a make up crew.)

After what seemed to be eons, Gordon-Forbes said, "I think we are on top of the balloons." The tail gunner (Goldberg) had stayed in the tail and reported that all five aircraft were still in trail. The formation headed toward home base, Station 153 at Parham.

The control tower had heard the radio calls and had the field lights turned on for the landing. Col. Jeffrey, Group Air Executive, met the crews upon landing. After hearing about the unscheduled trip through the balloon barrage at Norwich, he about exploded — but not at the sixty crew members who already needed new sets of underwear. Col. Jeff was mad at the GDF for not turning on the squeakers and the balloon lights.

The GDF sent a man to the base to evaluate the maneuvers the planes went through to avoid the balloons. They most likely added a few more balloons.

THE NERVOUS "P"

I was the skipper of the *Cabin in the Sky* crew. I had a malady at the start of my tour that I called my 16,000 foot nervous Pee. It didn't make any difference that I had that last call, before engine start; come 16,000 feet on the climb I had to go!! And I mean go!! Well all the guys know what that involved. Unbuckle, pull the connections to the oxygen, head phones and heated suit, crawl past the top-turret gunner and back to the bomb-bay to the relief tube (with walk-around bottle yet.)

So, after getting the word on my problem, our ground crew decided to do something about it. (God Bless them they were something of a wonder.) They put an additional relief tube in the aircraft, right next to my seat and of course a venturi tube on the outside to provide the necessary vacuum. Beautiful? Not quite. We made no arrangements for testing this new system. A boon to all aircraft commanders.

So off we go on our next mission, which one I don't remember, somewhere between the fifth and the eighth. We hit 16,000 feet and here comes the call. Gotta go! No problem: Just doing great until a yell from the ball turret gunner (Davidoff) "D — — N you, Skipper, you've just — — — — all over the front of my turret; it's frozen and I can't see a thing". Now what do you do? You can't abort. How would that look on the abort report. So on we went. We got jumped by fighters and all poor Duke could do was track the calls and bad mouth me. Now, that's not the proper relationship. But what can you say when your bladder has effectively wiped out one of your best gunners.

We got back OK (as well as the rest of the Group) and Duke grabbed a maintenance stand and pulled that venturi tube out with the greatest of satisfaction. I couldn't fault him.

P.S. I never had the 16,000 feet "bladders" after that HONEST!

Front:
W. Kubitsky, ROG; S. Widetsky, LWG; J. Poulin, BTG; J. Dolan, TG.
Back:
G. Wharton, N; E. Heitlage, RWG; W. Cabral, Pilot; D. Ferris, B; L. Wamble, TTG; R. Perry, CP (Pinch-hitting for J. Wenzel).

Fortnight in the Life of the *Eightball* Crew

by Richard H. Perry

Co-Pilot, 570th Squadron, Eightball

THE *EIGHTBALL* crew was only one of many B-17 crews that participated in the air armadas that eventually brought the enemies of the free world to their knees. This report covers only two weeks — the first two weeks of October 1943 — of the air war fought so valiantly by the allies.

The *Eightball* crew was one of the original crews assigned to the 390th Bomb Group — one of the most famous bombing groups based in England during 1943-1945. This crew and their B-17 (Flying Fortress) airplane (No. 42-30337) was commanded by Lt. (later Captain) William Cabral.

In October 1943, the 8th Air Force was suffering heavy

22

losses on most of their daylight bombing missions on the continent. Fighter escort was limited. The German Luftwaffe was desperately trying to protect the fatherland. On to this scene, the *Eightball* appears.

Nose art of Eightball.

On October 2, 1943, the 390th Bomb Group was ordered to bomb the port area in Emden, Germany. The *Eightball* with its crew on their ninth mission, was assigned an important position in the 390th formation that morning. The completion of this mission would mean that the Cabral crew would be two-fifths done in their determined path to complete the required 25 combat missions before they could return to the state side.

As the *Eightball* came up to the target, the No. 3 engine was hit by flak. The *Eightball* slipped out of formation and made a solo run on the target at Emden before heading for home. The lone aircraft attracted about 20 Nazi fighters. While the gunners went into action, Lt. Cabral dove the airplane into cloud coverage 16,000 feet below. Coming out of the cloud near the coastline in Holland, the No. 3 engine caught on fire. Alerting the crew that they may need to abandon the ship, the pilot dove for the North Sea. The Luftwaffe still taking turns making passes at the crippled fort. It was not possible to feather the prop. The airplane shuddered and shook as Lt. Cabral made violent turns to avoid the firepower of the attacking fighters. The crew claimed three destroyed enemy aircraft.

Lt. Cabral flew the *Eightball* so close to the whitecap waves, that the salt spray could be tasted on the crews' lips. This maneuver worked. The fire went out. Plane Number 337 limped back to the base at Parham. Upon landing, the unfeathered windmilling prop spun forward, digging large holes in the runway, as the plane hit the runway and slowed down.

The *Eightball* was outfitted with a new engine within a day. Holes in the fuselage were patched also. The ground crews were great.

After the Emden raid, the crew was assigned to a special secret mission for about four days. It can now be told that this assignment involved the possible use of B-17s to haul gliders. The necessary parts did not arrive from the states so the crew was placed back on combat operations about October 8, 1943 just in time to be assigned to one of the Eighth Air Force's longest missions on October 9, 1943 to Marienburg, East Prussia. The Focke-Wulff factory at Marienburg was wiped out due to the "most perfect

No. 3 engine after removal from *Eightball.*

example in history of the accurate distribution of bombs over a target." Lt. Cabral's crew was in the air about eleven hours. Very little fuel was left when it returned to the base.

The next day (October 10, 1943), the *Eightball* crew was sent to Munster, Germany. Just after dropping its bombs, the airplane was hit by an aerial rocket from a Messerschmitt 110 on a frontal attack. The right wing was about sheared off, 12 feet from the tip. The *Eightball* was again knocked out of formation. The airplane appeared destined to go down. The right wing had lost its lift capability. By using the trim tabs, excess rudder and help from the Co-pilot, Lt. Perry, and the bombardier, Lt. Ferris, Lt. Cabral was able to get the bomber headed home. The Luftwaffe continued their attack on the lone crippled Flying Fortress. The gunners went to work. The result was five enemy aircraft destroyed, two probably destroyed and one damaged. The 390th Bomb Group that day lost eight planes and destroyed a total of 62 enemy fighters — the top score for a Heavy Bomb Group in the ETO.

As the *Eightball* proceeded across the North Sea, the enemy fighters left, but trouble still loomed. The engines were run very hard in holding altitude and escaping the

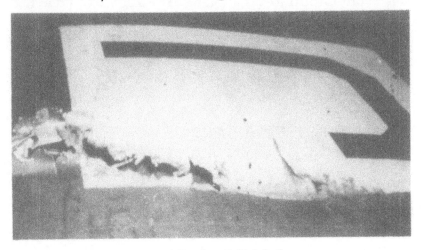

Hole in right wing of *Eightball.*

Nazi fighters. As the aircraft approached the 390th home base, the weather socked in with almost zero visibility. After making one unsuccessful pass, the control tower ordered Number 337 to proceed to Thorpe Abbotts, the home of the 100th Bomb Group. Before landing at the 100th, one engine needed to be feathered and another engine was providing minimum power. The landing was rather rough, due to lack of visibility and adequate power from the engines. The plane ended up in a small ditch off the runway. The *Eightball* crew was very happy to be down with no one harmed.

As a matter of note, the crew was debriefed by the 100th Bomb Group intelligence officers before being returned to the 390th base by truck. The interrogation room was rather grim. The 100th Bomb Group had only one airplane return to the base from Munster. All of the others were shot down.

After two days of rest and the normal ground school at the base, Lt. Cabral's crew was assigned to bomb the ball bearing factory at Schweinfurt, Germany, on October 14, 1943. Since the *Eightball* was still being repaired, Lt. Cabral's crew flew a replacement aircraft, No. 42-3557. Out of the 291 aircraft dispatched by the Bomber Command, 60 heavy bombers were lost. Most of these to flak and fighters. The 390th Group lost one plane. The *Eightball* crew had

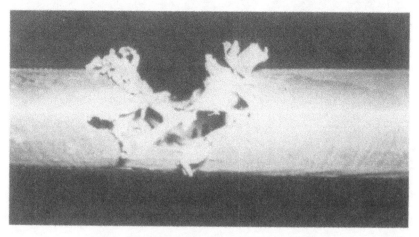

Side view of hole in right wing of *Eightball*.

many enemy airplane attacks. A chunk of flak hit the door on the ball turret knocking it loose. Sgt. Poulin, the turret gunner, stuck to his turret with only a small strap holding him from a very long fall (about 25,000 feet). Joey knew that if the turret did not move, the Luftwaffe would spot a dead turret and would pick on the plane. This decision proved to be a good one. The crew returned safely again. The next mission for the *Eightball* crew was a two-day leave to London for relaxation before taking the *Eightball* on many more thrilling episodes. Success came from sheer courage, a well-trained crew and a great aircraft.

During this thirteen day period, the *Eightball* crew flew four very successful combat missions. Two of these missions, Munster and Schweinfurt were considered, with the August 12, 1943, Regensburg mission, as "The Big Three". These three stood out above the rest of the 301 missions completed by the 390th Group.

Lt. Cabral's crew finished their 25th mission on 30 December 1943. Another crew was assigned to the *Eightball*. The battle-proven B-17 numbered 42-30337 (*Eightball*) was shot down on 10 February 1944 on a bombing mission to Brunswick, Germany.

In the 3 February 1944 Stars and Stripes article entitled *The Screwballs and the Eightball*, the *Eightball* was reported as, ". . . just another flak-battered Flying Fortress— her crew just ten more average Yanks in the bombing business in Europe."

The *Eightball* crew received no special recognition, or special medals other than the DFC and several air medals awarded routinely as specific numbers of missions were completed. There were a few newspaper articles reporting on their heroic deeds. It will be left to the reader to determine the extent of their contribution — they completed twenty-five combat bombing missions and left their toll on enemy aircraft. They were a crew made up of dedicated Americans eager to do their part in this very important phase of World War II.

Five Minute Hero

by Leif Halvorsen

Navigator, 570th Squadron, Liberty Belle

IT was our first mission — "Big B" — a tough mission, lots of flak — but we finally landed. The crew left the plane and finally I staggered out, my face covered with blood, and collapsed on the ground. The pilot Don Hassig, called the ambulance. As we waited, I could dimly hear the crew in the background saying that I had finished the mission — even though I had been wounded — implying I was a hero. Not so! I had put my hat on, stood up, hit the roof and drove the fastener that secured my insignia to my 50 mission hat right through my forehead!

Back: Cecil Holliday, BTG; Raymond Leveille, RO-G; Edwin Pearce; RWG; Harry Powers, TTG; George Jahnke, LWG; Fred Smart, Tail TG; Front: Fernie McEwin, CP; Victor Baker, N; Harold Erickson, P; Vincent McDonald, B.

Patches, a Plane; Its Name; and Its Fame

by George P. Jahnke

Top Turret Gunner, 571st Squadron, Patches

IN early 1943, a B-17 type Aircraft, serial number 229991, was signed for by Harold J. Erickson, a flight officer. This plane was to become the Army Air Force property of him and his crew of ten men. After training, this crew was to become a combat crew fighting for the AAF.

When this group of men started flying as a crew, the plane was not named, and was known only as Aircraft Number 229991. The plane was already a veteran of the skies, and had many hours of air time, with other training crews. It was intended to be used only as a training plane, since it was one of the oldest planes in the squadron.

Hours and hours of training was conducted in that old

plane with no accidents or major malfunctions. The plane and crew were assigned to the 571st Bomb Squadron, of the newly formed 390th Bomb Group that was activated to help the Army Air Force against Germany.

Training was accomplished at Ephrara, Washington; Great Falls Air Base, Montana, and at Salina, Kansas, prior to going overseas.

A few of the incidents and happenings remembered by the crew were:

Once, while on a training flight, a high pressure line broke. It caused a lot of excitement aboard our ship. We were forced to make an emergency landing at night on a strange field in the fog and on a very short runway. The plane got a mud bath and had to be pulled back onto the runway. The crew had its first real scare.

Another time while the unit was being transferred to Salina, Kansas and was flying over the Black Hills of South Dakota, one of the engines began to run wild and finally stopped. This caused everyone to get excited, and to make things worse someone accidently bumped the "abandon ship" switch. The pilot radioed the Squadron Leader for instructions. The instructions were, "Land at nearest Air Base". The crew however knew that if we were not able to keep up with the rest of our Squadron airplanes, we would not be able to go overseas with the 390th Bomb Group. So, for some unknown reason, on purpose, our radio went dead, and we continued on to Salina on three engines. We landed OK and found that all the other crews were being processed to go on leave. We parked our plane, went through the necessary processing, and then went to our homes for a short time before going overseas.

When we got back from leave, instead of having a new plane, as was rumored, we found our old plane and it had all four engines replaced. Well, to make a long story short — we didn't get our new plane, but we did get new engines. We were not at all that disappointed, as we had sort of learned to love and like that old plane, with its loveable ways. It seemed to be taking good care of us.

They were asking each crew to name their aircraft. No one on our crew could think of a suitable name for our plane, so we just called it "We'll Never Know". It wasn't a good name, but it did have a good ring to it.

We flew to England, through Newfoundland and Scotland and on to our operational base near Framlingham, England. In August 1943 we became operational and flew our first mission.

When we landed after our first mission, our plane was a mass of small flak holes and a few bullet holes. After it was repaired it looked rather odd, as all the patched holes made it like a mass of patches. We then and there re-named our plane *Patches*.

We painted a dumb looking duck on the side of the plane, carrying a bomb. It had a halo over its head. It looked dumb and stupid. It identified, however, our crew from other crews. This dumb duck was even painted on the backs of our B-15 jackets. A bomb was added for each mission that was made by the crew.

Patches was forced once to land at another English air base, when a fire was started by enemy fighters on the way home from a mission. We were forced to land almost before the ball turret gunner could get out of the turret and secure the turret for safe landing.

Once the oxygen system was knocked out a few inches above the heads of the two waist gunners, nearly taking a couple of heads with it.

Another time the plexi-glass was blown out of the nose of the plane, causing a lot of discomfort to the crew due to the 200 mile wind rushing through the plane. The only place a new or replacement glass could be found for such an Aircraft was in an Army Air Force junk yard.

Patches flew twelve hard missions over Germany. It participated in three of the biggest and toughest raids of World War II. (They were: Regensburg, Munster, and Schweinfurt.) These three raids stood out above the rest. For the Schweinfurt Raid the Group was awarded a Presidential Citation.

The "luck" of *Patches* ran out on the 14th of October 1943 on the Schweinfurt raid. This plane had paid its price in full. It had trained well; it had flown twelve combat missions, it had never been grounded because of mechanical failure, it had never aborted a mission or flight that was not aborted by the whole group, it had never failed to drop its bombs on the target.

Patches blew up that day; but not before she allowed her crew to clear the ship. Shortly after dumping the bombs at 22,000 feet, *Patches* was hit by flak and fighters. The No. 2 engine suffered a direct hit which started to burn. The right wing tank was ruptured also, causing the loss of gasoline, which started to burn.

While trying to keep up to the formation on three engines, it became a hopeless cause. Once we were out of the formation, and the protection of the other planes, the fighters hit us at will and from all angles. They were dealing death and destruction to a struggling plane and its crew.

As the problems increased, the crew knew it was a hopeless cause. It was either abandon the ship or die. It seemed like *Patches* had told her crew to jump. After the crew had jumped, *Patches* went into a step dive, maybe to catch a breath of life, but it blew up in a big black puff of smoke.

One of the crew members, hanging in his parachute saw *Patches* blow up — he cried that day — when *Patches* blew away.

Hugh McCarthy,
Bombardier and Gus
Mencow, Navigator

The Flak Depressor

by Gus Mencow

Navigator, 570th Squadron, **Pistol Packing Mama**

$\mathbf{I}$T is difficult to recall the happenings of 35-40 years ago. So many events took place, that it all becomes a montage, and only certain incidents are recalled, when an old song comes through the radio or a familiar sight or odor is stumbled upon.

One's mind tends to shut out the fear, fright and frustration of combat, and rest comfortably on the lighter side of warfare. As John Winant, the wartime ambassador to England put it, "It is all part of the soldier's faith, to have seen and done great things and to be content with silence". So be it — we have put aside the tools of conflict and we are left with friendships and memories that somehow sustain us

33

through our daily tasks.

Each combat crew was an entity in itself. We were a complete family — living and dying together, worrying over each one's welfare and yet still wrapped up in our own individual concern about getting out of the war alive. And as we lived — happy in our own way — at the end of the runway —.

How many of us, when turning into the bomb run, have looked up to the heavens, and said to himself — "Why me"?? — and yet we would not have it any other way!!!

To zero in on any one event is almost impossible, but the comic relief of combat always come to the fore. What may now be just another dull story, in the heat of battle was a very funny incident. The present generation can not comprehend what to us would be a funny tale.

"Bombs Away!" on to a Nazi fighter base. Flak bursts above and below the nearest 390th Fortress sending shrapnel flying through the air.

It all happened in late '43, when we were being equipped with the latest radar gadget — called "gee". This was a system to make navigation easier. — We were on our way to our airplane, when I overheard our bombardier, Lt. Hugh McCarthy, discussing this "gee" equipment with our Squadron Operations Officer, Major Bill Jones, who was flying with us that day, as Command Pilot. — They came to the conclusion that the scientists could invent anything that would make it easier for the combat crews. — It so happened that our target for that day was located in Bonn, Germany, right in the heart of the heaviest of flak areas. — As we turned into the bomb run the sky was literally black with the smoke from the flak bursts. We were all in awe, and full of apprehension as to our chances of getting through to the target. Through the inter-com, McCarthy said, "Hey Jonesy, will you please press that big button next to the altimeter."

Jones said, "What button?"

McCarthy said, "The one that those scientists put there."

Jones said, "What the hell are you talking about?"

McCarthy said, "Didn't we agree that the scientist could invent anything?"

"Yes," said Jones.

"Well," said McCarthy, "I think they've invented the button that tops them all — It's called 'THE FLAK DEPRESSOR'.

Needless to say, the tension was broken, and by good fortune we had a successful mission.

But for days after, Jones had a silly grin on his face anytime the word "button" was mentioned.

It all was so long ago, and yet the event still remains very vivid. McCarthy and Jones are gone to their eternal rest, but their warm personalities and brotherly friendship will be with me until I join them.

Crew of *Virgin Sturgeon*

Virgin Sturgeon's
First Combat Mission

by R. Rowland

Pilot, 570th Squadron, Virgin Sturgeon

IT was August 1943. We were a new Group
(390th) having just arrived at Station 153 at Parham,
England. It was our first raid, not only for the Group but my
first as Aircraft Commander of a B-17 named the *Virgin
Sturgeon* from the rhyme. We liked the name as the
Sturgeon is a very rare fish and eggs from it make a rare dish.

At briefing that morning, we were told the raid was to
Bonn in the Rhur Valley of Germany. The main defenses
were the anti-aircraft batteries that saturated the entire
valley. We were told that the black smoke from the anti-
aircraft bursts was a psychological weapon and to treat it as
such. Also, we were told we would have Spitfire escorts over

36

England and they would leave us at the Channel.

Our Group formed over England without incident. My Squadron, the 570th, was High Squadron in the Group. We flew across the Channel and the coast of the main land. As we approached the Rhur Valley and the anti-aircraft batteries opened up, I was completely demoralized at the sight of the black smoke of the shell bursts. As we entered the valley, I received a shell burst just under my left wing which knocked me out of formation. I lost about a thousand feet of altitude before I recovered. Scared as I was, my only thought was to get back to my position in the formation. So with a lot of maneuvering and fighting prop wash I was able to get back to position. I was so scared I never realized we had completed our bomb run and started our return to base. This is one raid (my baptism of fire) I know I will never forget. I know I had a wonderful crew with me but I felt like I was out there all alone, trusting no one for the operation of the plane. However, I soon got over this feeling and we went from there as a fine trained team with a great aircraft *Virgin Sturgeon*.

A crew arrives at the hardstand after briefing.

Front:
E. Jones, TG; R. DeRycke, RO; S. Smith, LWG; A McMillin, BTG; E. Gallagher, RWG.
Back:
R. Wilson, N; R. Winspear, B; F. Stoll, CP; C. Harmon, TTG; K. Harris, Pilot.

Spot Remover — Landing Gear Jinxes

by Stan Smith

Gunner, 570th Squadron, Spot Remover

WHEN we were assigned to our B-17 aircraft Number 230246 at Geiger Field, we were chagrined to see that all the other ships lined up nose to tail *looked* new. *Our* plane had paint scaling off the big vertical fin and, in general, looked a little seedy. We kept mumbling to each other as we walked around the ship, giving it the critical eye, "Are they sure this is a *new* B-17?"

But it was new, and as we began our series of break-in flights in the Washington and Montana area, we all became thoroughly familiar with 246's quirks and idiosyncrasies. That is, we *thought* we were getting to know our big fin bird until one day on a training flight near Lewistown,

38

Montana, we came in for a bit of surprise.

We were approaching the postage-stamp sized field, referred to as Lewistown Air Base, when Lt. Harris and Lt. Stoll, our pilot and co-pilot, gave us this message on the intercom: "The gear won't come down, gang!" Well, we were all a bit scared, since none of us were exactly old Air Corps veterans in 1943. Lt. Harris asked the crew if we wanted to bail out over the field rather than chance a belly-landing. Since the Montana real estate didn't appear very inviting, we all opted to stay with the ship. Meanwhile, Sgt. Harmon, the flight engineer, continued to work with our pilots to crank down the gear by hand; a tough job under any conditions. After a lot of elbow grease and perspiration, the main gear did come down and the flight ended without further event.

However, in the fall of 1943, even our trusty hand crank wouldn't do the trick and *Spot Remover's* main landing gear wouldn't budge from its retracted position. We were on final approach to Parham (England) Air Base with twelve 500-pounders and almost a full load of fuel aboard. The mission had been scrubbed and we were on our way for a little relaxation and some Red Cross coffee and donuts. But this was not meant to be, for once again the landing gear was giving us fits. Only this time, the hand crank would not engage and the gear was up to stay.

Down goes the ball turret into the English Channel.

The tower told us to get out of the pattern and head for the North Sea to fly off the gas load. We were instructed also to salvo the bomb load. While we were doing this, we were asked by the tower to attempt to jettison the ball turret. That way, the risk of tearing *Spot Remover's* belly would be lessened — and just incidentally, would lower the risk of the turret's column knifing through the flimsy plywood radio room door and tearing into the crew, crouched in crash-landing position.

Well after about thirty minutes of tinkering, the last bolts holding the turret were removed, and the turret plunged down into the North Sea.

After several hours, Lt. Harris and Stoll began the final approach for our wheels-up landing. Once again we had been given the option to bail out, but as before, we elected to stick with the ship. (Old sea-fearing tradition).

Lt. Harris brought old *Spot Remover* in slick as a whistle. No bounce, no jounce — she just slid along the runway, losing speed until Lt. Harris was able to rudder her off the runway onto the grass. As soon as the *Spot* had come to a full stop, we all climbed out and ran, but there was no fire or explosion and surprisingly little structural damage.

Spot Remover and her crew came thru another misadventure, not too much the worse for wear. After new engines and some dent-straightening, our big bird came back to us, ready for more escapades. Sadly enough, *Spot* seemed to be jinxed from that time on. Broken oil coolers, broken push-rods, oxygen problems, etc. After the belly-landing, *Spot* acted like an automobile which had been in a bad wreck; her "frame" seemed to have been sprung. At any rate, she held together long enough for us, Lt. Harris' crew, to finish our missions.

Spot Remover attracts plenty of attention after its belly landing.

Marshall B. Shore, 1944

Target Berlin

by Marshall B. Shore
Group Navigator

THE 390th Bomb Group (H) went to Berlin many times. On March 6, 1944, we went there for the first time.

I was scheduled to be the lead Navigator of the 8th Air Force Task Force on the first daylight mission to bomb Berlin on March 1, 1944. This was a deep penetration to one of the most heavily defended targets in Germany and of course the heart of all flyers skipped a beat when assigned to cover Big 'B' as we called Berlin in those days. The first schedule was scrubbed in the briefing room. The second one, a day later, was scrubbed with engines running at the end of the runway. The third mission was scrubbed in the

41

air by radio message from Headquarters, 8th Air Force encoded to all Air Commanders. The 95th Bomb Group (H) apparently did not receive the recall message and with thirty-one B-17s and twenty-three escort fighters continued to the target area. Although badly hampered by clouds they dropped their ordnance in the Berlin area, and thus became recognized as the first heavy bomber unit to bomb Big 'B' in daylight. The rest of us returned to base and our lead of the Division was rotated.

On the 6th of March, it was still my turn to fly and I went as lead of the 13th Combat Wing with a Pathfinder crew flown from Alconbury. Lt. Colonel Bob Tuttle was the Wing Air Commander. I was the Command Navigator and Major Gene Willms was the Lead Bombardier. We stayed on course that day and caught a lot of German fighter attacks.

Since we were the lead aircraft of the 13th Combat Wing on the planned route, we were the first to see the onslaught of German fighters at Heseluenne. We looked ahead to a solid stream of ME 109s in Hermichen's attack formation lined up in trail boring in on us from dead ahead. With the rate of closure around 450 knots the forward pointing guns of all B-17s in our formation were lined up on each fighter as it approached firing range with its 20mm cannon blazing away at us.

I remember holding my 50 caliber hand operated machine gun with the ring sight tracking each fighter for any deflection. I pulled the trigger until the fighter went out of sight through our formation. As many as ninety-one of our gun barrels were pointed at each fighter as it came through. It was very unhealthy for a German ME 109 pilot to attack head-on like this, but they did it and their losses were pretty high on this day. (66 destroyed for a loss rate of 20 percent.)

We could count from ten to fifteen fighters at a time in sight in trail out in front of us. All coming in headed for the center of our formations. More were swarming to get into position to keep the prolonged head-on attacks going as

View of Berlin from bombing altitude.

long as they could. ME 109s went through our formation every ten or fifteen seconds, with their 20mm cannon flashing brightly. They were easy to take aim at even though the time was a split second at best.

As they went by we could see our 50 Cal. bullets racking the windshields, the cowling, and the fuselage of the ME 109s. We worked like hell, sweated and cursed, and when not hit ourselves, managed to navigate to the Initial Point to begin our bomb run.

Our Standard Operating Procedures (SOP) called for bombing the primary target visually if we could see the target. Gene Willms was a cool dude in combat. He was a highly successful bomb aimer and we felt confident of real success on this mission. From the IP we could see the primary target real well. However, after turning at the IP and heading for the primary target, it became obscurred from our view due to scattered cloud cover below us.

It was too late to begin a bomb run by radar on the secondary target. Radar runs took longer and the Micky (radar) operator couldn't line up on the secondary target after we left the visual IP. Looking out of the nose of the B-17 over Gene's shoulder, I spotted the tertiary target which was visual. I pointed it out to him. Gene immediately placed his cross hairs on the aiming point and the pilot was asked to center the PDI (Pilots Direction Indicator). This was used by the pilot for following the Bombardier's course to the release point determined by the Norden bomb sight.

Word was quickly passed by the Air Commander, Bob Tuttle, over VHF radio to the rest of our crews that we were on the bomb run and for them to tighten up the formation and prepare to open bomb doors for the drop. The word came over interphone from Gene, 'BOMBS AWAY' and the Red Red flares went up from our plane. The entire formation dropped their bombs on this signal.

After bombs away we pulled off to the left, climbed 500 feet to get out of the flak that was coming up all around us and exploding generally at out bombing altitude. We headed for the Rally Point. At the RP, we had been briefed to take the lead of the Task Force bomber stream on the way home. We made the RP on course and on time. There was much confusion due to the combat situation. Over the target the flak was heavy, persistent and annoying. German fighter pilots didn't fly into the Berlin flak with us. They waited outside the flak area, regrouped and got into position to hit us again on our withdrawal from the target area.

Once on our way home from the heavily defended target area of Berlin we felt better. We had hit our target as briefed and still had four fans turning. We kept in good tight formation for defense against any further fighter attacks. The fighters pretty much left our formation alone as we were flying good and tight that day. They picked on the individual stragglers who had lost engines over Berlin and couldn't keep up with the rest of their formation. Stragglers were always in deep trouble from individual fighter attacks as German pilots were interested in making a confirmed 'score' and chalking up another B-17 to their credit. They obviously preferred to take on wounded stragglers rather than hitting large well defended formations.

We returned to base, landed, and had our shot of whiskey before debriefing. We were the lucky ones on this mission of March 6, 1944. Our Group lost only one aircraft on that day. The total loss for the 8th Air Force was sixty-nine bombers for a loss rate that day of 10 percent. The fighters lost eleven aircraft with pilots for a loss rate of 1.33 percent. Of the 701 men aboard the aircraft lost in action, 229 were killed or missing, 411 were taken prisoner, and thirteen who came down in the low countries evaded capture. Another eight were picked up from the North Sea and another forty landed in Sweden. In the aircraft that returned to their bases, three men were killed and twenty-nine wounded. Four who bailed out over Holland were taken prisoner. Our baptism of fire over Big 'B' had begun.

Wing damage.

Front:
Henry Dayton, Pilot;
George Benton, CP;
Howard Jones, N; John
Reichardt, B.
Back:
Don Keohane FE; Charles
Loomis, LWG; Harry
Schneider, RO-G; Robert
Hurley, TTG; Charles De
Arman, RWG; Richard
Mooers, BTG

Dayton's Crew - Plus Two

by Don Keohane
Flight Engineer, 570th Squadron, **The Skillet**

APRIL 13, 1944. On this date we are flying our third mission, the Group's eighty-sixth mission. We are new "kids on the block" and three in a row is an exceptional request. This is the one mission that our crew will never forget — the Messerschmitt aircraft factory at Augsburg, Germany. At the briefing when the target was announced someone in the back of the room, in an unconscious reaction, exclaimed, "the dreadful Augsburg". After the detailed briefing the crews drifted to the trucks and jeeps that taxied them to their assigned airplanes. The Dayton Crew, that's how we were usually tagged and we loved it, arrived at number 42 hardstand before 5 am. We were met by the crew-chief, Athanasis Cummings and several of his ground personnel. Richard Luke, the hardstand armorer and his assistant were checking the ten five hundred pound bombs. John Reichardt joined them with a watchful eye. Each of us went about our individual pre-flight duties. The mood at the hardstands before a mission was generally solemn. Chuck, "Moe", "Tex" and Bob loaded a few extra boxes of 50 caliber ammunition into the plane. The Luftwaffe usually made an appearance on such deep penetrations. Harry checked his radio frequencies. John placed some extra flak jackets around his and Howard's positions. Howard studied his mission maps; they looked like an "AAA" tour route. Henry and George had begun their pre-ignition check-list. The sun was peeking over the horizon. It was a chilly English morning and a thin frost covered the ground. High in the sky the green flare from the control tower indicated the mission was 'on'.

I positioned myself behind the pilot's seats and participated in the pre-takeoff check list. The planes on the east perimeter track appeared in perfect silhouette. "Pop" Cummings pulled the chocks and elevator locks himself. He stepped to the side of his favorite plane, *The Skillet,* and gave Henry his best military salute. This B-17 was a part of "Pop" and soon it would be a part of every man in Henry Dayton's crew. From this mission forward, we would realize that our part in this war was a combination of men and machines and that the men on the ground, no matter what their job might be, deserved much more credit than they received for their effort in putting 504 heavy bombers over Germany that day. As we taxied out to the perimeter track, towards the East-West runway, we were greeted by the local farm families that surrounded the air base. They knew when the base was readying for a mission. There was no way to disguise the crescendo of 180 B-17s engines as the takeoff time approached. The 'neighbors' were mostly elderly and their faces reflected the pain and sorrow of the war. They waved to each plane as it past by their vantage point along the hedgerows. As they waved they gave the Winston Churchill — "V" for victory sign. I'm sure that they knew from past experiences that they might not see the same planes or faces ever again. We appreciated their heartfelt expressions for a safe return. This was a different method of war.

The combat wing formed perfectly and we proceeded towards the continent of Europe. As we crossed the coast the German "AA" gunners greeted us with several bursts of flak. We were at 21,000 feet altitude, in a cold gray sky. Richard Mooers, from the ball turret, gave us a running report of the ground activity Some very useful information for the de-briefing session upon return to the base. Bob Hurley, from the tail position, confirmed some of "Moe's" sightings, without the Boston accent. The search for enemy fighters was a constant vigil from every crew position. We scanned the sky looking for that small dot that would suddenly grow into a ME 109 or a FW 190. Often John in the nose would report a flash from an "AA" ground position and then momentarily see the flak burst around us.

As we approached Augsburg the weather was clear. The bomb-run would be visual. Shortly we were turning toward the target. Henry turned the plane's control to John, the bombardier, for the bomb-run. About the moment John opened the bomb doors all hell broke loose. The flak was all about us. At the morning briefing we were informed that 170 AA batteries protected Augsburg. They had the facts. The sky was filled with puffs of black smoke. Chuck Loomis, from the waist, reported he could taste the stuff. Reports of flak penetration came from every position. From my position, in the top turret, I could actually see the skin of "927" being pierced by the shrapnel. Our number 2 engine's gas tank took a heavy hit. Moe from the ball turret reported that the gas was pouring out of the left wing. Henry ordered him out of the turret, knowing if a shot were to be fired into the spray of gas we would have "bought the farm". When we were on the bomb run I could see the bombs dropping from the planes above and to the side of us. Then I felt a sudden slight lift and I knew John had done the job we came to do.

George reported that number 2 gas gauge had stabilized at the 1/4 mark reading. Number 3 engine was losing power, the supercharger quit working. The number 4 engine was showing a high temperature reading and it was dropping oil pressure. We began to lag behind the Group. Another B-17 came off the target hurt and we teamed-up but we could not keep abreast and we fell further behind. Engine number 4 began to vibrate violently. At this time Henry came on the intercom. He had a big decision to make. Henry asked Chuck to assess the damage in the rear of the plane. Chuck reported that there were many holes and tears in the fuselage — some the size of a nickel, others as large as half-dollars. All the crew members were unhurt, although "Pop's" *Skillet* was hurting.

Switzerland was about one-hundred miles away. The easy decision would have been to turn towards Lake Constance but Henry asked Howard for a compass reading for home. We had come off the target at 24,000 feet altitude and now we were striving to maintain 19,000 feet. The right wing was flopping like a diving board. Number four engine was running away and completely out of control. George was trying to feather the prop but the oil pressure appeared to be too low. Finally, by being persistent, George got number 4 prop to feather. The right wing calmed down and we all breathed a sigh of relief. I transferred all the gas from engine number 4 to the other tanks; but kept number 2 tank below the 1/4 full reading. Without number 3 engine at full power and number 4 engine dead we were having trouble maintaining altitude. I checked the main fuse panel and found that the fuse to number 3 supercharger had blown. I replaced the fuse and number 3 engine regained full power. Henry had a smile a mile wide.

The Skillet continued to limp home. John sat close to the nose looking for enemy fighters or our little friends to escort us home but neither appeared. Howard's calculations followed the return route as briefed. We held altitude at 16,000 feet. West of Brussels we caught another burst of flak. It ruptured the oxygen system in the waist of the plane. Henry decided to drop to 12,000 feet altitude. The fuel capacity that remained was marginal. Our luck was running out. Henry and George agreed that we should prepare to ditch in the English Channel or land at the first field of opportunity; if we cleared the English coast. Harry was instructed to send out a "Mayday" signal when we crossed the Belgium coast line.

It was about this time that Henry went on the intercom to all positions. He requested that the whole crew join him in prayer. He recited the twenty-third Psalm:

"The Lord is my shepherd; I shall not want. He maketh me to lie down in green pastures: He leadeth me beside the still waters. He restoreth my soul: He leadeth me in the paths of righteousness for His name's sake..."

Henry recited the complete Psalm. The crew was refreshed by his action. This added a new dimension to our pilot. We crossed the channel at less than 2,000 feet altitude. Harry's "Mayday" alert was in effect.

We spotted a P-47 fighter base. The runway was clear and we took advantage of it. We made a straight in approach. Upon hitting the runway number 4 propeller fell off the engine. We taxied off the main runway and number 3 engine quit. Number 1 and number 2 engine gas tanks were almost dry. It was a very eventful mission.

Back at the 390th they had listed us as "missing". By actual count we had over 200 flak holes. "Pop" was not happy with us but he treated us like a father and his prodigal sons.

We flew our next mission on April 19th. The 5 days rest was appreciated. "Pop's" *Skillet* was repaired by the men of the 458th Sub-Depot. The damage was too extensive to be done at number 42 hardstand. *The Skillet* was back in service on May 29th and Dayton's crew made the trip to Leipzig, Germany. We flew 13 of our 32 missions in *The Skillet* and that's a love affair.

The Dayton crew may have been typical of many and most heavy bomber crews, however, I believe we shared a special ingredient in having Athanasis "Pop" Cummings as our crew-chief and the use of his beloved *Skillet* to complete the combination of "10 plus 2." Like so many other bomber crews, we passed through once.

I'm proud I was a "Dayton crewmember" in the 390th Bomb Group, 570th Squadron of the Eighth Air Force. I'm sure you will agree that the world is a better place because they served together in the cold skies, very far from home, in a new kind of warfare that is now obsolete; the four engine B-17 and B-24. I trust that my son will never have to go to war, but if he were to; I wish he be a man like Henry Dayton or be able to serve with a man like Henry Dayton.

Probably the most widely used picture of B-17s and their protective fighters was taken from the waist position of a 390th plane.

Arthanasis "Pop" Cummings.

Crew Chief's Description of *The Skillet's* Missions

by Arthanasis *"Pop"* Cummings

Crew Chief, 570th Squadron, The Skillet

YOU asked if the old *Skillet* (B-17) saw the war through — man she not only saw the war through (90 missions) but after VE Day she flew all over the continent hauling POWs. They put flooring in the bomb bays so that they could haul thirty POWs a trip. The ground crew got in on these trips since they only flew pilot, co-pilot, navigator, radio man and one ground crew. You may be sure I was with old *Skillet* every opportunity I had. Sure was great to get over there and see the results of the "fly boys" work. Then to top it off we got to fly to the USA with the planes. Since we had two planes on our hardstand, the Engineering officer asked me if I had any choice. I told him that if I didn't get to

52

fly on 927 there would be hell to pay all around. I was assigned to old 927. We had to put up with all manner of insults as the last time the old girl came home after three months AWOL she had sixty some patches on the left wing which was still the original wing — one unpainted bomb bay door and all the stabilizers were new and unpainted — so you can well imagine what others had to say about her.

The day the Group flew their 300th mission she was the only painted wagon among all those silver jobs. They formed low and flew over the base — you can imagine how she looked up there among all those silver jobs. So all in all she saw the war and came home with 90 missions — 1,100 hours (better than 800 of those hours were combat hours). We figure the taxpayers got their money's worth out of her.

While I'm still on the subject, you might like to know that of the Group's 301 missions we had 273 missions done by planes from our hardstand. There were only two abortions, one for oxygen and the other 'cockpit' trouble. There were six that failed to take off; one for carburetor failure and the other five taxiing into mud, snow, etc. So all in all it was quite a "clam bake."

The above was included in a letter from Arthanasis "POP" Cummings before his death in the early '50s'.

Henry Dayton with "Pop" Cummings.

Back:
Roy Shultz, CC-G; Mel
Adams, RO-G; M. L.
Moody, BTG; Ray Floyd,
WG; Emil Kosich, WG;
Roland Stottlemeyer, Tail
TG.
Front:
Bob Longardner, Pilot;
Harry Senior, CP; Bill
Robinson, N; William
South. B.

A Replacement Crew's
First Missions

by William J. Robinson
Navigator, 570th Squadron, G. I. Wonder

WHEN I was assigned to the Longardner
crew as navigator at Alexandria, Louisiana, it completed
the make-up of the crew. They had been in training for some
time before I arrived. We became a tightly-knit group very
quickly and soon completed training and were sent to
Kearney, Nebraska where we picked up a brand new B-17G.

We flew this plane across the northern Atlantic route
from Newfoundland to Northern Ireland on June 6, 1944.
We did not know that it was D-Day until we neared the Irish
coast and the radio operator picked up an announcement.
We had been told not to break radio silence to report anything that we saw while crossing, and that was the only hint

54

we had of the importance of the day.

After giving up the new B-17, we were escorted through Scotland to England along with other crews who had also flown across, and were assigned to the 390th along with the Clay Perry crew, with whom we had been in training.

We were assigned to the 570th Squadron to *G. I. Wonder,* a B-17F which had been converted to a G. She still had the camouflage paint job while most of the new ships arriving were the bare metal ships.

It took approximately two weeks to complete the special training that taught us the particular things that made the 390th great, especially the very tight formation flying. We were anxious to get started on our tour, though and eagerly awaited our first mission.

JUNE 28, 1944

The C.Q. woke us at 2345 and informed us that we would have breakfast at midnight and briefing at 0100. This was the big day, our first raid after all this time. Our target was to be an underground storage for rocket planes near Paris and we would carry two 2,000 pound bombs. We took off at 0345 and took about three hours to assemble over England and then headed for the target.

We were over almost continuous solid cloud cover. When we were about eight miles from the French coast there was a solid front up to about 40,000 feet. At that point, Colonel Robert O. Good,, who was flying the 390th ship leading the Wing that day, turned around and headed home. It is the policy to not bomb French targets with PFF. Since the front was too much to go through, Col. Good decided to turn back. We got in six hours of "Form One" time.

JUNE 29, 1944

This morning we were awakened at 0045 for breakfast at 0100 and briefing at 0200. This would be our day — I could feel it rolling out of the sack very sleepy.

At briefing we discovered our target was deep in Germany — a synthetic oil refinery south of Leipzig. The whole

Eighth Air Force was hitting various targets around Leipzig, and we were leading them — the 390th leading the whole Air Force — 1750 heavies! We were flying number three in the low squadron — Purple Heart corner. After about two hours of getting into formation after taking off at 0500 we headed out across the North Sea at 20,000 feet. We were at our flight level, 24,000 feet when we lost the undercast that had been below us across the sea. We were then across the Zider Zee in Holland east of Amsterdam. We had on our flak suits, but no flak as yet. I changed from dead reckoning navigation to pilotage in order to watch for the P-47s that were to be our fighter protection. All was pretty quiet, but I was excited and so was everyone else. The interphone was busy constantly.

About three minutes before we were to hit the I.P. I was to tell the Radio Operator to start throwing out chaff. As I was looking all over for the I.P., I saw the lower ball in the squadron lead ship cut loose at about 11 o'clock low. I looked down and there were two ME 109s coming hell bent for election spitting fire. Neither South, the bombardier, nor I got a chance to open up on them before they were by. Flak started bursting all around us and right at our level — they had our height down perfect, but the bursts were off the wing aways. I knelt down on the step below the top of the chin turret and put on my flak helmet. It was now South's plane, we were on the bomb run! I watched the flak off the left wing — each burst coming nearer and nearer in stepping-stone fashion. Then it hit the wing and I crawled up into my flak helmet and started praying, "Keep it away from us."

I was more afraid of it hitting South or I rather than of the ship being knocked down, and I couldn't see how it was going to miss the way each burst crawled up to us closer and closer. And then a ping and we were showered with plexiglass and I prayed even harder. I was afraid that South had been hit so I turned to look, but his hand was all set to salvo the bombs, twenty 250-pounders, so I knew he hadn't been hit. I was afraid to look and see where the flak had hit.

Then it was "Bombs Away," and South had to holler several times over the interphone before Adams, the radio operator, said the bombs were away okay. We rolled over and started our turn to the rally point. I could feel the flak hitting the right wing. Then the tail gunner cried over the interphone that he was hit and the interphone went dead and all was deathly still except the engines purring, or rather alternately roaring and then getting quieter. The pilots were having a rough time staying in formation. We turned on course for home and the flak stopped. I looked back at the target and all I could see was bellows of black smoke rolling up — we must have really hit it.

I looked all around for where the flak had hit our nose — it was right in front of South in the plexiglass. It had broken the silica gell tube. South had a little cut under his right eye, but was okay outside of that. As we flew by Leipzig I could see plenty of flak bursting at our level, but quite far away. When we were a little south of Berlin, I again took up pilotage mixed with looking for fighters, but I was still scared. South punched me a little later and motioned for me to look back at the tail. There was another 109 about 100 yards off shooting at us — and I dived for my helmet again and was able to get off a few bursts as one fighter flew by.

The interphone came on about an hour later and we discovered that the tail gunner had been hit in his earphone and his head and ear were torn, but Floyd, the waist gunner, had bandaged him and he was back at the gun. Both of the first 109s that hit us had blown up. A P-51 got one, but they didn't see who got the other. A B-17 behind us blew up in flames and our number 5 ship had an engine knocked out. A piece of flak had bounced off our substitute waist gunner's flak suit. The radio room had a large hole in it. The bomb bays were full of holes.

On the way back we saw B-24s on a bomb run. Our two formations nearly collided. We saw others headed home and the fighters out there looked wonderful. There were many bursts of smoke with trails winding down to earth — I couldn't figure out what they were. The number 5 ship in our squadron had another engine failure. The prop was just windmilling. The ship flying the right wing off us had one engine feathered. They dropped their lower ball to lighten the load. Number 4 in the lead squadron was gone — two engines shot out. We saw 5 parachutes going down just before the Zider Zee, but that was all. The trip back to the channel was terribly long, but it was at last over and we started down, still safe. We leveled off at 400 feet and were soon home. Number 2 wasn't to be seen nor number 5. Three planes gone in our group of 13. We landed after 8 hours and 35 minutes — what a day's work! Both number 2 and number 5 had crash landed okay and were safe, but Moody, pilot of number 4 lead, and his crew had not returned. They took our tail gunner to the hospital.

Adams told the story of seeing the flak hit the bomb bays and decided he'd better sit down in his own seat, and then a big piece of flak came through and knocked out the interphone and he then decided they were after him. The flak had been intense all around us and we had about 50 holes in the ship. The right wing had taken a beating. Moody, our ball turret gunner, had climbed out of the ball and asked Adams (he was so scared he was whispering Adams said) if he should stay in the ball with no interphone. Adams showed him the big hole in the radio room and Moody immediately got back into the ball. Flak hit the ball twice. Everything else was okay, but everyone had been scared to death.

We discovered today that the tail gunner was okay but had also been hit in the neck. Moody, the pilot, had ditched 10 miles from the Holland coast and was picked up by Air-Sea Rescue, but Jerry strafed their ship and killed the ball turret gunner and the navigator. Official bombing results were "good" for the 390th. It had been considered a tough mission. Number one was over — how could we stand 34 more?

JULY 6, 1944

After several days rest we were briefed the last two days for the same target — a battery of four 155-mm. guns south of Bologne, 500 yards from the coast. Both times the missions were scrubbed.

We were awakened this morning at 0130 for breakfast at 0200 and briefing at 0300. The target was to be the oil refinery at Bremen and there were plenty of flak guns protecting it. We just finished navigators briefing when they said the mission was scrubbed, but another was planned. We sat around and soon discovered our new target was in the Pas de Calaise area — some flying bomb installations north of Abbeyville. Abbeyville is noted for accurate flak — a short mission but certain to be rough.

We took off at 0630 and assembled and left the English coast at 0854. At 0915 we were at Abbeyville where we saw the first flak bursting behind us. The sky was full of big bombers, but no fighters, either ours or Jerry's. I've never seen so many bombers in the air at once! The whole Eighth Air Force was hitting this little area. Targets were everywhere and bombs were bursting all over. The flak stayed with us until after the turn to the rally point, but not so thick or accurate. I didn't see much of it, only that aimed at other groups. I worked like everything to keep my mind busy and wasn't half as scared as Leipzig. The plane was hit on top of number 1 cowling, in the bomb bay, and a few holes in the tail, wing and stabilizer. One piece sheared off some rivets from the main fuel tank — nothing serious. We encountered no fighters and were over enemy territory only 20 or 25 minutes, but that was plenty!

We saw one B-17 spin-in on fire, and two others explode. Davis, on his 30th mission, above us (we were number 2, low) was hit bad. They had to feather their number 2 engine after it caught fire. They lost their hydralic fluid, so they had no brakes. They had read in *Stars and Stripes* about a crew urinating in the hydralic system and getting enough pressure for brakes. They tried it and it worked.

A piece of flak missed Davis' foot by 6 inches. He landed plenty scared and glad it was over.

The afternoon mission was scrubbed, but everyone is to be in bed by 7 tonight. I believe tomorrow or the next day will see us invading Pas de Calaise.

JULY 11, 12, 13, 1944

Three times we visited the same target, Munich, Germany, attempting to hit the BMW motor works which produce jet motors for the rocket bombs. Each time the sky was overcast and bombing was done by PFF. The flak was intense, but not very accurate on all the missions, and we received only a few hits. The missions were all 10 hours long, and we sweated out the gas supply every time. We carried 500 pound bombs and incendiaries mostly.

In the third raid number 2 of the lead squadron was hit in the control surfaces and driven into the tail of the lead ship. The props completely hacked off the tail turret, and the nose punctured the vertical stabilizer. Number 2 started down out of control, but recovered and got back okay. The lead ship stayed in formation and also got home okay.

JULY 14, 1944

The fourth straight day found us really sweating. Were we going back to Munich? The flak there was terrific and if it was a clear day they would really try to get us. The undercast is all that had saved us before. Well, we were a spare and the target very secret. We were to drop parachute containers of guns and supplies to French guerrillas in an area east of Bordeaux. We were going in at 18,000 feet and down to 500 feet over the target and back home at 18,000. If there was any flak near the target we would get it — all calibers! We broke out of the undercast before the target and found Southern France a very beautiful place. We found the target area and flew around in search of a triangle of fire which was to indicate the field where the guerrillas awaited our supplies. We soon found it and there were people everywhere waving to us and all seemed very happy to see all those bombers — 385 of us — I imagine very few people enjoyed seeing us. We came in 500 feet over the ground, and South had asked if I wanted to toggle out the load, so I did, and it landed in the field okay. It really made me feel good and plenty close to the war — giving guns to the French who were waging their own little war. Their guerrillas had held back a division of Panzers from the beachhead. They had so disrupted transportation in France that two German divisions had to get to the beachhead by bike.

JULY 18, 1944

After a 48-hour pass our next target was Kiel, Germany — an overwater flight until we were near the target. The target was an experimental station for the flying bombs, it was completely overcast so we dropped bombs by PFF. Flak was heavy over the target. It burst all around us for 16 minutes and we also had some at Helgoland. The ship was not hit bad though, but number 4 lost its power and was just supplying enough power to pull itself. Perry's plane had to land by auto pilot as his control lines had been hit. No planes were lost and only 6 ships damaged, we learned the next day.

—England, 1944

Our crew survived the tour and *G. I. Wonder* survived the war. She must have served at least three crews, or possibly more, well.

Bob Longardner tells me that he found *G. I. Wonder* in one of the large groups of "war wearies" awaiting destruction after the war. He shed a tear for us all.

Canisters of supplies and weapons drop in a designated area for use by the French Maquis. The Maquis can be seen gathering the canisters as soon as they land to load them into the trucks gathered to carry them away.

Richard H. Perry in 1944

One Mission Without Bombs

by Richard H. Perry

Pilot, 570th Squadron

ONE of the 43 missions I flew with the 390th Bomb Group did not involve the dropping of destructive bombs. On 25 June 1944, we were briefed to drop containers full of munitions to the French Maquis in Southern France in an area known as Area "5".

Our planes were loaded with 300 pound containers. These containers were ruggedly designed to withstand considerable shock. Each container contained many machine guns, ammunition and other material useful to the Maquis who were making a gallant effort at resisting the well equipped Germans.

I was a Command and Formation Officer in one of the

eleven B-17s from the 390th B.G. that joined 25 planes from other bases. We hit the continent at about 20,000 feet and after flying past Paris, still in the hands of the Germans, we let down to minimum altitude (near 3,000 ft.). We were very excited to find markers and bonfires exactly as briefed. We made our pass over the marked field dropping the containers as planned. The ball turret and tail gunners reported that our drop was exactly on target. As we pulled up and turned to the right I could see people running from under trees beside the field where the containers dropped.

After reorganizing the formation and climbing to higher altitude we returned to our home base. We obtained a great deal of satisfaction upon landing and learning that a message had been received before we were back saying, "Supplies from American planes received in good order. Many thanks. When may we expect you again?"

Crews in briefing session for mission of 6 August 1944.

Front:
Harry O'Hanesian, RWG.
Back:
Will Richarz, RO-G;
"Hap" Hallek, WG;
Angelo Martin, BTG.

A Mission

by *Wilbert H. Richarz*

Radio Operator-Gunner, 570th Squadron, **Cocaine Bill**

IT is usually very early — about a quarter to three to be explicit — when the night C.Q. comes in to awaken us. He stands there in the dark, flashlight in hand, as he somewhat apologetically calls for Myers, our engineer. At Myers' unintelligible grumble he sonorously begins to read the news that falls so heavily on our sleep-prejudiced ears: "Breakfast at three, briefing at four" he says and his face lighted to a ghostly grimace by the glare of his flashlight seems to my fogged vision to be wreathed in a triumphant smirk. After a few moments hesitation in which he seems to either savor the telling effect of his words or to be sure we are going to get up — I've never figured out

65

which — he snaps on the light and quickly exits.

We lie there for awhile, still groggy, squinting, and wondering at the miraculous change that has come about in our G.I. sack. It has become a haven of warmth and comfort — no longer is it cold and lumpy. Somebody across the barracks rolls over noisily and with an interrogatory grumble says something to the effect which when interpreted can be put on paper as "Why in the hell can't they fight this war in the daytime?"A movement here, a groan there, and we slowly begin to come to life, to reluctantly emerge. Snake lights up his ever-present cigarette. Hap, the ball turret gunner, comes out of bed almost fully dressed — including his socks — then it's out of the sack for me, a quick wash, shave, and on to the mess hall.

Breakfast ordinarily holds no appeal for me, especially early in the morning — early being defined as any time before nine, but fresh eggs sunnyside up go good on a cold misty morning — if you're awake? I'm never awake, but it's always cold and misty and after that bone-chilling ride to the mess hall I look forward to my eggs. The mess hall scene is one of sleepy-eyed crewmen eating their eggs and each thinking how nice it would be to have such a breakfast at a reasonable hour — and each with the resigned look of those who realize that you can't have everything.

After breakfast trucks take us to the briefing room and by that time we are almost chilled to consciousness. By four o'clock we are assembled with the rest of the gunners in the long narrow curved-ceilinged gunners' briefing room, at the front of which is a black-cloaked war map. On one side of the map is a blackboard on which is given the flight formation plan for the day, engine starting time, take-off time, etc., while on the other side of the room the briefing officers sit along the wall, waiting for their cue to step before us — each with his bit of information to be tossed to our hungry, eager minds. It is amazing how really eager one becomes in a game where their life can be the pawn. As we sit there, waiting expectantly, some nervously, some still too sleepy to really be interested, we find ourselves trying to guess what the target of the day will be — what secrets the sombre-cloaked war map will disclose when the curtains are thrown back and the course to the target marked there in black ribbon revealed.

When everyone is seated and all late-comers have been ushered in, the briefing officer formally begins the briefing with the command "hats off, cigarettes out, attention to roll call." After roll call the tension runs high and we all sit up expectantly. The curtains over the war map are thrown back and amid the "ohs" and ahs," a few derisive whistles, and general awe, we see the course of black ribbon that leads to the target of the day. If it is a notoriously rough target or a particularly deep penetration, the more whistles. The newer gunners unconsciously regard the general reception of the target as significant. The other briefing officers then take the stage and each in turn gives us the facts covered by his department that are considered necessary for the success of the mssion. Such things as weather, rendezvous points, time over target, and most important of all — flak — the number of guns and where to expect them. The uppermost question in our minds is always "how about the flak?" Other information such as the number of fighter escort, enemy fighters expected, and anything else considered important is given and then we are shown pictures of the target and course on target charts. At the end of the briefing the officer in charge calls for the radio operators and while the rest of the boys go to dress I stay with the other static-chasers to receive additional information on the communications of the day and to draw my "flimsy." A flimsy being a small case containing all the necessary information on communications — call signs of stations, frequencies, weather information, and navigational radio aids to be used — all of which is a very important part of the mission's preparation.

On leaving the briefing room we go to the dressing room, draw our equipment, and start to dress. This dressing for a high altitude combat mission is something that even the knights in armor of King Arthur's day would gape at. Starting from the inside out you have G.I. longies on and heavy socks — over which go electric flying pants and vest and shoes. Then comes the heavy flying pants and jacket, heavy boots, and winter flying helmet. Thus decked out — parachute, parachute harness, and Mae West life preserver in one hand and flimsy in the other — I'm ready to go out to the ships. Half of the trucks go to the right side of the field and the other half go to the left side. The problem is to get on the truck that is going to the side of the field that our ship is on. When a truck pulls up it produces a scene reminiscent of a Chicago fish market — "Which way you going' — left or right?" "Hey Joe, hard-stand 46" — "Pull 'er up a little" — "Help me up Mac." With all their cumbersome flying clothing on everyone looks like clumsy little old men trying to bundle themselves and their kit bags into the truck. Once

Ships line up along the perimeter taxi way awaiting their turn to take off on mission of 28 September 1944.

in the truck the driver takes over and despite the confusion in the back of the truck, he always seems to deposit the right guys at the right ships.

The first thing we do when we get to the ship is to place our equipment in our respective positions — the second thing is to clean our guns. Each man cleans his own guns and puts them in. The guns are coated with oil and this must be wiped off of all parts to prevent freezing at high altitude. Those guns are mighty cold so early in the morning.

After the guns are in, the ship is pre-flighted. I check all the radio equipment, the antennaes, the emergency equipment, and the first-aid equipment. Hap checks his lower-ball turret, Snake checks his upper turrett and curses his guns because he is usually still putting them in, Ange, the waist gunner, and the bombardier fuse the bombs, the co-pilot checks the oxygen supply, Ennis the navigator checks his navigation equipment, the pilot checks the ship in general, and the ground crew pulls the props thru. All this while Dixie is in the tail busy building himself an airborne pillbox with flak suits.

By about seven o'clock it is time to start the engines. Everyone gets in the ship — Dixie, Hap, Ange, and I are in the radio room, and as the pilot starts the engines I fill in the preliminary information on my log. One by one the engines roar to life and rise to an ever increasing crescendo under the expert hands of Jack and Tex. The ship strains forward and seems to be impatient to be off. In a few minutes our big ship lumbers forward to take its place on the taxi strip, in the long line of ships waiting to take off. Big silver birds of prey lined up in a seemingly endless line in the twilight of early dawn, as one by one they take to the air in quick succession. We move slowly down the taxi strip, take our place on the take-off strip, and we are on our way. The engines roar and tremble with power, the ship strains forward, and we speed down the runway. Gradually, as we gain speed, the strain seems lifted, the engines quieter, the ride smoother, and we realize we are airborne. We are free of the bonds of the earth and the nose of our ship points skyward — the realm of the not-so-mythical wild blue yonder.

We circle the field in wide climbing turns and the ground fades through the clouds as we climb above them. Above the clouds we find the sunrise waiting for us and I find myself thrilled somehow to think that we've met the sun half-way. At 10,000 feet Tex calls us on interphone to tell us to put on our oxygen masks. The putting on of the oxygen mask always seems significant of the fact that we are really on our way.

We join our group formation at the pre-determined place and altitude and the lead ship leads us to where we are to rendezvous with the other ships. What a sight it is to see those hundreds of silver ships, all gathering in uniform formations one group behind the other. When the formations are completely formed, the caravan heads out over the channel. I record the time we pass over the coast in my log — everyone is in their position and we are Germany-bound.

If it is a nice day the clouds below us are dazzling white against the endless sky and the pink tint of the rising sun colors the horizon to the various shades of red and gold. There are ships all around us, above us and below us, all in orderly procession and gleaming bright. The channel below is a solid bank of blue when seen through occasional breaks in the clouds.

Our arrival over the enemy coast is announced when Tex calls out over the interphone, "Flak ahead." I record the time over the coast in my log and we gaze with no surprise, but casual interest at the black, angry-looking puffs that appear as if by magic off our wing. The flak over the coast is rarely accurate and we grow to regard it as a futile but defiant gesture on the part of Jerry.

Once into enemy territory everyone is on the alert — Dixie in the tail, Ange in the waist, Hap in the ball, and Snake in the top turret. The navigator in the nose is busy checking his course and keeping the pilot informed. Jack and Tex have their hands full keeping our ship in formation and the bombardier keeps watch out the front. Occasional "oxygen checks" are about the only bits of conversation over the interphone. We have the oxygen checks every ten minutes or so on the way to the target just to be sure no one has been overcome by lack of oxygen. The bombardier usually calls the check by calling "oxygen check" and this is the signal for the crew to call in, starting from the tail. The answers are usually the same each time and somehow rather typical of each individual. Dixie drawls, "Okay — I guess," Hap, trying to sound pathetic, says "Okay — so far." Angelo's voice comes over the interphone in a business-like way as he says, "Waist okay — radio okay." Ange usually answers for me as I am usually busy copying my log and listening to both the radio and the interphone simultaneously on my two-way headset. Snake always sounds tight, though trying hard to be casual. The navigator's hurried "Navigator okay" makes his sound as if he were being disturbed from his work — as he invariably is. The co-pilot calls out, "Cock-pit okay" in his laconic tone of voice and we all settle back and wait for the next one. The panorama of Germany unfolds beneath us.

As we near the target and flak is sighted ahead we put on our flak suits — a heavy cumbersome affair that hooks over the shoulders and hangs like an apron protecting both front and back from the neck to just below the crotch. It's made of steel plates fitted together in a heavy cloth and weighs about 70 lb. I look back at Ange and laugh to myself at the picture he makes standing there in his modern armor and looking very much like a baby tank. On top of all of this goes the flak-helmet and we are as ready as we can get for the barrage that we must fly through.

When we start down the bomb-run to the target, our "little friends" — the fighter escort — pull away from the flak and it seems that as if by some unseen, unheard signal a million things begin to happen at once. The sky is filled with black puffs of flak, talk flows quickly and tersely over the interphone — the pilot fights to keep the ship level for the bomb release and time has changed from a slowly passing doldrum to a speeding, racing thing, while the bomb-run becomes the longest ten minutes imaginable, a ten minutes of sheer fantasy — as unreal as a highly imaginative movie — a ten minutes in which the physical discomforts of a few minutes before are forgotten. You forget how your oxygen mask has been clutching your face like a live thing, daring you to tear it off and try to face the lethal lack of oxygen of high altitude without it. You forget the cold of 60 below, the all but unbearable weight of the flak suit, how tired you are — you forget these things and yet remember their necessity. You remember that in the beauty around you lies the proof that death is also there and I find myself struck by the thought that how often it is that we find beauty and death so close together. The condensation trails that stream out behind the engines like flurries of new-blown snow are evidence of the intense cold that point as accusing fingers our course to the enemy guns below. The tracings of the fighter escort planes as they range across the trackless sky in watchful vigilance over our formation are indicative that enemy fighters are expected. Enemy fighters that can come and go in a matter of seconds leaving havoc and destruction behind.

As I'm throwing out "chaff" that is supposed to confuse the Jerry aiming devices, I can hear the interphone dialogue of quick excited talk — "Flak at 3 o'clock level," "Fighters passing over," "B-17 going down at 9 o'clock," and as I look out my window to watch the ship go down I'm greeted by a sky made dirty with the splotches of black flak; there off the left wing a little low to us is the stricken ship going down in wide spirals with flame and smoke pouring out behind. We watch for the "chutes" that we hope will surely come. Up ahead a "fort" receives a direct hit and blows up in a huge orange bellow of flame — we expect no chutes from that one. The bomb-bay doors swing open and soon the bombardier calls "bombs away" — the ship lurches at the release and I check to see that all the bombs are away. Our formation swings off the bomb run and an unspoken sigh of relief is felt throughout the ship. It is very much like being able to pull away from an aggressive opponent in a boxing match who is getting much too hot to handle.

We head for home — fewer in number perhaps than when we started, but leaving behind us a job well done — a mass of smoke and flame where before stood our "target for today." The tension lifted, the interphone fairly burbles with the excited talk of the crew as they recall what they've seen — how close the flak was — how lucky we were today! To quote an English phrase "We've had it" for today and we are eager to get back to the base, to put our feet on the ground again.

All the way back to the base we sweat out the weather and I get the latest weather reports from the ground station. By the time we reach the English coast the ground is hardly visible and this means an hour or so of circling the field waiting for a chance to land. We watch for the flares that come from the ships with wounded aboard. When our ship finally gets permission to land all of us in the back of the ship are slightly sick — Dixie and I just sit and look at each other. When Jack has landed the ship and taxied back to the hard-stand we find the ground crew waiting to meet us. They greet us with a casually spoken, "How was it?" and we answer, trying to be equally as casual, "Not bad." Together we count the holes in the ship and amid the jokes and bantering air we feel that the ground crew is almost as glad to see us back as we are to be back. We take our guns out, clean them, re-oil them, and replace them in the racks in readiness for the next mission. By this time there is usually a truck waiting to take us back to the dressing room. We shed our flying equipment and then go to interrogation.

At interrogation the first thing we do is to get our refreshment — Dixie, Tex, Snake, Jack, Hap, Ennis, and Ange — in fact everyone but me — get their double shot of whiskey — I mentioned Dixie first because he always takes

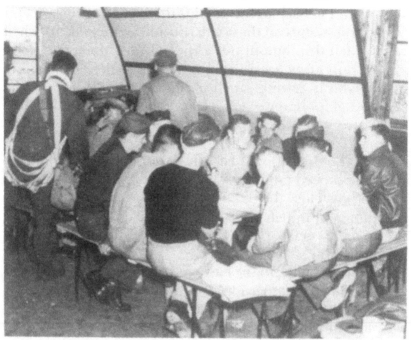

Intelligence officer takes a crew's statement about the mission after their return.

mine too. I grab a doughnut and take my "Flimsy" to the communications department. After the "refreshment" we have our interrogation, which consists of having an intelligence officer question us about the mission — what we did, what we saw, and everything which might be helpful to the intelligence department in their trying to out-guess the Jerry. After interrogation we are officially through with the mission for today. We get on trucks and go to the mess hall for supper. It's been a long day, but in completing another day of war we are just that much closer to going home.

—*England, 1944*

A Time I Remember

by Wilbert H. Richarz

THE day before the mission we had corned beef for lunch — semi-congealed faded pink and mottled gray chunks of indeterminate origin. I still think of it as dogfood and since I still blame it for my subsequent condition later that night I still won't eat it.

By midnight I was too sick to care much about anything except the impending decision. If we were designated to fly the upcoming mission should I go ahead and try to tough it out or should I cancel out and go on sick call? If I tried to fly I knew I would be hard pressed to hold my own even if I made considerable improvement in the next two hours. If I cancelled out I knew that I would most likely have to make up the mission with another crew and in that regard I was faced with the unwritten rule that we all tried to live by. Always fly with your own crew. As crew members we knew each other very well, perhaps better than anyone would ever know us for the rest of our lives, and we knew on what we could depend and on what we could not. No one wanted to fly with another crew. So, when the alert call came I staggered out.

The briefing was ominous — Giessen again. The pre-flight preparation was almost overwhelming, especially the on-loading of 14 boxes of chaff — big cardboard boxes filled with small bundles of tinsel strips. This was the stuff that, upon the radio command "Rainy Day," the radio operator dispensed through a small port located low on the left wall of the radio room behind the chair. The objective was to confuse the enemy radar and thus protect us from the flak.

By the time we were over the continental coast I felt no

better and had even acquired a corking headache to add to my problems. Fortunately, things were relatively quiet and it was a beautiful bright sunlit day at 26,000 feet so I just sat at the radio table in a stupor and hoped that no further demands would be made upon me. But, then things began to get rough. We began to be buffeted by flak and we got the "Rainy Day" call. "God," I thought, "How can I possibly get all that stuff from all those boxes through that one little hole the way I feel." Then, after I managed to put my flak vest on, about 75 pounds of small steel plates in a kind of two-piece cape, and my huge flak helmet, which was made big enough to go over the headphones, I felt like I was going to collapse from the sheer weight of it all and never get up.

I laboriously opened up the first box, got down on my knees behind the radio chair, opened the port and started feeding the bundles into the opening. The slipstream sucked them out where they broke open and the strips scattered. The flak was thumping all around us and the plane was pitching up and down and wallowing from side to side. It was obvious that the flak gunners had us bracketed. Several pieces of flak ricocheted around the radio room and one of them about the size of an egg came to rest on the radio table. I remember thinking that it was a tough way to collect a war souvenir, and so much for chaff as a flak deterrent.

The combination of my kneeling head-down position, my being overbalanced by the heavy helmet and the motion of the aircraft really got to me. I thought "The hell with it." I had to stand up, get rid of the weight and get some more oxygen. I struggled to my feet, dumped the helmet and pulled the flak vest jettison tab. The vest separated into two pieces at the shoulder and fell to the floor. I switched to 100% oxygen, leaned forward with one hand on the table and the other on the back of the chair, and hung there like a skid row derelict.

After a minute or two I felt enough better to raise my head and look out of the small left side window. At first it didn't register but then I noticed that the plane off our left wing was out of formation. Instead of being just behind us in the overlapping wing position, it was slightly ahead of us and drifting away as if out of control. As I concentrated on what I saw, flak bursts, close enough that I could see the orange flame centers, began to appear in a tracking pattern just ahead of the aircraft. First one, and then a second, then a third, all in perfect rhythm and in a direct line leading to it's nose. Then, as if by magic, as if cut by one giant stroke of an invisible knife, the ship was in two pieces. Where an instant before there had been an intact aircraft there was now a wing with the nose section, the engines and the radio room in one piece, and the tail section with the waist attached in the other. Both pieces were suspended in space and time and pointed slightly upward and toward each other as could be expected from a powerful upward cutting stroke.

I could see into the rear of the radio room at a distance of no more than 30 to 40 yards and in the gin-clear air every detail was vividily distinct. The radio operator was on his stomach facing in my direction and I could see that he was desperately trying to pull himself over the raw edges of the torn bulkhead. His oxygen hose was ripped loose and his mike and headset cords were hanging free. His chest pack chute was fastened to his shoulder harness by one hook on his left side and it seemed to be hung up on something beneath him. His gloved hands were clawing at the twisted edges of the bulkhead and his face was contorted with the effort to pull himself free.

A second later gravity took over and the wing over-weighted by the four engines knifed down in a swift clean arc. I watched as if hypnotized as it and its one visible passenger became smaller and smaller as they sped toward the 8,000 foot cloud cover in an ever accelerating rate. Then they were gone. It didn't seem possible that it had really happened.

I looked back up at the tail section and only then had it begun to move in slow sweeping circles, first in one direction and then in the other, like a falling leaf. It took several minutes for it to reach the clouds and the last thing I saw was the 'Square J' tail as it swirled under into its own vortex. There were no chutes. Where there should have been a plane and a ten-man crew there was only empty sky. I was struck dumb. Then I reacted. We could be next. In just seconds I had the flak vest back together and on, the flak helmet in place, and I was trying feverishly to figure out how to hook my chest pack chute onto my harness over the flak vest. Failing in this I dedicated myself to shucking out the chaff — all 14 boxes of it — and went back to work on the radio with enthusiasm. My sickness was cured.

A short time later we made the bomb run and dropped the load. As I leaned out over the bay to check if all the bombs were away a burst of flak hit just below us and the blast seemed to funnel up the open bay. The concussion lifted me up and back and weighted by the vest and helmet I hit the floor hard. I was nearly unconscious, had the wind knocked out of me and hurt all over. I wondered if now it was my turn. Angelo Martin, our waist gunner, saw what had happened through the open radio room door and called to me over the interphone and asked, "Are you all right?" Since I was out of breath and my mike cord had pulled loose I couldn't answer right away. Because of the weight on me and the fact that the plane was in a steep pull-up I was pinned to the floor so all I could do was to wave weakly at Ange over my shoulder. I heard him say, "I think he's hit." Again I waved and then there was a dead silence on the interphone. When the pressure let up I managed to roll over and get up. I checked myself over and after finding nothing drastically wrong I plugged in my mike cord and reported to Ange that I was "all right." Then the interphone started buzzing with talk again and we pulled back up into formation and back to routine duty. We were lucky.

A Low Crossing

by Wilbert H. Richarz

COMING out of Hamburg over the estuary the B-17 took a hard hit of flak and immediately went to the deck and hung on. As they were following the waterway to the sea the pilot ordered the crew to throw out everything they could to lighten the load. Just as the waist gunners were about to throw out the waist guns a Gunboat on the estuary opened fire. The gunner held up on their jettisoning long enough to return the fire and when the big fifties began to center their patterns the Gunboat literally came apart in the water. Then the gunners threw the guns out.

Over the channel with the aircraft at about 200 feet the radio operator frantically sent his SOS to his designated Air Rescue Control Station. Luckily, he got an immediate response. He was glad that he had so carefully tuned his transmitter to the emergency frequency before the mission on his frequency meter. The Air Rescue Control Station called its two satellite stations and the three of them zeroed in their radio compasses on the aircraft, triangulated, and then radioed back the course to steer to the aircraft. Meanwhile the pilot was having even greater difficulty in keeping the bird aloft. By the time they sighted the English coast they were below 100 feet.

The radio operator switched to voice transmission and relayed the message from the pilot, "I don't think we can make it." The English operator immediately replied, "Good show, Yank, you can do it." Then he said, "I've got you in sight — good God man you're flying at a 45 degree angle. That '17' is quite a bird!" Then "You can make it."

The pilot worked harder.

The aircraft skimmed over the coastline and just inched over the threshold of the emergency runway. On impact the plane collapsed and began to come apart, shedding bits of metal as it skidded to a stop. It was the last landing that aircraft would ever make. Fortunately, no one was injured and the crew gratefully climbed out to the cheers of the English audience who gathered to watch the show. Together they counted the holes and marveled at the durability of the Big Gas Bird.

Later, in the dining hall, the camaraderie ran high and after a few unauthorized drinks and countless retellings of the story of the low crossing the crew was driven back to their base to get a new airplane and try again.

Two Square J ships in formation over the English countryside.

George Zadzora

Merseberg Mission — Fall 1944

by George Zadzora

Radio Operator-Gunner, 568th Squadron

I'D like to begin by recalling a mission that we flew in the summer of 1944. The target was a synthetic oil refinery in the Merseberg area.

As we approached the I.P., one of our engines went out but we continued maintaining our position in the formation during the bomb run. Flak was intense but we kept in formation and dropped our bombs. Shortly after "bombs away" the second engine went out and our oxygen system was also shot out. That left us with two engines and no oxygen. The pilot, Paul Goodrich, did the only logical thing and that was to drop down to a lower altitude since with two engines out we could not hope to keep up with the formation. So down we went to 15,000 feet and found ourselves alone in a clear sky.

A conference was held on the intercom and it seemed like the best thing to do was to head for a cloud bank to the northwest which was estimated to be about one and one-half hours flying time.

In the meantime, we made tentative plans that if another engine should quit, we were prepared to lighten the ship by getting rid of the guns, ammo and anything else that was not absolutely essential.

We continued northwestward, expecting to be attacked by enemy fighters at any time. We had no fighter escort, so we were on our own all the way. The navigator, Bill Nordling, steered a course clear of any major cities that in all probability would have a heavy concentration of flak guns.

Onward we flew, the crew on extreme alert looking for enemy fighters. Tension built up within us with each mile that we flew as we neared the cloud bank. So far, so good. No fighter attacks and no flak. Finally we reached the cloud bank. Some of the tension left us but we were still over Germany and had a long way to go to get to England.

The pilot, Goodrich, decided to stay just under the clouds and in case of attack we could climb a few hundred feet and hide in the overcast. As we flew on, the cloud base lowered and Goodrich kept the ship just below the clouds. We descended for some time until the cloud base levelled out at about 300 feet.

The land was practically flat so Goodrich leveled out the plane and on we flew at this altitude over northwest Germany and Holland. Tensions lessened a bit more but we kept our hopes high that the two engines wouldn't fail us.

We flew over one small town at this altitude and I remember looking down and seeing a woman and child crossing the street. They stopped suddenly and looked up, no doubt startled, and I could see their faces. A moment later a church steeple passed by about 150 feet below the ship.

On we flew until we reached the coast line and then out

over the North Sea.

The pilot called the radio operator and informed him to be prepared to call the base for a Q.D.M. (A course to fly to reach the home base).

As we progressed toward the English coast, a Q.D.M. was sent to home base to which they responded immediately and gave us a course to fly.

Our hopes kept getting brighter with each passing mile and eventually we crossed the coast of England and landed without further mishap.

After the pilot parked the ship on the hardstand, we got out and looked at the ship and examined the damage. The thought in my mind was that we made this mission but there will be more to fly. Will we be as lucky on future missions as we had been on this one?

390th Formation at "Bombs Away"

Back:
John Eusner, N; Keith Wilcox, Mickey Operator; Ted Wosczyk, B; Lloyd Taylor, CP; Jim Kenny, Pilot.
Front:
Raymond Winn, WG; Fred Techmeyer, Engr.-Gunner; Don Brouman, RO-G; Joe Laden, Tail TG.

A Slight Delay in Return From One Mission

H. James Kenny
Pilot, 570th Squadron

AN unusual thing happened on the December 24, 1944 mission to Zellhausen, Germany. In the target area our Number 1 and 2 engines were hit. I had to feather both of these props. As I recall, it was quite a haul back to England. After some discussion with the crew, we elected to make an emergency landing at a small emergency strip called Laon near the Belgium border. As we were letting down through the overcast, I could see in the distance a tremendous amount of plane traffic. We really had no other place to go. I was anxious to get our wounded bird on the ground. We decided to go ahead with our plan to land. I contacted the control tower to tell them of our situation.

It was very hard to keep the right wing up. It was easier for us to turn right than left. We were faced with a problem because of the very heavy traffic, 25 or 30 troop transports were making left turns in the traffic pattern to land on one strip. The other strip was being used for takeoff.

As we found out later, the transports would land and taxi to the end of the runway where trucks were stationed. When the airplane stopped, infantry soldiers, fresh from England, would get off the plane and jump into the trucks and be transported immediately to the Battle of the Bulge. This was a continuous operation. As soon as they were unloaded they would taxi back to the other strip and take off for England to load up again.

During the time we were approaching the field, we saw a couple of airplanes shoot red flares which we assumed was to obtain landing priority possibly due to low fuel.

As we approached turning right, we continued to shoot double green flares. Since it was almost dusk, these flares made quite a sight.

After making two turns around the field, they signalled us to land. Just as soon as the wheels touched down, the left tire blew. It had been sliced by flak. All I could do was apply the right brake and slow the plane down. We were moving down the runway at a rather good clip with two engines in-operative on the left side and a flat tire on the left side.

Thank God the ground was frozen. I recognized that I couldn't block the runway and disrupt this very important troop transport operation. I gradually eased the plane about 25 yards off the runway on very hard ground where I made a ground loop. As the plane came to rest, we all piled out. We were all safe and sound despite a very badly damaged aircraft.

We had to obtain some transportation to another allied base where we were able to obtain a ride back to England. We arrived back at the base on December 29, 1944 and flew our next mission on December 30. This was a very busy and eventful period in our young lives.

An Unforgettable Sight

H. James Kenny

ONE of the most outstanding sights that stands out in my memory happened on the 26 February 1945 mission to Berlin. The 100th Group led the 8th Air Force that day. The 390th was the second group in the bomber stream over the target. My crew was in the lead aircraft in the 390th formation. On the bomb run we kept very close behind the 100th Bomb Group. This was a good position for us. The 100th Group encountered very heavy flak. The group behind us also experienced a great deal of flak. We had very little. I assume this was due to the time required on the ground to reload the AA guns. They didn't have time to reload and fire at us since we were so close to the first group.

Although we did not know it immediately, the lead aircraft of the 100th was hit by flak over the target. They continued to go straight east rather than turn to the left after dropping their bombs as they were briefed. We followed them for a short time, but then realized that something was amiss. The 100th Group planes attempted to reform on the deputy group leader. Recognizing that we were proceeding in the wrong direction, we made a left turn to get back to our briefed return route to England. At this time we took over the leadership of the entire 8th Air Force.

As we turned, I looked down and recognized the Oder River. That was the eastern front at that time. Each group behind us turned left slightly inside of us.

On this particular day, the visibility was excellent. There were no clouds or haze at our altitude.

After several minutes, I looked back to my left at the trailing bomber groups. I don't think I have seen or ever will see such a sight. I could see the entire 1,500 B-17 airplanes of the 8th Air Force stretched out in echelon behind us. This was a real sight — once in a lifetime!

A Miracle

H. James Kenny

THIS unusual episode happened on one of our missions while flying at about 25,000 feet over Northern Germany. We were on our way back from the target this day heading for home base in England. A rocket about three feet long and six inches in diameter with two yellow rings around the nose came up just in front of our right wing tip. It reached the top of its trajectory as we flew underneath it. It tilted over and pointed toward the rear of the plane. The rocket fell over the back part of the wing without exploding. Thinking back, I can only call it a miracle. It just seemed to hang there in space waiting for us to pass by. I was told that some of the rockets were programmed to blow up when they hit the top of their trajectory. Thank God! This one didn't blow up.

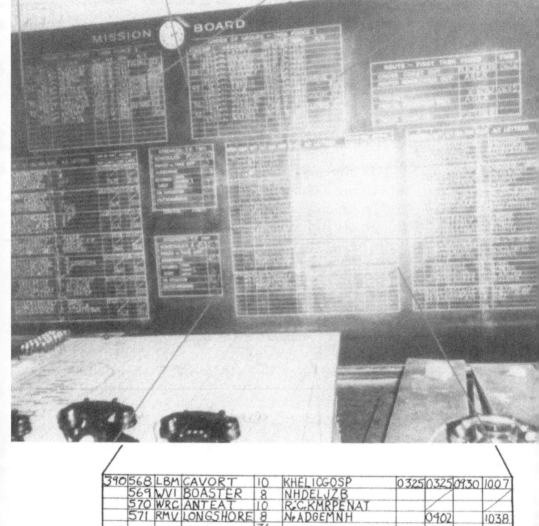

| 390 | MAJ GEMMIL | WRQ | B | 570 | " | GREEN |

| 390 | COL GOOD | RRKI | RP | 570 |

THE 390th WAS THERE ON D-DAY

The Mission Board of the Eighth Air Force shows two of the three missions flown by the 390th that day. Note that take-off of the early mission involved 36 ships of the 390th and started on time although the return was delayed.

390	568	LBM	CAVORT	10	KHELICGOSP	0325	0325	0930	1007
	569	WVI	BOASTER	8	NHDELJZB				
	570	WRC	ANTEAT	10	RCKMRPENAT				
	571	RMV	LONGSHORE	8	NPADGEMNH		0402		1038
				36					

Back:
Roy Schultz, CC-G; Mel Adams, RO-G; Ray Floyd, WG; M.L. Moody, BTG; Roland Stottlemeyer, Tail TG.
Front:
Bob Longardner, Pilot; Harry Senior, CP; William South, B.

Lamentations: Dusseldorf, September 9, 1944

by Robert L. Longardner

Pilot, 570th Squadron, G. I. Wonder

THE 390th suffered one of its greatest losses on a mission to bomb an obscure factory at Dusseldorf — six crews and nine airplanes.

The saga of *G. I. Wonder*, the forceful B-17 manned by the Longardner crew was leading the low squadron on this eventful day.

G. I. Wonder was well experienced with combat before we arrived at the 390th shortly after D-Day. This rugged B-17F had been modified to a "G" model at Cambridge. When she was assigned to our crew, she had already logged 38 successful bombing missions.

Probably this modification and the fact that the cockpit

had been shrouded with at least 1,500 pounds of special steel armor was the reason she survived the blast effects of the bomb explosion in Hobbie's airplane which was flying immediately behind us.

Though she outweighed her sisters, there was not a better rigged and balanced aircraft in the Group. Phil Chute, our crew chief, knew her special place in the sky and intimately attended daily to her needs and cultured her spirit. After our crew had completed seventeen missions, we were selected to lead the low squadron. Our pattern of flying the low lead was to swing the squadron back and forth under the Group lead squadron in a fashion to evade the barrage of flak that those 88s would agonizingly throw at the Group.

Clay Perry, a 43 J classmate of mine, assigned to the 568th Squadron of the 390th, and I studied the German 88 and calculated a probability of accuracy that their rifle had at various altitudes. At 25,000 feet the 88 was most deadly with accuracy of better than 50% chance of hitting the target with four rifle batteries firing sequentially. At 28,000 feet, the accuracy of the 88 fell arithmetically and was rendered to firing a barrage pattern. Based upon the muzzle velocity of the 88, a four-barrel battery firing sequentially to 25,000 feet would explode in track approximately 100 feet apart. Therefore, by kicking the rudder at the first flak shell explosion away from the burst, the following burst would trail off target. With this knowledge, and by swinging the squadron back and forth under the lead squadron, we had been successful in avoiding any serious battle damage in the low squadron position since we started leading August 16 on a mission to Liepzig.

At the briefing on the morning of September 9, 1944, we were given a bombing altitude of 26,000 feet. The combat crews erupted in vexation, grumbling about the severity of such low altitude in "happy flak valley." Surely the targeted factory could have been hit from 28,000 feet as well as from this defenseless altitude of 26,000 feet which meant that the low squadron would be flying at 25,000 feet until the initial point of the bomb run.

The following chronicle is lifted verbatim from my mission diary, and without edit, it depicts the intensity of the battle and the impossible attitude that *G. I. Wonder* was thrown into by the exploding bombs in Hobbie's bomb bay that was hit with an 88 shell:

Something different for the Eighth Air Force today. We had our early morning briefing as usual. The target was Dusseldorf, Germany, in the center of "happy flak valley" where there are 1,000 flak guns but only 150 guns could be brought to bear on us provided we stayed on the briefed course in and out. The target was a small arms and tank factory 4 miles east of the city employing 35,000 workmen. Everyone dreaded the target, including me, because of the low bombing altitude.

We were to bomb with the pathfinder, provided the target was 9/10 to 10/10 covered, if not, we were to bomb our secondary to keep from being shot up too badly. We reached the bombing altitude of 26,000 feet just before the I.P. and started a run in toward the target which was 6/10 covered. The flak didn't look too bad. Over the target before "bombs away", a direct burst caught Hobbie's ship in the bomb bay which was loaded with 12 x 500 pound bombs. It blew him and eight other ships out of formation. Hobbie was flying the slot element directly below *G.I. Wonder*.

When the explosion occurred from the direct hit, we had not yet pulled the low squadron out from below the lead in order that we could bomb on the pathfinder drop. At the instant of the explosion, *G. I. Wonder* was tossed tail high, riding the ball of overpressure while the bottom of our aircraft was battered by debris and shrapnel. The intense heat and noise of the explosion drowned the senses of the crew, and it seemed an eternity before I was able to command control of *G. I Wonder*. After righting the aircraft from the dive attitude, I observed an engine nacelle at ten o'clock to our aircraft. The sky was full of other exploded aircraft debris that was avoided by some of the wildest maneuvers ever flown in a B-17. Had *G. I. Wonder* not been shrouded with all of the armor steel, the cockpit would never have withstood the effects.

It was dreadful. I won't try to go into details for it's too horrible to recount. There were many buddies of mine in those nine crews.

It was a sorry sight. Of the twelve ships that went in, only three ships of our low squadron were left. We pulled into formation on the pathfinder aircraft. The battle damage was intense among us.

Immediately we got the hell out of there. Nothing really seemed to effect us, for we were in a trance all of the way home. I know that one time on the way home we were in flak for nearly ten minutes, but due to the disastrous previous moments, it did not phase me.

Out of the nine ships that were knocked out of formation, one managed to get to Paris, another landed in Belgium, and one struggled into our field after we had landed. The battle damage cost us six complete crews and nine aircraft. I was never so shocked in all of my life, losing 55 buddies in one second was more than I could take. Because I was in a trance, shocked because of the loss, I did not write this until September 10. That made us twenty-four missions, but only by the Grace of God will we complete the tour.

Epilogue

The shock of the mission caused great mental stress for our crew, but most of us regrouped and flew to Liepzig on September 11 in a replacement ship while *G. I. Wonder* went in for two weeks of intensive battle damage repair.

This plane flew for miles with the nose shot off and the Top Turret Gunner still aboard.

Back:
Louis Kiss, Tail TG; Lester
Boettcher, N.; Robert
McCormick, LWG; Art
Dix, BTG; Mathias Biehl,
RO-G; William Poythress,
CP; Walt Byrne, RWG;
Perry V. Row, Pilot.
Front:
James Fitzsimmons, B;
Eric Bennett; Top TG.

Talk About Thirteen

by Walt Byrne

Waist Gunner, 568th Squadron, **Phyllis Marie**

IT was the 13th of November, and the raid was
Bremen, Germany (13 letters). It was the second time that
the target had been hit by the 13th Combat Wing.

Briefing turned out as usual with a few outbursts about
flak and how rough the mission would be. It's not that any
of the gunners were afraid. No, a combat man is very seldom
scared to go on any mission. It's not that a gunner is
superman, or that his nerves are iron, but if "Jerry" will
come up and meet us with such odds against him, we'll
certainly take any mission assigned to us.

After a few remarks from Captain Zelman, our well-liked
Squadron Surgeon, about frostbite and the expected

temperature at flight altitude, which incidentally, was 46 below zero Fahrenheit, the men began to file out of the briefing room. As usual, the radio operators stayed behind to get last minute information. T/Sgt. Biehl received his Flimsey with that good luck number on it again (13). He proceeded with the crew to the ship *Phyllis Marie* (713).

Takeoff was at dawn. As the great fortresses taxied to the line-up position for takeoff, it began to drizzle. There weren't many of the ground crew around that day, possibly because of the weather. The brakes screeched as we came to a stop. Lt. Row and co-pilot Lt. Poythress began to run up the engines. They checked out O.K.

"Unlock tailwheel."

"Tailwheel unlocked," replied the co-pilot, as we pivoted for the last turn before taking off into the wild blue yonder.

We were airborne now. It wasn't long before the formation was on its way. Crossing the North Sea was uneventful, except for the usual test firing of guns. The check-in was nothing new and in a short while, there could be heard, "Tail guns O.K.," "Right waist gun O.K.," "Left waist O.K.," "Ball turret guns O.K.," "Radio O.K.," "Top turret guns O.K.," and finally "Nose guns O.K."

The German coast was spotted soon. It was just a few seconds later that the navigator called to tell us to put on our flak suits. The pilot asked T/Sgt. Bennett of Georgia, T/T operator, to assist the co-pilot, Billy Boy, and himself with their suits. The radio man and tail gunner struggled with their heavy pieces of protective armament as the waist gunners helped each other.

Upon crossing the coast, we could see a German airfield. High winds were blowing us off course rapidly. For a minute it was expected that we'd drop our bombs on it and return home. It seemed that Bremen would never be reached that day. Ah, but no such luck. We weren't going to put in such a milk run. In we went. A few bursts of flak came up off our tail and to the right of us, but it wasn't accurate.

Midway from the enemy coast to the target, the left waist

gun froze up on S/Sgt. McCormick. I cursed and proceeded to check my cal 50. It also failed to fire. The radio operator's heated equipment cut out, as a result "Mack" took over the radio gun, leaving me to *sweat* out the rest of the mission in the cold waist section. I mean sweat, put yourself in this predicament. Two waist guns dead, all I could do was stand by and watch.

Now the bomb bay doors were opened. However, they were closed shortly. As a result of the target being overcast and general bad weather conditions bombing would have been inaccurate anyway. The Nazis really threw up the flak that day. However, it wasn't as bad as the first raid.

Meanwhile, out about 1,500 yards, a formation of fortresses were being attacked by those sons of Hitler. It was hard to say what did it, but in front of my eyes, the two end panels of a B-17 blew off. She went into a spin gradually, pulling out into a vertical dive towards earth and crashed with a terrific explosion. Much to my regret the true facts are no chutes were seen. A short while later, F.W.'s attacked a Liberator formation. One heavy went down, much like the B-17 described previously. On the next attack, the Liberators gunners hit three enemy fighters simultaneously, all exploding and going down out of control in flames.

On the way back, more enemy fighters were seen. Lt. Row called out a formation of 12 F.W. 190s attacking from the nose. One in particular was heading for our ship.The attack was at eleven o'clock low. "Top Turret to Pilot — Top to Pilot, drop your left wing a little."

As I said my prayers beside dead guns, the chatter of 50's could be heard. They were at it hot and heavy: navigator, bombardier and engineer. "Hit him, Bennett, hit him. Get that son of a you-know-what before he gets us," could be heard from someone probably closer to the action than I.

In the excitement, and because of the bank we found ourselves a bit out of formation. Jerry peeled off and went down in smoke into the cloud bank below us. Some say the pilot was dead because he stopped firing at us, but others think he was surprised at the presumed attack on him. You see we turned into the attack. Credit for damages was given to the engineer.

On the way home, the bomb bay doors were opened again. This time the incendiaries were released to spread fire and destruction upon the enemies of all allied nations. The papers say, "Forts Libs Hit Target in Northwest Germany Today," but to be more explicit, our Combat Wing hit canals. Reports are that the raid was successful.

At interrogation, a short while later, Tail Gunner Kiss, reported 13 F.W. 190's had attacked us in that first pass. The pilot called it 12, probably because that's all he wanted to see (if you know what I mean). At any rate, there's one Jerry that will never be home for supper.

> 13 F.W. 190's attacked
> 13th of November
> 13 Number of Flimsey
> 713 Ship number
> 13th mission for most of the crew
> 13th Combat Wing
> Formation Formed at 13,000 Ft.

A Pal Goes Down

---

by Walt Byrne

FRANKIE was a nice fellow, quite a bit older than I. He shouldn't have been flying anyhow. How he got into this so-called racket I don't know. Some fellows are like that, willing to do anything to fulfill their patriotic duty.

A whole gang of young fellows like myself, trained on the West Coast. They came from all walks of life. Frankie was one of them. Yes, they were from Ohio, Georgia, Washington, New York, California, Arizona, Utah and nearly every state in the Union. Frank Bongiovani was from New Jersey.

After leaving the States, our squadron broke up. We were only a Provisional Group anyway, so that was expected. It was only a coincidence that we met in England.

Frankie was put in a hut next to ours. You'd never think he lived there though. He was always in our place playing cards, arguing, or just laying on someone else's bunk. After his crew was knocked down this was more true. Unfortunately they were missing in action after their first mission. Frankie was in the hospital at that time.

We'd wake Frank up just before a mission, take him to chow and briefing. He was the sort of fellow who didn't have to wish you "Good Luck" you knew he meant it. "Why make a sortie look tough," must have been his psychological view point. When the big bombers came back to base, there he was with the ground crews, waiting for us to hit the landing strip.

One of his self-imposed jobs was helping us clean our weapons.

The crews in his quarters didn't have any luck. Up until the time I left the European Theater of Operations, every man who slept in that shack was eventually knocked down.

I recall the day our Commanding Officer gave us orders to move across the road. Our hut was too crowded to be healthy. We lived with a couple of radar mechanics, a hell of a nice bunch of medics and, of course, only one combat crew — crew 7. Move! "Like Hell we'll move, our luck's been good so far and we don't intend to change it." An order is an order though, it had to be obeyed or we'd subject ourselves to disciplinary action. All the bitching in the World couldn't help us unless we saw someone with rank. The bombardier, superstitious Lt. Fitzsimmons, went to see Major Good to settle the affair. Yes you guessed it, we didn't move.

To be frank about the whole thing we weren't superstitious, just too darn lazy to be inconvenienced by moving.

It was a quiet, clear day in England, which I'll grant was unusual. No mission was called because the quick change didn't allow enough time for preparations. The loudspeakers blasted away with their usual common, but monotonous tone, "All combat crews report to ground school at 1330, repeat, all combat crews report to school at 1330."

A notice had just been placed on the bulletin board by Colonel Wittan to the effect that flying personnel missing three classes would have to fly an extra operational mission. This was probably the reason for so many being present at school that day.

It was late in December 1943; the class was armament. The instructor, the squadron bombardier, had just finished a very interesting lecture on bombs. He was now demonstrating the power of a *non*-explosive incendiary. It was only about twelve pounds, nearly burned out, when it happened. The darn thing exploded. Fortunately, no one was killed, but it injured 14 men four of which were on our crew.

Our new co-pilot was hit above the eye. He was definitely out of action for a couple of weeks. The navigator was ready to fly the next day. The tail gunner, S/Sgt. Kiss, was hit solidly in the pit of the stomach. It made an ugly mess. The left waist gunner was taken to the hospital with a fragment deep in his leg.

This unfortunate accident left positions open on our ship. We got together and decided to ask Operations for Frank Bongiovani. Customarily, requests of this type were granted. Of course, Frank was no fool. The way he put it, "If they're going to fly me anyhow, then I'm with you, otherwise I'll not tempt fate by asking." In the words of our ball turret gunner — "It only takes one" —.was his motto.

Briefing was scheduled for 0630, breakfast at 0530.

No one likes to get on the wrong side of a Major, so there was no fight when I told the boys of my decision to argue for Frank.

The scene changes, the men are seated in their chairs, some half asleep, others speculating over the possible target. Could it be Berlin?

"Men, the target for today is target number 51, in the 'Pas de Calais area' (France)." The speaker continues, "I needn't remind you of the necessity for security. The Captain will give you the rest of the information on ground batteries, possible enemy planes encountered and what to do in case you bail out. Remember, men, if worse comes to worse, name, rank and serial number, *that's all*. Good luck and good hunting." We were finally given our position in the formation after which the Major asked if there were any questions. That was my cue. I jumped to my feet and said, "Sir, if it's all right with you, we'd like S/Sgt. Bongiovani for our left waist instead of our original replacement." In a quiet, very puzzled and questioning voice, the Major replied, "Does it matter that much, Sgt.? The list is already made up, besides it's an easy mission. But I'll tell you what we'll do; we'll fix it up for the next mission." What could I say, he was saying NO to me in a nice way.

We were to paste approximately 52 different targets that day. The most unusual raid to date. The planes were to form as usual. At a given latitude and longitude the groups were to peel off from the combat wing and head on their own course. At another position we were to separate again, break up into six plane squadrons and go after our own individual targets.

The raid was to be made from 12,000 feet, which was the lowest attack over Europe by heavies to date. The flak guns would be very accurate at this altitude. We had to depend on the element of surprise to help pull us safely through this raid.

After the Major finished the explanation, one fellow jokingly asked, "Sir, when does the ball turret peel off?" The whole congregation broke into laughter. It showed how much we defied the German fighters. The mission was also an excellent present from the Eighth Bomber Command,

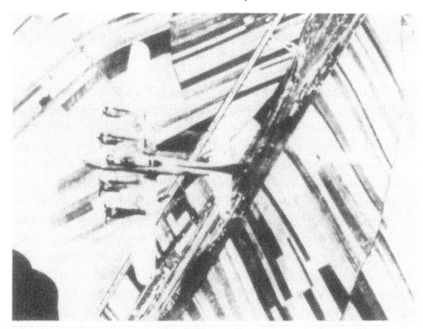

A fire is burning in the right wing of this plane and two crewmen who have bailed out can be seen. One is below the left wing and one is behind the tail.

for we considered it soft. You see, today was Christmas Eve, 1943.

Weather conditions scrubbed that mission, however. The next day we were briefed on the same target with plans changed very little.

Fate finally had it's way. "A B-17, passing underneath us, number 3 engine on fire, going down." I cannot express in writing the feeling that came over the crew when it was discovered that Frankie was in that plane."Oh God, let them live." "There's one, two, three chutes." "I see three more," someone said. We're sure that six or seven got out. A seven out of ten chance to live. The fate of the rest lies in God's Hands.

An Act That Will Never Be Forgotten

by Jim Horan

Ball Turret Gunner, 568th Squadron

THIS is about a mission to Merseburg in November 1944.

We had just come away from the target. I turned the ball turret toward the rear to view the target damage. All at once the plane slowed down, like it had run into a brick wall. We dropped out of formation. I noticed that the tail wheel had fallen down. I turned the ball turret and found that both the landing gear and bomb bay doors were down.

I wondered what the heck was going on. You don't put the wheels down for fun. It turned out that our electrical system had been hit by flak.

In a short time the interphone started buzzing. I

remember hearing Ralph (Spence) our waist gunner say, "I'll do it."

All he did was hang an oxygen walk-around bottle on his chute, go into the bomb bay, straddle the open doors and turn the large crank 109 turns to bring up one door. After this he moved over to the other side and did it again. His final act was an easier job. He went back to the rear and cranked up the tail wheel. He did all of this at 20-25,000 feet, only 10 minutes away from Meresburg, at 50 degrees below zero with no heat in his flight suit.

It is easy to see why I have always said Ralph K. Spence was the *Greatest*.

Formation from below.

The Middle Missions

Chaplain (Captain) Marshall R. Shickles shows the E6B Navigation Calculator to a

Back:
C. Medeck, RO-G; L. Baumgartner, WG; S. Hoffman, Top TG; P. Morris, WG; D. May; Tail TG; C. Puckett, BTG;
Front:
J.R. Geary, Pilot; H.J. McCarthy, B; N. Mencow, N; R.H. Perry, CP.

The Real Thing — Not a Training Mission

by Richard H. Perry

Co-Pilot, 570th Squadron, Pistol Packing Mama

ON the morning of 17 August 1943 we were awakened very early. When we were told to bring our mess kits along with our flying gear we knew we were in for a strange mission. At the briefing the ribbon that marked our intended course on the map stretched a long way from England to Africa. We were to bomb Regensburg, Germany and then continue on in what later became known as the famous "Regensburg Shuttle Mission to Africa".

As we entered the Continent we were attacked by a group of FW 190s. From their brightly painted engine nacelles we knew they were the group known as the "Abbeville Kids". This German attack was very intense with some FW 190s

View of the Alps taken from a 390th plane on the Regensburg-Africa Shuttle mission.

being flown right through the B-17 formation. During one fighter pass, an armor piercing bullet, smaller than a 50 caliber, hit our waist gunner (Sgt. Leonard Baumgartner) in the head. When the fighter action slowed up, I went back to the waist of the plane using a portable oxygen bottle. Baumgartner died in my arms. This was my first real test of war. I knew then that we were "not on a training mission."

We continued to have fighter attacks until we had dropped our bombs on the Messerschmitt factory at Regensburg and proceeded south toward Africa. We were running out of gas as we reached Africa and, therefore, we landed at the first opportunity, which was a steel mat runway at Bone, Algiers. We were briefed to land at Telergma.

We proceeded later on to Telergma where we gassed up and loaded our plane with bombs. On 24 August, we returned to England, after dropping our bombs on the Bordeaux/Merigmac airfield.

*The death of Sgt. Baumgartner was a sobering experience for the **Pistol Packing Mama** crew piloted by Lt. Geary. This was a closely knit combat crew that had trained and worked together. The loss of this very important member of this team drew this group even closer together. The remaining crew members completed their required number of missions leaving their mark on the enemy from their bombs and guns.*

A breifing officer points out the first leg of the 21 June 1944 shuttle mission to the crews before the flight.

George Von Arb and
Gene Willms rest
awhile awaiting
refueling at Poltava,
Russia.

Russian Shuttle —
"Operation Frantic"

by George W. Von Arb
Commanding Officer, 571st Squadron

THE Charge of Quarters awakened the flight
crews at 0200 on June 21, 1944.

The previous night's 'alert' had predicted a bombing
mission, for either a "Milk-Run" or a deep penetration run
over enemy territory, and now it was confirmed.

It was not until the very early morning briefing that
orders revealed that units from the 390th Bomb Group were
to fly an unusual 7000 mile shuttle bombing mission to
Russia.

We lifted from the runway with a last look at Station 153
knowing we would not touch down again at Framlingham,
England for a period of at least two weeks.

107

The bomber stream (for primary and diversionary targets) consisted of approximately 2,500 8th Air Force B-17s and P-51s ordered on the "Operation Frantic" shuttle mission, bombing strategic targets in Eastern Germany enroute. The plan was to land at Soviet bases, refuel and complete the shuttle run to Italy and back to England. The first diversionary force was sent to bomb Basdorf, Germany, and returned to assigned British stations.

Twenty-seven aircraft of the 390th Task Force continued on, joining the full Group and bombing the Ruhland industrial works near Berlin.

From Ruhland the 390th Bomb Group continued the shuttle mission, landing at the assigned base in Mirgorod, Ukraine, Russia. German fighter planes failed to intercept the Task Force.

As we approached our landing pattern over Mirgorod, Lend-Lease P-39s provided protective top cover. To our amazement the pilots were Russian women!

Peace and tranquility did not last long, as German reconnaissance planes located the Poltava airfield loaded with B-17s. The information and photos were quickly forwarded to German Headquarters. That night the Germans bombed the Poltava airfield. Fifty eight B-17s were damaged or destroyed.

For our protection the 390th Task Force was ordered to fly immediately to a satellite field in Zaporozhe, Russia on the Dnieper River on 22nd of June.

We rapidly learned the interpretation of the word "halt." A Russian guard succeeded in getting our undivided attention by shouting "Stoi" punctuated with a rifle shot between the crew and the about-to-be boarded aircraft. With proper clearance to board our own planes, we departed for Zaporzhe, 150 miles from Mirgorod.

Upon landing at the Russian flying school field at Zaporozhe, the Russian Commander met us at "Field Operations" and through an interpreter, told us that our bed rolls and "K" rations would not be necessary, for he had

Russian water tower and scene in Mirgorod.

adequate accommodations for the crews of the 390th Bomb Group.

All the crews were loaded on the back of a familiar 2-1 2 ton Lend-Lease American truck, and were given a short ride to the dining hall. The hall was very small and seated only three flight crews at a time.

Our food consisted of borscht, dark wheat bread and butter, a tender meat, and a salad with fresh boiled eggs, and no vodka. The dessert consisted of cooked plums served hot.

We thought the meal very good and indicated to the Russian Commander the dinner was far superior to our "K" rations. Later we found out that our flight surgeon had checked the preparation of the food and found the butter, eggs and meat all "imported" from the United States and that we were eating American food from Wisconsin.

Our transportation reappeared after supper, as darkness had arrived along with a light sprinkle of rain. The journey to the "dormitory" was only a short distance, and with limited light, a three story building appeared to be our place of lodging for the night.

As we entered the structure, candle light was sufficient to indicate that our bed was one long sheet, placed on a platform covered with straw for the full length of the building.

We found out later, when the candles were extinguished, that the building contained no window glass, no second floor and no roof! Fortunately, the light rain had stopped and a good nights sleep ensued.

On June 27th we flew to Poltava for logistical support to continue our shuttle mission. We were guided carefully to the remaining paved surfaces. Great care was required to park the aircraft. The earlier German attack had not only destroyed B-17s and support group buildings, supplies and fuel, but many anti-personnel butter-fly bombs were scattered in the grassy areas of the airfield. Russian soldiers cleared these by locking arms, carefully walking until they found the butter-fly bombs. This procedure appeared to be more hazardous than a bombing mission.

We were briefed in a building with only one wall standing and no roof for the shuttle flight to Italy via our target of Drohobyzez, Poland.

Two Russian military officers from the Red Air Force boarded the flight as observers. The Russians did not have a daylight strategic bombing capability, and were most observant during the bomb run, especially the "hit" on the oil target at Drohobyzcz, Poland.

The last leg of the mission was from Foggia, Italy to England, bombing the marshaling yards in Beziers, France. We returned to England Station 153 on July 5, 1944.

The 390th Bombardment Group, as part of "Frantic II" Strike Force from England, had participated in and completed the first of three historical shuttle bombing missions into Russia during World War II.

It Had To Be Gremlins

by Robert Banta

Radio Operator, 568th Squadron, Hot Rocks

I always thought those mischievous and sometimes sadistic little rascals attacked only planes and equipment. No way! They got after us, I know it! It had to be them! Judge for yourself.!

Somehow, the "powers to be" left our crew out of the first two missions the Group flew. It was a matter of utter frustration since we were sharp and I personally was frantic to be off on combat missions.

We were finally scheduled for the third mission on 17 Aug. 1943. When we found out our first mission was to be the greatest ever scheduled, all through Germany to Regensburg then to North Africa, I was beside myself with joy and forgiveness! We waited patiently at the plane until the green flares showed. Everyone scrambled aboard and one by one the engines were started. I felt the engines run-up and suddenly the brakes were released. As we moved forward I slapped my hand on the desk and yelled "Yahoo!". Immediately, as if the result of that slap the bomber jolted to a stop and leaned to the right. The engines roared as the plane bumped and shook, but it didn't move. A voice said we were stuck. We in the back got out to help. There it was, the right wheel sunk into the cement! We pushed and lifted on the wing, but to no avail. A shout. "Hey!" and someone pointed to a bomber going by on the taxi strip. It was the supernumerary. They were taking our place and were waving and shouting to us.

I stood by *"Hot Rocks"* full of fury and disgust with tears in my eyes. The foul things I shouted after them came back to haunt me. They died over the target in our place.

« « « » » »

On another day we were over the target and as yet there were no fighters and little flak. I heard the bombardier say "Bombs away" and turned to check the bomb bay to make sure there were no hung bombs. I called an all clear as I continued to watch the land below through the open bomb bay. After they closed, I turned back to my gun and was confronted by another B-17 flying directly overhead. I couldn't figure why he was there or why it didn't move off to the side. As I watched, the bomb bay door opened and a 'hung' 500 pound bomb hung there over my head. I became frantic as I realized what the next step was. Salvo the errant bomb! As my left hand wildly waved the Fortress off, my right hand grabbed the mike switch and I yelled to the pilot to move fast. Nothing! It seemed as if we were suspended in time. I screamed into the mask mike again. Nothing! Then, I realized that the mask mike may be frozen and banged away on my oxygen mask. Nothing. I was never so absolutely full of fear in my life. I started to shrink back to cower in the corner as if I could get away from a determined 500 pound bomb. Only then did the bomber ever so slowly sidle off to the side. The bomb dropped along side of the plane not even as far out as the tip of the wing.

The thing that really made me sick was that when I later jumped both crews about it — nobody saw anything. Impossible! The Gremlins did it just to make me think I was crazy!

« « « » » »

Then they attacked me personally. I was a good operator, and I knew I would normally have not done such stupid things on my own. Consider!

They were all local training flights. On this one, the tail gunner reported a fighter plane heading up from six o'clock

Formation over the North Sea.

low. It was mean looking! It came in close and just sat there. Someone suggested that it may be a night fighter. Finally a voice questioned if the IFF was on. I started to say something when I realized I hadn't turned it on. I reached inside the waist and flipped the switch. Two long minutes later the mean one swung away and out of sight in a flash. There were strong words for a guy who would do such a thing to his buddies.

« « « » » »

It was getting hot in the radio room. So, I figured I would remove the plexiglass hatch cover. With a hand gripping the hatch I unlatched one side and pulled down slightly. Then I unlatched the other side. The end to the rear of the plane was hitting the stowed gun. I lifted the other end lightly to free it and the slip stream caught it and whipped it out. The only problem was I was still hanging on. I was at least two feet off the floor heading out before the brain waves traveled to my gripping hands. With absolute gratitude I fell into a heap on the floor. Some voice on the intercom asked what that was. I told them that it was the radio hatch and that they were lucky. What would they have done if they had seen it go by with me still hanging on. In the end I paid a price. They made me restring the transmitting antenna high onto the tail that the hatch broke off. Pure torture it was.

« « « » » »

Finally, we stepped from the plane after a local flight and one smart aleck asked what was all that wire under the plane. My face reddened. It was what was left of the trailing antenna I had forgotten to rewind.

I tell you I was innocent! It was those Gremlins for sure.

Back:
Steven Przepiorka, CC-G;
Harvey Burr, Jr., WG;
Charles Richardson RO-
G; Samuel McGee BTG;
Jefferson Fuller, Jr., WG;
Rogelio Sanchez, TTG.
Front:
Raymond Strate, Pilot;
George Curnes, CP; Neal
Payden, N; Victor Estes, B.

7,000 Mile Shuttle Mission to Russia

by Raymond E. Strate

Pilot, 571st Squadron, Good 'Ol Yank

THE Shuttle Mission to Russia from June 21st to July 5th, 1944, covered 7,000 miles and was the first mission of this kind from England.

At 0520 hours, June 21, the *Good 'Ol Yank,* number 673, B-17G, was off on its fifteenth mission, piloted by Raymond E. Strate. It was one of 27 planes that departed the 390th home base at Framlingham, England on the first leg of the Shuttle Mission.

We had been issued Russian language cards and special prisoner of war kits. Some of our planes carried wing tanks for the fighters on the initial leg, for use on the flight from Russia to Italy, as none were available in the Eastern

115

Command. The Eagle Squadron, commanded by Col. Donald Blakeslee, age 26, was to fly fighter cover on the entire trip. The greyhound sleek Mustangs with Red Noses planned a 7-1/2 hour trip to Russia. They joined us enroute to Ruhland, an oil refinery target, just south of Berlin.

The Bomber attack on Ruhland was commanded by Col. Archie J. Old, Jr., with 27 aircraft from the 390th and the balance of planes from the 45th Wing — a reported total of 120 aircraft.

All 27 of our planes bombed Ruhland, dropping 214 x 500 pound general purpose bombs. One plane was reported M.I.A.; however, the pilot landed over the Russian lines, returning later by the A.T.C. route. Over Ruhland a flock of Yellow Nosed ME 109s and a few FW 190s rose to give battle with little effect. Later, over Warsaw six Germans were destroyed by the Mustangs. None of the Bombers were lost to flak or enemy fighters on the trip.

Enroute to our bases in Russia the towering cumulus clouds nearly broke up the formation, leaving only small areas of open airspace for us to maneuver. The 390th landed at its assigned base at Mirgorod, while the ships from the

Mess line at Mirgorod.

45th Wing landed at Poltava.

The arrival was scouted by German reconnaissance planes and that night, shortly after midnight, a force of approximately one hundred German planes heavily bombed and strafed the Poltava base leaving anti-personnel bombs scattered for miles. Approximately 72 Bombers were destroyed that night. Nobody has ever given an accurate figure on the destruction for reasons unknown.

The *Good 'Ol Yank* logged 10:40 hours on the journey from England to Mirgorod, Russia, that day. The red lights in the cockpit were flashing when we approached the field. We landed with very little fuel in the tanks.

The following day, June 22nd, the 390th, fearing a like attack at our base at Mirgorod, moved approximately 150 miles southeast to a Russian fighter base near Zaporozhe, which had about 4,000 feet of metal landing strip. The flight that day took 1:50 hours logged time. We were housed in an underground manger type building with rough wooden beds and straw. The first night we slept in a bombed out building with only the walls standing. One of the adobe-like houses still standing was the "Mess Hall" where

End of the mess line at Mirgorod.

we enjoyed dark bread and Russian borsch on rough hewn wooden tables with candles for light. Older women and little children were the only people who had survived the terrible onslaught by the German Army as they swept through the Ukraine. Very few buildings remained, all bombed by the Luftwaffe or shelled by German tanks, some of which could be found destroyed in the area. Trenches used by both Armies were visible from the air. We talked with a Russian pilot who flew old U.S.A. P-39s, apparently a gift from the "Yanks." We saw some "Yaks" flying about and they looked like "Ruddy Ducks."

We stayed at Zaporozhe until June 25th and went swimming in the Dnieper River, near the Sea of Azov. The river was a slow, meandering stream in the heart of wonderful agricultural country. Some of my men broke open the emergency "K" rations and cooked them over an open fire with one of the Russian guards. Col. Ott of the 390th chewed me out for disregarding orders on the rations. After dark on the 24th all pilots met in the middle of the field for a briefing. We were briefed about flying to Poltava the next day and using some flare pots for runway guidance lights.

Typical Russian apartment home at Mirgorod.

On our return to our aircraft we were challenged by the Russian guards, who had been recruited fresh from the front to guard our planes in the open field, by a loud bellowed "STOI" (STOP). We froze in our tracks like champion pointers. Somebody shouted "Americanski Soldat" and the rifles were lowered slowly from our heads. The Russians played for keeps throughout the area.

We flew to Poltava on the 25th and saw firsthand how our aircraft had been destroyed at that base. The Russians were recruited to walk through the fields and clear the anti-personnel bombs dropped by the Luftwaffe. Lanes were made for our troops to walk from flight line to mess hall or barracks, using string with tiny bits of white cloth as markers.

We stayed at Poltava overnight and then flew back to Zaporozhe on the 26th, as bad weather scrubbed the proposed flight to Foggia, Italy.

On the 27th, we flew back to Poltava, loaded up with fuel and bombs. Then the 26 planes of the 390th headed for Drohobycz, Poland, an oil refinery where we dropped 391 x 250 pound general purpose bombs, with good results, on

Russian women sweeping the runway.

the oil storage tanks, gas holders, roundhouse, and rail yards. We landed at Lucera, Italy, near Foggia. This flight took nine hours flying time and was uneventful except for a German anti-aircraft gun in Yugoslavia. The Red Nose fighter planes had landed long before we settled in and all the "RED NOSE" Mustang Pilots were flat on their backs in the bunks, having consumed all the good drinking brandy available.

We stayed in tents at Foggia from the 27th until July 5th, having one "Milk Run" to Arad, Romania, a marshaling yard, dropping 174 x 500 pound general purpose bombs. I missed this flight due to engine problems. Had we completed this mission, it would have saved me a nightmare later on when that "extra" mission turned out to be a really tough one.

While at Foggia we attended a Rodeo staged by some Yanks on the 4th of July. We also hitched a ride in a DC-3 to Bari, Italy, for a dish of ice cream and to see the city sights. I drew straws with my companions for a ride "Piggy Back" in a P38 back to Foggia. The Command Pilot of this machine, a Colonel, had about three hours in the plane but was a super pilot. I never did get his name. He demonstrated why he thought the P38 was a great combat machine. He dove at the end of the runway for a landing, pulled up about 200 feet above the ground into a steep climb, dropped his wheels, and came out of a loop for a landing. I never told him that was my first blackout.

On July 5th we were briefed for a target at Beziers, France, a marshaling yard, where we dropped 256 x 500 pound general purpose bombs. Photo reconnaissance revealed extensive damage. On this leg we logged nine and a half hours of flight time. We landed at Framlingham, "Tightboot," without incident.

The record book states "They had flown the greatest bombing operation in history — a trek over most of Europe which had taken them about seven thousand miles."

A View of Russia From Human Interest Side

by Paul J. Argenio

Staff Sergeant, 569th Squadron

THE following is a brief account of some of the interesting human interest experiences I had in Russia. I was on two shuttle missions to Russia in 1944. The first was June 21 and the second August 6. At this point in time, I can no longer distinguish many of the events that occurred. In other words I am not clear as to whether a given incident took place on our first trip or second trip.

During our stay in Russia, non-commissioned officers and commissioned officers saluted us everytime we passed. Although I was a Staff Sergeant, I received salutes from higher ranking Russian officers. I suspect that they were not familiar with our uniform markings just as I was not

121

familiar with theirs.

A slightly built Russian soldier, named Alex, and I established an immediate rapport the second day we were there. I was near our ship, performing some trivial chore when Alex approached, smiling broadly. He greeted me in his native language and I smiled and replied, "Hi!" He placed his hand on his chest and said, *Ah*lex." I did likewise and said, "Paul."

Alex then placed his hand on his head and called out the Russian word meaning "Head." He then touched his eye and called out a word, he touched his nose and called out a word, working on down his face to his mouth, chin, shoulder, elbow, wrist, finger. Reading his expression, I took his cue and again did likewise, calling out the English words as I touched my head, eye, nose, mouth, teeth, chin, shoulder, elbow, wrist and finger. We each repeated this routine several times and then moved on to comparing alphabets.

Thinking of Socrates as I drew the 26 letters of the alphabet in the dirt; I came to a stop after drawing the Z some ten feet to the right of the A. I then returned to a standing position and gestured to Alex, conveying to him that this was our alphabet. He frowned, thrust out his index finger, and counted each of the 26 letters. He turned to me quickly and thrust out one full hand, asking in Russian, "Where are the other 5?" Because the Russian language is one of the non-Roman languages, their alphabet, like Hebrew or Arabic, contains 31 characters. We were at an impasse. There was no way I could break the language barrier and explain to Alex why we had 26 and Russian had 31.

The next day at about the same time, I saw Alex running toward me, again smiling broadly. His teeth were beautiful; and they were his own. As he got within ten feet of me he slapped his head and yelled, "HED!" Then as he pronounced each word, he touched that part of his body. "NOZE ... I ... MOUT ... TEETH ... CHEEN ... SHOL-DEHR ... ELBO ... REEST ... FINGAIR." I was overwhelmed, and especially after he gestured for me now to recite the same thing in Russian. I could only remember the word for "Head." I thought to myself that Alex, this naive peasant, could not be smarter than me. I was quick to rationalize that he was more motivated than I. I was not as interested in learning Russian. He had been practicing, while I had not. I would not admit to myself that he was the superior student and/or superior in intelligence!

Before Alex left that afternoon, he was amazed when I lit a cigarette with a ZIPPO lighter. He showed me his lighter. A piece of flint, a rock, and a four or five inch piece of rope. He would strike the rock against the flint which would ignite the rope held in precisely the correct position. Once the rope smoldered slightly, Alex would begin to blow on it until it ignited more strongly, then he would light his cigarette

Crews at the briefing for the second England-Russia shuttle mission, 6 August 1944.

from the burning rope. I believe the ZIPPO lighter was the first cigarette lighter Alex had ever seen. Alex and all other Russian smokers carried their rock, flint and rope to light their cigarettes. They also carried a small bag, or other improvised container for tobacco, and a piece of newspaper from which they rolled their own cigarettes. No doubt, the neatly made American cigarette was a novelty and the lighter was a treasure. I gave my Zippo to Alex and won a friend for life.

The next day Alex appeared again, with five friends. Their short visit cost me ten cigarettes. Alex lit all the cigarettes with his ZIPPO lighter.

Several of us wondered about Alex and his duties in the Russian army. We assumed he had drawn easy duty as an airfield guard. When we questioned him and he was finally able to figure out what we were asking, we learned he had been through the German campaign. He showed us a healed bullet wound in his lower back. He showed us a bayonet slash below his right rib cage that he had received at Stalingrad. He showed us a second bayonet wound also received somewhere on the battle field. It seemed that after Alex bled three times for his country, he received easy duty!

I could relate stories of battles in the sky with German fighters, or how heavy the flak was over Berlin. I could tell of wounded crewmen praying for their safe return to base. I could tell of seeing Lt. Wayne Dyer going down in flame. Wayne was a good navigator. So good that he was pulled from our crew to fly lead navigator to Merseberg July 20, 1944. We were attacked straight on the nose by one-hundred plus enemy fighters. Wayne's ship nosed down burning and he never got out. Three other ships were hit suddenly; this all happening in front of us. I could go on with such stories but I know that we all had similar experiences. The things I would rather not remember all seem to blend into one bad dream, they are vague. Most clear in my memory are those happy moments, and I spent many of these with the Russian people.

Many of the 390th crewmen were anxious to learn phrases like: "Let's go for a walk.", or "How about going for a walk?", or "Would you like to go for a walk with me?" One afternoon, a pretty little native girl was peppered with such phrases by a group of eight or nine gunners completely surrounding her. She was finally able to convey to them that her boyfriend was a Russian flyer and that she was true to him, faithful, and unavailable to anyone else.

Shortly after our arrival in Russia, Colonel Ott, commander of the 390th Bomb Group, called us together to tell us that the Russians were giving us a party in the square in the little village that evening. While explaining some of the local customs to us, he emphasized that in case a Russian girl asked us to dance . . . then we must dance, as it would be an insult to refuse. That evening while we all assembled around a circular cement area specifically built for dancing, the small Russian ensemble broke out into a fast Russian dance, reminding one of 'The Sabre Dance.' One of the more attractive Russian girls across the dance floor started our way. I believe most of us swallowed in unison. She ran straight to Colonel Ott and extended her hand, asking HIM to dance. The Colonel never looked more ridiculous, but it was a sight we shall never forget.

After we all stopped laughing, I reached for a cigarette. At least ten Russian soldiers surrounded me screaming, "Seegaret . . . Seegaret?" I almost quit smoking 38 years ago!

When we left Russia, Alex was at the plane to bid me goodbye, and as I entered the waist door, he yelled, "Paul . . . Boom, Boom, Berlinski!" He then clasped his hands over his head, squeezing them tightly together, and yelled "Roosevelt - Stalin!" or was it "Stalin - Roosevelt!"?

Hope you enjoyed the above short story. Because of the language barrier, I also *could not* convince a Russian Officer that our Colt 45 Automatic Pistol was an automatic as I could not demonstrate the action loaded. He was convinced his six shot pistol was the superior gun because he could squeeze out six clicks while his gun was empty.

Front:
Goodrich, Pilot; Thomas,
CP; Nordling, N;
Shipplett, B.
Back:
Thomas, FE-G; Berry,
TTG; G. Zadzora, Ro-G;
R. Spence, WG; J. Horan,
BTG; L. Losch, TG.

Warsaw Shuttle Mission

by George Zadzora
Radio Operator-Gunner, 568th Squadron

ONE of our missions was the one known as the "Warsaw Mission". It took place on September 18, 1944.

The bombers took off early in the morning, formed-up and headed east by northeast, generally speaking, and out over the North Sea. The formation climbed steadily and crossed the northern part of Germany just south of the Danish border and continued eastward over the Baltic Sea and then changed course to a southeast heading which took us over Poland and towards Warsaw.

Approaching Warsaw, the formation descended to a lower altitude so that the supplies the planes carried would have a better chance to reach those for whom the supplies were intended — The Freedom Fighters of Warsaw.

When the navigator located the area for the supplies of guns, medical supplies, ammo, etc., to be delivered, the bomb doors opened, the supplies dropped by parachute, bomb doors closed and we flew on into heavy concentrations of flak.

During this encounter with flak, there were two flak bursts near the tail of our ship, one immediately after the first. A few moments later the tail gunner got on the intercom and said that "they were too damn close".

We continued on and landed late in the evening at Mirgorod, in the Ukraine, on a perforated steel plate runway that was laid down on a long flat field. The moment the wheels touched that steel plate runway there was a loud rattling of the steel plate runway that diminished as the plane slowed down. The plane then taxied to a parking place and the engines turned off.

The first thing that we did when we got out of the plane was to examine the damage and there were many flak holes all over the plane.

We then gathered at the rear of the ship having the new larger tail gunner enclosure. The tail gunner Leonard Losch, explained what happened over Warsaw when the two bursts of flak exploded near the tail position. Lenny said that when the first burst occurred it was very close and he then bent backwards until he was flat on his back. The second shell burst almost immediately after the first and sent a piece of shrapnel thru one side of the plexiglas and out the other leaving holes about the size of a baseball. Had he been in his normal position his head would have been at the place where the shrapnel came thru the plexiglas. Lenny escaped without a scratch.

The Maintenance Officer came over, examined the plane and said that it was grounded due to flak damage and would not take off the next morning with the rest of the planes on a mission that would take the group to Italy. So for the time being we were not sure how long we would be in the Ukraine and not certain of how and when we would get back to England.

As it turned out we spent four days at Mirgorod taking life easy and not having any duties to perform, just soaking up some warm early autumn sun.

We then received word that we were to go to Poltava some sixty miles southeast of Mirgorod. On the fourth day we got a flight to Poltava.

Again we were in a waiting situation with nothing to do. On the second day, just waiting around got to be monotonous, so the ball turret gunner, Jim Horan and I walked over to the motor pool and to our surprise no one was around. So he got into a "6x6" and I got into another one, we started the engines and headed for Poltava just a few miles away. The city itself was severely damaged but the main streets were cleared of rubble. He drove one way and I went the other way on the same street.

There was no other vehicular traffic except the trucks we took from the motor pool. People were walking along the street as there were no street cars or buses. When we saw people walking we would stop the vehicles, point to the back of the truck and they would climb aboard. Then we drove until we saw more people walking and picked them up as well.

When our passengers wanted to get off, as they reached their destination, they would pound on the roof of the truck with the palm of their hands. Now we had a system going. When we saw people walking, we picked them up, when we heard thumping noise on the roof of the the truck, we stopped to let those who reached their destination get off.

We continued this taxi service for several hours. Then when the fuel supply was getting low, we let off the last passengers and headed back to the motor pool and parked the vehicles. Again no one was around the motor pool so no questions could be asked.

The time came when we were notified that a B-17 was ready for us to take back to England via the Air Transport Command route: This plane was prepared for us by American mechanics who were at Poltava to service the planes.

And it was a gem. The fuselage and one wing was olive drab, the other wing natural aluminum color, the tail assembly a combination of both. The engines no doubt came from different planes. It had no guns, no oxygen and no windows at the waist positions and some radio equipment was lacking.

Came the morning for take-off to Tehran, we had a short briefing and were told that a Russian navigator and Russian radio operator would also be going along. No doubt to fly a course that the Russians wanted us to take.

We climbed into the ship along with the Russians with their gear and luggage. The engines were started, we taxied to the end of the runway and took off for Tehran.

Shortly after take-off the Russian radio operator indicated to me by writing on a piece of paper the frequency that he was to use to give position reports to the ground stations during this flight. Since he was not familiar with American equipment, I proceeded to set the transmitter to the frequency he indicated. I turned on the radio equipment and motioned to him that the equipment was ready for use. He tapped out a code signal to the ground station and received a reply. It brought a smile to his face. And for the remainder of this flight to Tehran only the Russian operated the radio.

The Russian navigator was in the nose of the ship along with our navigator but the Russian did all the navigating. He had his maps before him and since the day was bright and clear, all navigation was done by pilotage. He spoke no English and our navigator spoke no Russian. So they communicated by hand signals.

At one point in the flight, it was necessary to make a 10 degree turn to the left. The Russian navigator, by means of hand signals to our navigator, pointed to the left and then held up the fingers and thumbs of his hands. Our navigator then called the pilot on intercom and said to make a 10 degree turn to the left. This is the way we flew all the way to Tehran.

Several hours into the flight, we felt just a bit hungry. We had an ample supply of K-rations. The Russian radio operator also brought along some food. He had a large roast duck, a large round loaf of bread and a chunk of butter that weighed about a pound or more. He shared the duck, bread and butter with the others on the plane. We had no utensils so we just tore off a piece of duck, same with the bread, and with the bread we would scrape butter on to it. What ever number of K-rations we started out with was the same number that we had when we arrived in Tehran.

The next leg of our trip back to England was to Cairo. Most of the flight was over Biblical lands; arid and desolate but beautiful. We flew over the Dead Sea, Jerusalem, nearby Bethlehem then westward over the Suez Canal and on toward Cairo. As we approached Payne Field, the pyramids were seen. We later took a tour and visited them, including a trip into the Cheops Pyramid, the largest of the three.

Then on to Bengazi. It was early afternoon when we approached the field which was located about a mile or so from the Mediterranean Sea and we could see a beached transport ship listing heavily and a circular concrete fortification nearby just prior to landing.

Shortly after landing the upper turret gunner, Jim Thomas; waist gunner, Ralph Spence; ball turret gunner, Jim Horan and I, the radio operator, decided to take a hike and visit the ship and the concrete fort. We decided to take a direct route across the sands. This we did. Approaching the concrete fort, which had been abandoned for some time, we noticed a doorway and walked inside. The walls were about two feet thick with square or rectangular openings around the periphery. A stairway led to the roof so we went up to see what was there. And there was something: a rusted child's tricycle without tires.

We then went over to the beached transport. We climbed aboard and walked around the sharply sloped deck holding on to handrails or whatever else we could grab. It was extensively rusted so it no doubt had been resting there for many months.

Now it was getting time to get back to base. We climbed down off the ship and headed in the same direction from which we came. Walking was slow because of the hot weather and loose sand. At one point I saw a projectile lying on the sand so I picked it up, tucked it under my arm, and carried it like a football. Later I learned it was from a German eighty-eight and that it was a live shell. Whether or not it was dangerous to handle a shell like that I do not know.

As we approached the edge of the base, a Sergeant was standing there waiting for us. He asked where we were and we told him. He then asked which way did we go and we told him; a direct walk to the ship and fort and about the same way coming back. He then said, "I'm glad to see that you made it. The four of you have just made two trips through an uncleared mine field,"

Our next destination was Rome. The flight was uneventful with the exception that one engine was not performing properly. After landing at Rome, inquiries were made to find where the engine could be repaired or replaced. It was learned that facilities were not available in Rome and that the plane would have to be flown to Naples for this maintenance.

This was done and we prepared for the next leg of our trip to an airfield near Marseilles in southern France.

Prior to our flight to Marseilles, a briefing was held and the pilot received a frequency for voice contact with the control tower. The radio operator received a different frequency for code communication with the control tower in case that was necessary.

Two American infantrymen asked if we were going to England and we said that we were. They then asked the pilot if they could ride along and Goodrich said, "Sure, climb aboard."

We took off and headed out over the sea towards Marseilles. It was late in the morning so that we were aware that it would be dusk when we reached the airfield.

And so it was. As we reached the area of the airfield, the sun had set and objects on the ground were almost indistinguishable making it difficult to locate the field. The pilot attempted voice contact with the tower — no response. The pilot then called the radio operator to try code contact — again — no response. It was now almost totally dark and the pilot and radio operator could not get the control tower while circling in the general area of the field.

As we circled, the pilot began switching the landing lights on and off continuously. After about fifteen minutes this strategy worked. Lights could be seen on the ground in two parallel rows. The plane descended and landed between two rows of army vehicles with their lights turned on. We then learned that no radio communications were authorized after 6 PM as the night before JU-88s had attacked this field.

The next morning we took off with our two G.I. passengers. The plane lifted off the runway and began a slow turn to the left at no more than one hundred feet above the ground. This was an unusual take-off. The pilot continued to make a full 360 degree turn still at very low altitude, and lined up with the direction of our take-off. The pilot then opened the throttles and we were headed for the control tower located in the middle of the field. The control tower was a temporary two-story structure.

As we crossed over the edge of the field, the plane dropped to about fifty feet above the ground and then turned slightly right to miss the control tower. At this point I looked out the plane's window and saw two men who were in the control tower jump from the second story window and flatten themselves on the ground. The plane then made a steep climbing turn to the left and headed for an airfield just outside of Paris where we stayed overnight. The next morning we left for England and landed at our home field.

D.N.I.F.
Duty Not Including Flying

Turkeys are prepared for a holiday feast.

The smile on this Radio Operator's face is indicative of the attitude of the men of the Eighth Air Force.

Its Greatness Was Its People

by Joseph A. Moller
Commanding Officer, 390th Bomb Group

EVERY American knows that the Eighth Air Force, based in England, was the greatest American Air Force ever assembled. Much has been written about it as an Air Force together with the contribution it made towards the winning of World War II.

While it had the best planes and equipment which could be provided at the time, there is no doubt that its greatest asset was its people. I think that among ourselves we correctly sum it all up by saying that essentially the entire Eighth Air Force was motivated and operated by a splendid team of dedicated and patriotic Americans, each of whom contributed his fair share and more to the overall team effort. In so doing, each member of that team earned the admiration and respect of every other member.

Every combat unit had its ground and its flight personnel. Neither could operate without the other. Each was dependent upon the other. Each had tremendous respect for the other.

Because of the close coordination and understanding among all our people in the 390th, we were able to achieve outstanding bombing results while holding down our losses.

We can all remember what an Eighth Air Force bomber base looked like during the war, especially at night. Few, if any, lights could be seen. But the fact was, especially on a night before a mission, men were hard at work repairing battle damage, tuning and checking engines together with all of the systems and various types of equipment carried on each plane. Supplies, from oxygen bottles to ammunition and bombs, were loaded aboard. The men worked under tarpaulins which shielded them from the weather if it was raining; and shielded their lights from enemy bombers if intruders were overhead.

All too often the fact that the results obtained by the crews working on the aircraft determined whether the flight crews made it back to base the next day. They knew it. The flight crews knew it. The flight crews completely trusted their ground crews.

Elsewhere the entire base would be a veritable beehive of activity. The intelligence, navigation, armament, radio, mickey and operational people were going strong. The combat mess personnel were getting ready to feed the combat crews a good breakfast, with real fresh eggs; the Military Police were taking care of our security. Splendidly coordinated teamwork characterized the effort of all the men in all the arms and services. The work was accomplished effectively, efficiently and smoothly.

When time came, perhaps at midnight, to awaken the crews scheduled to fly that day's missions, the transportation people were ready and waiting to take the crews to the combat mess hall for a breakfast of real eggs. After breakfast they would take the crews to briefing and then later to their hardstands where their planes were ready and waiting for the day's mission.

Much later in the day when the tower passed the word that the boys were returning to base, our people would gather to watch; and as soon as the planes were sighted, to count the returning planes to determine how many had made it back. On days when the count showed we had lost planes, the question then became first how many and then who was not returning. It was a time of strain and worry for everyone. As the planes came in for landing, signs of battle damage became evident, as feathered props, or red-red flares for wounded aboard, and flak holes in the surface.

Our ground people would wave and call to those in the planes welcoming them back from their missions as they taxied to their hardstand. Ambulances and medicos would be busy. The transportation people would take the crews to de-briefing so they could tell their story of the mission. The camera films would be rushed to photo lab for development so that a first quick assessment of the bombing could be made.

As soon as the flight crews left the airplane, the ground crews would swarm aboard checking and noting everything which had to be repaired or replaced to make the plane again ready for combat. Often this sequence of fighting and working was a round the clock affair, yet the men never waivered in their complete dedication in the performance of their jobs.

I can remember that within about two hours after each mission had landed, and the ground people had carefully assessed the battle damage to each plane, Major Al Engler would give me his estimate of aircraft availability for combat for the next day. He would tell me so many aircraft could be made combat ready within four hours, so many within eight hours and so on.

Working on the wing of their B-17.

I never tried to push him unless I had to, but I can remember telling him on more than one occasion that his estimate was not good enough and we would need more aircraft combat ready much sooner than he indicated. Somehow he always came through because he and his men could always be counted on to "go the extra mile" — to work the extra hours — to do the needed job.

Innumerable stories might be told of the countless instances wherein our service people, day after day and night after night constantly showed great dedication in the performance of their work.

Perhaps a personal story might give some small glimpse of the dedication and devotion of our ground people to their assigned tasks.

Early one night, during which I could not sleep, though it was my night to sleep, we had been alerted for a mission the next day. As I often did, I got into my car and drove around the perimeter track which leads to the hardstands. I would stop now and then to talk to the ground crews readying the planes for the next day's mission. It was an unpleasant evening. We had had a red alert earlier and a cold drizzle was falling. The men were working under tarpaulins.

Eventually I came to an empty hardstand, but as I was passing it I thought I saw a man sitting on a tool box. I turned into the hardstand and drew up beside the man, realizing as I did that perhaps he belonged to the ground crew of one of our aircraft which had not returned from that day's mission.

I greeted him and for the next few minutes he had very little to say. At first he may not have known nor cared who I was, yet I was driving the only sedan on the base, if that meant anything to him. But there he was, sitting on a box on an empty hardstand in the rain, answering my first questions and statements with but a word or two.

Somehow, quite suddenly he seemed to recognize who I

Ground crewmen relax at the Red Cross Canteen.

was and he began to talk.

He was the crew chief of an aircraft which had not returned. He had been sitting there since the mission landed some five or six hours before. After talking about the mission, he finally said, "Colonel, I have gone over everything that we did to that airplane last night a thousand times in my mind. I can't think of a thing we didn't do or check and double check — but still I wonder if somewhere I went wrong."

When he stopped talking, I told him, "Sergeant, I led the mission today. One of the aircraft lost was yours. I have gone over the mission in my mind as well as at de-briefing. I will say that I, too, wonder about many things." He said, "You wonder too, Colonel?" and I said, "Yes, I wonder, too, Sergeant."

Then, after a moment or two during which we seemed fully occupied with our own thoughts, I said, "Sergeant, let me give you a piece of advice which General LeMay gave me after I had led an especially rough mission in which we lost several aircraft and after which I had spent time flying and reflying that mission and wondering about a great many things.

General LeMay said to me, after we had discussed the mission, 'If you can think back to everything you said and did, and can honestly say to yourself that you know — beyond any doubt — that you did the very best you could under the circumstances as you knew them at that time, you have no reason to look back.' "

And then I said, "Sergeant, I am passing this on to you because if you believe this advice, even if you wonder about some things, you can go forward with confidence and a clear conscience."

Again, we were quiet for a minute or two. Then, thoroughly soaked and obviously cold as he was, he stood up, faced me, and though he seemed to break down, he saluted and said, "Thank you, sir," turned and walked away.

This has been a simple story of the dedication, of the devotion to duty and of the acceptance and discharge of an enormous responsibility — the safety of an aircraft and its crew, by a crew chief in our ground echelon.

It is no wonder, therefore, that the flight crews admired, trusted and respected the ground personnel; and that the ground people honored and respected the flight personnel.

These were the great people of the Eighth Air Force and they are the reason the Eighth Air Force was great.

You Can Always Learn

by Joseph A. Moller

AS I sometimes did, when the information for the next day's mission was slow in coming in, I would not call my driver but just get in my car and drive myself around the perimeter track, stopping now and then to talk to the men working on the planes. Of course, everything was blacked out. To drive we used a mere slit of light from the car's headlights to see the road.

One cold, rainy, dark night, I had circled the perimeter track and was heading back to the war room at headquarters, when I saw a G.I. walking not too steadily along the perimeter road. I stopped beside him, asked him where he was going and suggested he get in and I would take him there.

He settled himself in the seat, turned to me and, obviously thinking I was my driver, asked, "What do you think of that old bastard you work for?"

Somewhat startled, I told him that that old bastard was

really a pretty good guy.

His response to that was that because I worked for him I had to say that, and, after all, I was not walking in the rain as he was, but was riding in a warm, dry car.

So we discussed the old man and I did my best selling job when, to top off his argument, he said the old man really didn't know much, and especially about guarding airplanes. Now I had never thought much about that. I suppose I just assumed the MP's knew their job, and were doing it even though we did get reports of sabotage once in a while.

About that time we arrived at the 68th Squadron area. As he got out, I asked for and was told his name.

The next morning, after the mission took off, I called the Commander of the 68th Squadron and gave him the soldier's name and said I wanted to see both the C.O. and the soldier in my office.

Shortly thereafter they both were announced by my Adjutant Major John Williams, and came into my office. I suggested they be seated and opened the conversation by asking the soldier if my car had picked him up the night before. He said it had. I then asked him if he had said that the old man didn't know much — especially about guarding aircraft. His answer to that was "that damn driver talks too much."

I then told him I was the driver. He jumped out of his chair, shook his fist and said it was "damned unfair to fool a fellow soldier like that."

I agreed that I was unfair, but told him I also wanted him to tell me how he would guard aircraft.

He told me. He was right. He said that guards around aircraft should not walk post, they should not be visible. They should — in effect — hide out of sight, but where they could see and hear any one approaching the plane.

Later, I talked the idea over with Capt. Archie White of the MP's, and we adopted the idea of guarding our aircraft. At the next group commander's meeting I gave the idea to all 3rd Division Commanders. I heard later some were already guarding aircraft that way and that others then started it.

All because a G.I. told the C.O. he didn't know much, especially about guarding aircraft.

Little Friends

---

by Joseph A. Moller

IN the earlier days of daylight bombing, the fighters — our "Little Friends" — would go with us, perhaps as far as Achen, which would be the then limit of their endurance.

We, in the bombers, were the "Big Friends" whom they defended against the enemy fighters — the "Bandits." But when their fuel supply forced them to turn back, we would have to fight our way to the target and back to a rendezvous with our "Little Friends" who had refueled and came out to meet us as we returned to England. And, once again, they would take on the fighters who had been attacking us.

As time went on, external drop tanks were developed which extended the range of the fighters. More fighters became available which permitted relays of fighters to be used and which then protected us throughout the entire mission.

There is no way of knowing how many bombers made it back to base because of our "Little Friends" defending the bomber stream. But every airman who flew in bombers is well aware of the debt he owed our "Little Friends."

I recall one day when the mission had been a rough one.

A P-51 "Little Friend" off the wing of a B-17.

Our fighters had taken on the bandits. We were in de-briefing. A fighter pilot, having engine trouble, had landed at our base. I took him into the de-briefing room.

Word quickly passed throughout the room that one of the fighter pilots who had flown that day was in the room. With no word spoken, every bomber airman stood up. The room was silent for a minute or two as the bomber airmen paid unspoken thanks and tribute to the fighter pilot.

A moment later "as you were" was given and de-briefing resumed.

The incident illustrates the bomber airmen's feelings towards the fighter pilots whom they saw time and again, take on superior numbers of Luftwaffe pilots to protect their "Big Friends."

The fighter pilot was our hero.

The Three Musketeers and 'Doc'

by Joshua M. Perman, M.D.

Flight Surgeon, 570th Bomb Squadron

For many reasons, friendships during wartime developed into a special comraderie important to all. What was important to one became important to all! Those friendships left memories, shared by all fighting units, that have been told over and over again, or have been recalled in private moments at special times of remembrance.

This is part of the story of one special group. How did we meet? We were all in the 570th Bomb Squardon. Who was the organizer? "Stretch" Settles? Captain "Mac" McKnight? or Bill Corkrean? Perhaps it was the result of my rounds to all of the barracks, or the convenient location of my Squadron Dispensary. It just seemed to happen, we were

144

Sometimes you just want to get away from it all.

frequently together, sometimes as two, as three or all four.

There were the times we listened to Corkrean and his wonderful droll sense of humor, or quietly listened to his mountain music from his cherished fiddle as he sat by a tree across from my dispensary and played to the cattle that surrounded him. It was a memorable scene that warmed our hearts and our friendship. Do you remember the time Corkrean on liftoff grazed a fence with his landing gear, on one typically dark English morning? When I asked him, on his return from the mission, if he knew he had touched the fence with his wheels, he quipped in reply, "Did I hurt it?" One day, he failed to return from a mission!

Then there was "Mac" who always insisted that I accompany him to Sunday Services and took particular delight when I raised my voice with his to *Onward Christian Soldiers*. As we walked back to the Squadron area, we both chuckled at Padre's surprise on seeing me at his services, at which point I would say, "Mac, why do you insist on taking a nice Jewish boy to Christian Services?"

"Doc", he always replied, "It's good for your soul!"
McKnight was killed in Belgium when his chute failed to
open after he delayed his jump until all of his crew were
safely out of his plane.

Stretch, Mac, Corkrean and I had our bullsessions that
covered many subjects. We talked in my dispensary around
the warm stove, on walks around the area, or on bicycle
rides, or at the Officer's Club. Stretch completed his tour of
missions when tragedy struck his family in the States. After
a visit there, he returned to fly and to survive the war. We
still correspond at irregular intervals.

My experience as a Flight Surgeon left a deep impression
on me. After the war, I completed my residency training in
Pediatrics, but after a few months in private practice I
decided to return to residency training to complete what I
had begun as a Flight Surgeon. I became a Psychiatrist and
then a Psychoanalyst. That was the result of the total
experience. The personal experiences were special and left
deep impressions that were as Mac said, "Good for my
soul!"

Glenn Miller and his band play at the 390th.

Al Engler points out engineering change ideas to a Boeing Tech. Rep.

Reflections of a Group Engineering Officer

by Al Engler

Group Engineering Officer, 390th Bomb Group

Regarding aircraft weight: Various publications give the B-17 maximum gross weight anywhere from about 53,000 lbs. to 65,000 lbs. The actual Tech Order maximum was 64,500 lbs. The 390th held close to this number except for as much as 1000 pounds of extra ammunition for long range missions when fighters were to be expected.

In one case a B-17 was reported as chronically tail-heavy and high in fuel consumption. Inspection revealed a tail gunners position completely lined with multiple layers of flak-suits. The inspector estimated about 1000 lbs of flak suits were removed. The complaints of tail-heaviness

147

Inspecting an engine on a dolly.

stopped.

« « « » » »

A significant change from B-17F's and G's was the doubling of braking capacity. The E's had expander tube brakes only on the inside of each main wheel; the F's and G's had brakes on both the inside and outside of each wheel. The added braking saved many aircraft by permitting hard braking when landing on the last half or third of the runway when bad weather made any glimpse of the runway a welcome sight. The old brakes would have caused many overruns and possible collisions on the ground.

« « « » » »

Changing inboard superchargers (Nos. 2 and 3 engines) on B-17s was a miserable job because of extremely limited access. As a result each squadron tried to maintain at least one very small statured mechanic who could crawl inside the wing behind the wheel wells to help replace superchargers.

« « « » » »

Apparently many B-17G's were rushed to the ETO even though some important parts were not as originally intended. During the winter of 1943-1944 many crews reported frozen-over windshields and windows due to inadequate heat. In some reported cases, formation flying was performed with pilot and co-pilot looking out the open cockpit side windows because the windshields were frosted over. Some aircraft returned to base with frost still on the windows.

Investigation revealed that the new heating systems (heated air from passage over exhaust stacks in place of the former glycol heaters inside the exhaust stacks) did not have the fluted exhaust headers required for sufficient heat exchange. The headers were just straight pipe about 6 inches in diameter. A frantic call to the Boeing technical representative revealed that the proper fluted stacks were unavailable at the time. After some arm-twisting, the Boeing representative remembered that some experiments had been made in drilling holes in the exhaust stack and making small "scoops" to cause exhaust gas to leak out and pass directly to the air-to-air heat exchanges in the wing. He didn't know how big or how many holes were made in the stack. Group Engineering was very apprehensive about holes in the stack because excessive loss of exhaust pressure would prevent the superchargers from maintaining manifold pressure at altitude and thus cause "aborts." (For one reason or another Group CO's and Operations Officers seemed to frown on "aborts.")

Engineering guessed at a hole size and drilling pattern and modified about ten or twelve aircraft that same night for use the next morning — without notifying anyone or obtaining any approval.

We knew the planes would perform well at low altitude

but high altitude was a question mark. I don't remember drawing a deep breath for two or three hours after the mission took off for fear of multiple "aborts." No aborts occurred from this cause, however, and the crews reported much improved heating. We used this makeshift "fix" for quite a few weeks until we could obtain the proper fluted stacks. Very few people ever knew of the quick fix.

« « « » » »

When engine failures occurred on a mission, the aircraft was normally out-of-service at least one full day to change the engine and fly at least three hours of flight "slow time." When aircraft availability in the Group was low due to battle damage, an overnight engine change on an otherwise flyable airplane seemed like a minor problem provided the three hours of slow time flight could be arranged. One squadron (I believe it was the 571st) agreed to try the concept of installing four overhauled engines on a war-weary aircraft and slow-timing the engines so they would be immediately flyable upon installation on a mission-ready aircraft. This permitted installing a complete engine-propeller package in a few hours instead of eight hours plus slow-time. The concept proved to be feasible and did ease aircraft availability in a number of cases; however, the concept was eventually abandoned mainly because each engine had to be installed twice and the mechanics seemed to have enough to do without doubling engine changes!

« « « » » »

A humorous note (now, not then!): The single cylinder, two-cycle engine driven auxiliary generators called "putt putts" provided to check out electrical systems without running the aircraft engines, and for starting the engines, were great! — if you could get them started. No statistics were kept, but it occurs to me that the auxiliary power units in each squadron required the equivalent effort of a full time mechanic. The power units expanded the swear word vocabulary of many mechanics, and caused many a dripping sweat on cold nights from pulling on the starter ropes. Aircraft engines we understood and could cope with; auxiliary power units baffled us to the very end!

« « « » » »

On the first Russian shuttle mission, the 390th was reassigned to a Russian fighter field at Zaporozhye after landing at Mirgorod. One of the B-17s had a main gear wheel go through the light concrete runway to a depth that the underside of the wing was almost on the runway. We didn't have wing jacks to raise the aircraft and requested by radio that jacks be sent to us from Tehran, the nearest source. In the meantime we worked at trying to pave a path to pull the aircraft out. A couple days later the jacks arrived and we raised the aircraft in the late afternoon with the help of Russian soldiers who had been wounded and were recuperating at a local hospital. We found out later that all the local farm workers had planned to come to the field that evening after work to pick up the aircraft so we could block up under it. There were enough strong people around that I don't doubt they could have done the job!

« « « » » »

A "trick-of-the-trade" that might be of interest: The exhaust driven G.E.Co. superchargers were very reliable and durable; however, they occasionally lost one or two of their 250-300 buckets due to excessive stress or flak. The supercharger bucket wheel had to be in good balance to deliver full pressure at altitude because the wheel wound up to about 27,000 rpm. Changing superchargers, as required by Technical Orders, was a tedious, time consuming job. Some clever person discovered that if the supercharger was otherwise in good condition, we could rebalance it by deliberately breaking off a bucket directly opposite the missing bucket. Supercharger performance was unaffected and much time was saved. This was a very useful gimmick and a tribute to the rugged design of the supercharger.

John Quinn in 1944

Understatement

by John Quinn

Engineering, 571st Squadron

IT was early 1944, February or March when I received a letter from my father that contained my cousins' address in Coventry and asking me to pay them a visit.

From their letters to us in 1940-41, we knew that they had been through some terrifying times, but typical of folks in those days their letters usually contained some witty remark or a very large note of optimism. I recall one such. In a letter from cousin Rose around November or December of 1940, she wrote; "We had a bit, a wee bit of damage from the sky the other night, but thank God none of us were hurt, and now we have got some kindling for the rest of the winter."

Three and a half years later I would recall those words.

152

Coventry lies about one-hundred ten miles west of Ipswich. In those days, one had to get there by way of London, since the main line tracks were not always usable. As I recall it took seven or eight hours to make the journey. It was late afternoon when we pulled into Coventry Station.

From their letters I knew they lived across the square from Coventry's ancient fourteenth century cathedral. Getting directions from a railway employee, I started down the High Street to the town centre. As I walked I became acutely aware of what total destruction meant. For eight or nine square blocks only an occasional bit of a wall or the stump of a chimney still stood. There were countless mounds of brick and stone everywhere neatly placed, eventually to be used again. What had once been a crowded tenement district was now a wasteland.

After arriving at the cathedral square, I wandered about looking for Belvidere Court. Not being able to find it, I decided to seek help. After many, "Sorry, I don't know that street," I was fortunate in finding a constable who knew my relatives. Pointing down a nearby lane and across a meadow at smoke rising from a chimney, he said, "That is their home. I believe you will find them in."

Arriving at the spot I gazed in disbelief at what had unfolded before my eyes; the remnants of a chimney eight or ten feet high with sections of carved figurines still stuck to the brickwork, a small section of an inlaid mosaic tile and marble floor peered out from the dust and debris. A wisp of smoke curled out of the top of the chimney ascending into the sky until it disappeared from view. There were three small windows in what was the basement wall. All this framing had been the main floor of a once elegant home. On the side was a sloped cellar scuttle and all around neat piles of brick, stone and wood. And from within came the sound of laughter and voices.

In response to my timid knock, a young woman appeared who I instantly recognized from her picture as cousin, Rose. I introduced myself and was invited in. It was then that I recalled her words of nearly four years before when she said, "Welcome John, as you can see, we were damaged a bit but we were more fortunate than our neighbors. We still have our home."

London taxi.

Recollections — D.N.I.F.

by Wilbert H. Richarz

Radio Operator-Gunner, 570th Squadron, **Cocaine Bill**

FIRST TRIP TO LONDON

ON our first trip to London as a crew we were still at the stage of sticking together. After all we had weathered nine missions by sticking together and we had kind of gotten used to the idea. On the ricky-ticky train ride from Ipswich we had time on our hands and we nervously played cards and read and wondered what the big city would really be like.

The first thing we noticed about Liverpool Station was the bomb damage and the makeshift track system built over the bombed ones underneath. The second thing was the soot-loaded air from the train engines puffing their coal smoke under the girdered canopy that roofed the station.

155

With our B-4 bags in hand we went out to take our first ride in a real London taxi.

The fabled and ubiquitous London Taxi proved to be a stodgy, gleaming black little monster. The driver sat in the open while the passengers rode in covered comfort. The paint looked like it went clear through and was obviously as tough as it looked. The drivers were obviously proud of their machines both in terms of fact and legend. One of our guys accidentally scraped a fender with his bag and at his guilty look the driver nonchalantly remarked, "Think nothing of it mate, she's built like a bloody tank." Once in motion the driver drove with expert aplomb through the thick traffic accompanied by a constant tattoo on the saucy sounding horn.

Since we were big spenders on our first fling we had reservations at the Winston Hotel off Picadilly Circus. We got a couple of adjoining rooms and went down to eat in the hotel dining room. A dark, brooding waiter in a faded and worn tuxedo-type uniform seated us and presented our menus with a flair and a French accent. The menu was mostly in French, and the only thing on it that was at all recognizable was "Steak Neopolitan." I asked, "What is this Steak Neopolitan?" In pure Brooklynese he replied, "Hamburger Steak, Mac!" The "steak" was as phony as his French accent. It tasted like sawdust as did everything else. We learned the real meaning of "ersatz" and after that even the Mess Hall food was more palatable.

After dinner we walked around and watched the human drama taking place on the sidewalks. Prostitutes of all descriptions looking for business; sidewalk entrepreneurs selling every conceivable piece of merchandise both human and material, large and small; soldiers, sailors, and marines of almost every allied country looking for relief from the war; scammers and shysters everywhere, all dedicated to parting the servicemen from their money. Bombed-out buildings, air raid shelters, the blackout after dark, and the high tension sounds of forced bawdy laughter, loud

Picadilly Circus.

drunken voices, traffic and traffic whistles, and in the midst of it all the somber black-uniformed Bobbies patrolling and lending an almost ludicrous solemnity to the mad circus atmosphere.

Somebody had heard that the Regent Palace Hotel was the place to go for servicemen, so we wandered over wondering what the attraction was. In front on the street level was a large poster sign with a picture of a very formidable-looking red-haired woman. Beneath the picture was printed "Daisy Mae Skaggs and her violin playing in the dining room for your pleasure." Now, Daisy didn't look like a concert violinist, but I can tell you she played beautifully as she strolled from table to table. On the other hand, it just didn't wash that Daisy Mae was the attraction for servicemen on leave from the monastic war so we looked further.

Below the street level we found a ballroom replete with numerous bars strategically located so that no one need go too far to buy a drink. The ballroom and bars opened at 5 o'clock. Leading to the ballroom was a long hallway and when we got there at about 4:30 we found the answer to the question. Arranged along the right wall were women of every possible description from all over England: brunettes, blondes, redheads, some even purple haired, tall, short, ad infinitum — all painted fallen sparrows. Along the left wall were the servicemen — all allied countries represented. Each group appeared to be ignoring the other. At the time I put this down as some form of perverse British protocol, but I never did find out the why of it all. However, at 5 o'clock sharp the big double doors to the ballroom opened and immediately the two groups merged and the socializing began—tentative testing, bantering, conversation, and finally price quoting and bargaining. How many bargains were struck I don't know, but I got the idea that to the service men the game was the thing—to the girls it was economic survival.

We stood around for awhile and gawked and listened, but we were too wet behind the ears for that traffic so we had a drink or two and wandered back to the hotel. Everything seemed relatively normal, reasonably quiet, when all of a sudden it felt like the earth split. The walls buckled, the plaster flew from wall to wall, we were thrown out of bed onto the floor, and the telephone hit the floor and began to ding plaintively. Our heads were ringing and dust filled the air. It was only then we heard a sharp crackling explosion of awesome volume and force. Obviously a bomb of some sort had struck close by — but what kind and where?

The next morning we found the answer. A V-2 Rocket had struck the American Bar a few blocks away. A rocket that was as big as a boxcar and went up 60 miles before descending at tremendous speed to penetrate deep into the ground before exploding. It had scored a direct hit on the American Club by sheer chance and I believe it had killed over a hundred Americans. We happened to be just close enough to feel the blast and just far enough away to not be hurt. Luck!

The next night I rode the Subway or the Tube as it was called. The first thing I heard when I descended to the track level was the sound of the train stopping and a female voice saying "mind the step" and then the mass of humanity poured out onto the platform. As I looked down the platform I was struck by the rows of three-high bunks lined up against the wall. On the bunks were mostly small children and a few older people lying down. Other older people were sitting on the lower bunks, the women knitting or sewing and the men reading. A few had chairs and sat between the bunks. They seemed absolutely and completely oblivious to the bedlam of humanity and noise that flowed back and forth and up and down the part of the platform adjacent to the tracks. In fact, there seemed to be an invisible but unbreachable wall between the two groups. On one side the quiet old folks and children, sleeping and resting, and on the other side drunken G.I.s, English girls, loud voices, laughing, and singing of bawdy songs like "Roll Me Over in the Clover," and, of course, other humanity such as British night workers, air raid wardens, and an occasional older person going who knows where. Each group acted as if the other didn't exist. In fact, it was apparent that for each — the other did not exist. They didn't see each other. They didn't hear each other. I suppose it was a classic example of social adaptation in the face of overstress.

The next day we returned to the fantasy world of the air war. Behind us we left the fantasy world of a metropolis in a war. Both seemed strange and unreal. We weren't sure which was the furthest from reality. We did know we would be going back to London, but underneath the bantering, the spreading of wings, the sowing of oats, the relief from pure combat we all knew that we had seen a wounded city and a wounded but resilient people and that it had left an indelible mark on each of us.

THE FLAK HOUSE

About the time that our crew of 097 *(Cocaine Bill)* finished our 23rd mission we began to laugh at things that were less than funny and to brood about ridiculous things. It was then that our lower ball gunner Hap Halek went to work on the problem with his usual BTO suavity and skill. And it wasn't very long before we were on our way to the "Rest Home" at South Port for a brief respite from the air war.

On the train enroute, I met a Canadian Infantry man and in our conversation I learned two things: we really did deserve and need to go to the Flak House and once again I realized how lucky I was to have gotten out of the infantry and into the Air Corps. He said, "You chaps are the real heroes of the war. My heart goes out to you when I see you flying over and see your planes going down in flames." Then in response to my questioning, he told me that he had been wounded four times and was on his way back to the front for the fifth time. I told him that if we made it through the mission we returned to a warm meal and a bed — not C rations and a fox hole — and if we were wounded anywhere near severely we would be sent back stateside. In short, I told him, the words to the song applied "Live in fame or go down in flame" and that was the way most of us liked it. Then too, there were the three-day passes to London every three or four weeks to oil the machinery and when things

Crew of *Gloria Ann* plays croquet at the Flak House.

were just too much there was always the Flak House. Better than the infantry. He didn't understand.

When we got to the "Rest House" we found it to be a huge castle completely converted for the ease and pleasure of us war-weary airmen. Red Cross girls; English girls with pretty teeth, hose, and perfume; real cokes; fantastic food; tea time every day with non-ersatz sweets of all kinds; dances; girls with pretty teeth, hose, and perfume; movies; sports; and girls with pretty teeth, hose, and perfume. Around the walls in the dining hall were full color pictures — each depicting a different single line from the song "America the Beautiful" such as "across the fruited plain," "thy purple mountain majesties," and "from sea to shining sea." Nobody passed these without getting a lump in his throat.

Altogether it was an experience never to be forgotten — a time to regroup, reassess, and to realize once again that we were doing a good thing and that our country was worth everything we could give it. The only problem was that when we returned to the base the next mission was the toughest of all. We had been so vividly reminded of how much we had to lose if we didn't make it that every burst of flak seemed to have our name on it.

P-51s AND CYCLING

My boyhood friend Eddie Hyman flew P-51s and was stationed at the 357th at Saxmundham which was about 11 miles away by twisting, winding lanes. He usually flew the same days that I did since the 357th normally flew escort for us. As a result it was tough for us to get to see each other, other than to wave as he sideslipped over and under our formation at 27,000 feet. Finally, after careful calendar watching we found a day when we were both DNIF so I hitched a ride over on the mail truck.

Riding in the back of the truck I didn't get much chance to memorize the route, but I was acutely conscious that there were many turns, small villages, and little lanes. Later I was to regret not paying more attention.

Eddie met me and we talked over old times for a while and then he suggested we go down to the Flight Line and watch the planes come back from the mission of the day on which they had escorted B-17s. We watched the planes land and I was quick to note that all planes had returned safely. We then got into the "pick-up" truck and went to the various hardstands to pick up the pilots. After all were in, the conversation turned to the mission. I was sitting in the shadows and unnoticed when one pilot said to his buddy, "God, did you see those bombers go through that flak?" "Yeah," said the other pilot, "I really feel sorry for those poor bastards." At this I couldn't restrain myself and I asked, "Don't they shoot at your guys too?" "Hell no," he replied, "when that flak starts we get the hell out of the way."

That night when it came time to leave the fighter base and return to our 390th base at Parham near Wickham Market, there was no transportation. This was a considerable blow since I was fairly sure I would probably be up to fly the next morning. Desperate, I finally borrowed a bicycle and armed with detailed directions from practically everybody about which turns to take, short cuts, and places to avoid, I set out. I was not too sure of the navigation required, but I was supremely confident that I was equal to the trip. After all I had grown up on a bike and I was in good physical condition. I figured that even if I made a navigational mistake or two, if I left at 8 p.m. I could surely make the 11 miles before 1 a.m. — the earliest time that we were usually alerted for a mission.

Everything being blacked out, the usual ground fog, and there being no moon, it was dark as the inside of an Egyptian tomb. All I could see was the narrow road in front of me, an occasional house, lots of fog, and nobody on the road.

I had on my O.D. uniform and a raincoat, and I carried a Mussette Bag. For awhile I did fairly well and I thought I would arrive back in plenty of time. Then I got lost, the first time, then the second, then the third, etc. Finally, I saw a sliver of light from the doorway of a small farm house and I stopped to seek directions. I knocked and the door opened a fraction of an inch and a middle-aged woman peeked out. I said, "I'm lost. Could you direct me to the bomber base?" She said, "Have you got any cigarettes?" "No," I replied, "I'm sorry I don't smoke." She said, "So am I." "Where is the base?," I asked, She asked, "Which one? There are five nearby." Since I was very security conscious I decided I should not say "390th" and since I couldn't do that I was back where I started. Besides with no cigarettes with which to barter I wasn't too sure I'd get a right answer anyway. I left her standing in the door looking a bit puzzled while I continued down the road even more puzzled.

About midnight I was soaking wet all the way through, completely exhausted, and feverishly desperate to find the "base." By that time I knew I was somewhere near Wickham Market and if I could find it, I then knew the rest of the way. I thought I might have passed it in the dark and was on my way to Ipswich, 16 miles away, but had no way to verify such a disastrous thought. Time was running out.

Finally I saw a dim light approaching from downhill in front of me. When it got closer I saw it was a girl on a bicycle and as she got near she "ring-a-linged" the push bell on her handle bar and swept by me. Seeing my last chance hurtling by I called out, "Wait, wait please, I need help." To no avail — she raced away. The only thing that slowed her down was the steep hill I had just descended. Panicked, I turned my bike around and started after her calling to her to wait. She continued with a steady determined rhythm while as tired and raveled as I already was I was practically foaming at the mouth. Finally I overtook her and while gasping for breath between strokes of the pedals I asked her, "Where's the base out of Wickham Market?" Without missing a beat she gave me the precious directions and then zoomed away while saying in her impeccable English accent, "I say, you don't cycle much do you?" Talk about feeling inadequate.

I rode up in front of the Quonset Hut just as the rest of the crew was coming out on their way to the mess hall for the pre-mission breakfast. Amid all the jokes about where I probably had been, how bedraggled I looked, etc., I fell in line and trudged to the truck. That mission was the longest day of my life.

THE GROUND CREW

In the years that have followed the war, one of my greatest regrets is that I never sufficiently thanked our ground crew for the part they played in our completing 35 missions. Oh, I've thought about them many, many thimes and I have always been grateful, then as well as now. I just never told them exactly how I felt.

Maybe they knew or maybe they would have been embarrassed had I voiced my feelings in those days of dark, early morning encounters before the missions and the studied casualness of the after-landing comments: "How was it?" "Not bad." "Glad you made it back." "Thanks."

I remember our Crew Chief, "Ace" Brault, and the hours upon hours he and his crew spent in getting our "bird" ready, replacing engines, repairing battle damage, and making sure that airplane was battle ready and would not fail us. It never did. Most of all I remember the looks on their faces when we taxied up to the hard stand after a long mission. It was the look of thankfulness, relief, and fellowship, but I never fully understood what they really went through until I spent my first non-flying day out on the runway waiting for the survivors of the mission to return. It was an education in compassion.

About an hour before the estimated return time the ground crews would gather along the flight line to sweat out the return of "their" crew. The first clue was the feeling of an ominous presence — a feeling that something was about to happen — something was coming. Quite possibly it was the unseen, unheard but "felt" sounds of the engines from afar and it was awesome. Then, slowly you could feel the throb of the engines — then you could hear them — coming closer and closer. Then far off the end of the runway you could see the dark specks coming low against the sky from the channel. They grew in size as they came nearer, and everyone strained to see and then everyone began to count — one, two, three...

Off and on somebody would recognize and call out an airplane by the pilot's name — "That's so and so," "That's so and so," especially when the red flares began to appear indicating the presence of wounded aboard. Then they looked for damaged aircraft. And all the time the counting continued — fourteen, fifteen... It was seldom that anyone expected the full 36 to return, but from the ground crews' viewpoint it was first how many returned and then did "their" crew get back?

Ground crews watch the planes returning from a mission.

As each "bird" touched down it was counted again and identified for sure — "Yep, that's Jones — there's Perry." The ambulances raced to those with wounded. Their ground crews rushed to help. Fire trucks stood by for the planes on fire. The runway cleared for aircraft with disabling damage. And the counting continued. From Colonel Joe on down to the lowest ranking man, everybody counted.

When a ground crew recognized their plane and they knew it was safely down, they raced to the hardstand to meet their combat crew and to casually and as off-handedly as possible say the things they always said.

Unless the members of the air crews ever spent an afternoon meeting survivors they would never know how the ground crews really felt. I found out that "Ace" and his crew really cared. I hope they knew I knew and that I cared too. Flying the missions was tough. It was tougher to wait.

ENGLISH TRAINS

Back in 1944 while with the 390th the only way to get to London for a three-day pass was by train. The English train of that time was right out of a Class B movie about the Orient Express: Loose-jointed, noisy, dirty, and so slow they gave passengers plenty of time to play cards, sleep, or observe each other.

I remember one time there was a fellow Yank across the aisle and facing my direction. He was obviously day-dreaming. It was daytime but even so there were small bare electric light bulbs burning in the ceiling. The only time they were noticeable was when the train went through a tunnel.

As I was watching my fellow traveler with his vacant stare of daydreaming, the train went through a tunnel. He looked out the window at the blackness of the tunnel, his eyes adjusting to the dark, and then glanced across the aisle in my direction. The funny thing was that he didn't see me or anything else until I motioned violently in his line of vision. It was obvious that when we went through the tunnel he saw that it was too dark to see and then, not realizing that the little bulbs were burning inside the car, when he looked back inside, his mind told him he couldn't see because it was supposed to be dark — and he couldn't see.

Another time Dixie Anderson and I shared a compartment with an English lady and her young teenaged daughter and three English soldiers. At tea time the English lady offered to share her tea with us. To be polite we did and found it to be little more than wartime milky colored warm water. We felt we had to reciprocate in some way so we took some oranges out of our B-4 bags and passed them around. We were really surprised that none of the English people in that compartment had ever seen an orange and we had to show them how to peel them. We knew the war was tough on the civilians but didn't realize that most of them had also never seen a banana or many other fruits that we took for granted.

GOD, THE ODDS, AND CAMBRIDGE

The stove had been turned down and the lights had just been turned off. Outside the green of England was shrouded in fog. The inside of the Quonset was dead dark. Already, Tex, the waist gunner, felt the damp cold seeping up through the crack between biscuit one and two of his three biscuit English mattress. "Damn," he thought, "as long as we are helping the English fight the war you'd think the least they could do is give us a decent mattress. Next I'll feel those damn springs in my back and then there'll be no sleep for sure."

The other crew members in the Hut didn't seem to have Tex's problem. Their characteristic night sound patterns were already in full symphony. Pete was snoring loudly and vibrantly. Limpy was inhaling in long windy whooshes and then sighing contentedly. Ernie was grinding his teeth and snickering at the same time. Everybody else was breathing in regular sleep slowed cadence. All except Joe, the lower ball gunner. He was out chasing village girls and drinking Pub ale. Tex couldn't sleep so he thought about Joe.

Joe was a good man, but it seemed to Tex that the crew spent a lot of time taking care of Joe, seeing that he was on time, helping him get ready for a mission, helping him meet his responsibilities. Somehow, though, he always made it. "Maybe," thought Tex, "the problem is that in flying combat together for so long, sharing life-and-death situations over and over, you get to know one another too well." Certainly he and Joe knew each other better than any civilians. When you depended on each other for your life you got to know each other pretty well.

They were different, Tex and Joe. Tex, from a small ranch in West Texas, brought up to be self-reliant. Believed everybody should pull his own weight. Like a lot of people he was not formally religious, but from his upbringing he lived by a strict code of right and wrong. He thought of himself as a person of logic. Facts, figures, and reasons seemed to him to be more important than blind faith. He looked for concrete answers.

Joe, on the other hand, was from a different background. He was a big city boy of slavic and religious roots. He lived life to the fullest as he saw it and when he overstepped his narrow confines, which he did often, naturally he confessed, asked God for forgiveness, and started anew. He had faith and he believed. He prayed a lot.

"Oh well," thought Tex, "what the hell, who knows what's right and wrong." At that moment he heard the outer door open and then in a moment the inner door and he knew that Joe was back. "Just in time, too," he thought, since their probable flight alert call was only two hours or so away. Another long day ahead on too little sleep. Then he heard Joe clumsily making his way around the chairs and the long table which occupied most of the center of the room. Then around the stove and finally to his bunk which was just beneath Tex's. Tex lay still. No need for conversation, and he heard Joe take off his clothes and crawl noisily into bed while constantly talking to himself in low mumbling and slurred words. He was settling himself on the biscuits when with a sudden snort and an "oh hell" he got back out of bed and knelt down beside it. Then Tex heard him pray. "Dear Lord," he said, "tomorrow I'm going on a mission. Please protect me and bring me back safe so I can go back home to my mother and girl friend Suzie. Amen." Then he crawled back into bed and in a few minutes was fast asleep.

In the darkness Tex thought it over. To his logical mind it just didn't make any sense. "Tomorrow," he thought, "there will be millions of missiles of all kinds sailing through the air. Some aimed. Some flying around at random. Thousands of human beings will be killed, maimed, or wounded. The probability — the odds — of being hit is just that — a matter of odds. Then there is the probability of which Divisions, Wings, Groups, Squadrons, individual aircraft, and crews will fly tomorrow. By what system were they selected? How was it all decided?

"Then there are the problems of full load take-offs in the dark, the oxygen, the cold, the mechanical efficiency of the aircraft, its durability. Then there's the fact of whether the flak burst is behind you and has to chase your plane and strikes with low velocity or whether you run into the flak and the shrapnel comes back with its forward speed against your forward speed in which case even the best armor plate won't stop the penetration. Then there's the close formation flying, the fighters, and on and on.

"With all this going on," thought Tex, "you can't tell me that when that one piece of flak gets up to Joe that the good Lord is going to hold up his hand and say 'Stop, Joe prayed last night.' No," thought Tex, "if there is a God He's just got to be too busy to worry about Joe. It's got to be just mathematical probability — the odds — luck."

Thirty-eight years later Tex stood on a grassy knoll at the Cambridge Memorial Cemetery. It was spring and all

A formation against a cloudy backdrop.

around him was the green of England and he was stirred by a flood of old memories. He looked down at the row upon row of white crosses, 3,811 of them. And on the Wall of the Missing the names of 5,125 who gave their lives but whose remains were never identified or recovered. Most of them were from the Army Air Corps. He had known the losses had been high in those days of long ago — a lot of good men had not made it back, but the impact of all those crosses brought it home to him like nothing he had ever experienced. He had survived the war. So had Joe. So had the rest of the crew, but those under the white crosses and those whose names were on the Wall had not. What did it all mean? Who or what had decided who survived and who did not? Was it God, or the odds? Tex still didn't know the answer. He wasn't sure that Joe did either. But he had a haunting feeling that those at Cambridge did!

THE LAUNDRY WOMAN'S HUSBAND

Like most of the crews of the 390th ours always had trouble getting our laundry done when we needed it. Like many of the others we found a partial solution by locating somebody in the nearby village down the steep muddy path just behind our Quonset. We took turns delivering and picking up the laundry.

The woman was of undeterminate age — possibly between 40 and 50 — and her plain care-worn face was not enhanced by the fatigue of hard work and the drain of obvious poor health. Her hands were raw red from the constant washings in cold water and harsh soaps and the absence of soothing cremes. Her husband was a portly man whose every move bespoke of a life of hard work. His pale skin and general pallor suggested that he perhaps was a retired miner. He was often home when I brought or picked up laundry. Both he and his wife were always cordial but very noticeably reserved as if afraid to overstep the bounds of propriety. The woman particularly was reticent. This I put down to their past experience with the rigid English class system and ideas of the "place" of the woman in the household because as far as I could determine they liked us and liked to have us visit them.

One day when I dropped off our laundry I noticed the husband soaking his hand in a pan of plain unmedicated cold water and rubbing it with a small piece of flannel. He explained that he had cut his hand and that the flannel had medicinal properties and would heal the infection. When I examined the wound on his hand I was shocked. His hand was swollen to twice its normal size and the ugly red streaks of blood poisoning were already starting up his arm. The lymph gland under his arm was swollen to the size of an egg. Clearly he was badly infected. I tried to tell him that the water and flannel were quite likely contributing to the infection rather than helping cure it, but he seemed convinced otherwise. But then after a bit he said, "But it's all we've got."

I asked him to wait for me and I rode my bicycle back up the trail to our squadron and went to the dispensary. I explained the problem and they equipped me with disinfectant, sulfa, bandages, etc., plus instructions. I hurried back down and doctored the laundry woman's husband as best I could. However, I was somewhat doubtful that the "cure" would work since he was in such bad shape when he got the treatment.

About a week later I had a chance to go back and check on him, and I was met at the door by the woman. She walked up to me and very uncharacteristically took one of my hands in both of hers and with lowered eyes began to speak to me. Fearing the worst I listened carefully to understand her and I heard her say, "God be praised, you cured me old man." Then she began to cry softly. Once in a while it happens.

THE SONGS

It was a different time and we were different people. There was no "Rock" to assault our senses, and we were brought up to believe that even if music couldn't soothe the savage beast it could mold, shape, and influence dreams and thoughts and behavior — and it was good. We reveled in the emotional fantasies of love, heroism, and patriotism. The songs we listened to on the radio and at the public dances inspired us, gave us solace, and gave us hope. Their simplistic, perhaps overly sentimental, and often unrealistic themes helped give us the stability and the strength to persevere. Without them times would have been much more difficult.

And, like old fragrances, the music of that era need only be faintly sensed to stir memories, rekindle old feelings, and bring on a far away stare with tear-moistened eyes. The Glenn Miller tunes, *Moonlight Serenade*, *Tuxedo Junction*, and *Little Brown Jug*. Great songs like *I'll Walk Alone*, *The Shrine of St. Cecelia*, *As Time Goes By*. Stirring ones like *Praise the Lord and Pass the Ammunition*, *Coming in on a Wing and a Prayer*, and of course *The Army Air Corps Song*. Those funny, but close to the heart, songs like *This Is the Army Mr. Jones* and *Someday I'm Going To Murder the Bugler*. The ballads, the jump tunes, and the easy lyrics and pleasant and insistent rhythms.

There there were the parodies that were classics in their own right. *I Bombed Cologne* to the tune of *I'll Walk Alone, You Must Remember This — The Flak Doesn't Always Miss* to the tune of *As Time Goes By,* and *From Berlin to Bordeaux* to the tune of *Blues in the Night.* All guaranteed to bring a smile and tear at the heart strings at the same time.

And then there were, of course, the "folk songs" that were heard in pubs throughout the kingdom, like *Roll Me Over in the Clover* of English origin and *Wing on Three Ninetieth* and *Come On and Join the Air Corps* of distinctly American roots.

Yes, the songs played a very important part in our lives. They helped us through some difficult times and gave us a memory bank to draw upon with pleasure for the rest of our days. I wonder what the aficionados of Rock will look back on.

Phil Hilson

No Purple Heart — But...

by R. P. Hilson

30th Station Complement Squadron

AS a teletype operator one doesn't see much battle action. When I was transferred after the war to Straubing, Germany (a Nazi fighter base) for occupation duty, I was on night duty and while catching a few winks on the cot I was bitten on the finger by a mouse. (I don't believe there is anything in the rules that entitles one to receive a purple heart for that.) We had enough beer and cognac there so no medical treatment was needed.

Shot Down Stories

A B-17 goes down in flames.

Exploits of Jack Bass On His Last Mission

by Quentin R. Bass

Bombardier, 570th Squadron

OUR crew was assigned to the 390th Bomb Group as a replacement in February of 1944. We were known as Crew number 42 assigned to the 570th Bomb Squadron. We stayed with this assignment until we flew our last mission which was on May 28, 1944. Our first pilot was A.J. Matthias, co-pilot was Henry Gerards, navigator was Joseph Freiland, and I was the bombardier. We had gunners in the name of Abbott, Oliver, Walker, Wolfe and Deal and one other replacement gunner that I cannot remember.

We flew 24 missions. Our last was on May 28, 1944 to some sort of oil installation near Magdeburg, Germany.

176

The Squadron was in the group lead. We flew number 3 position in the lead squadron. That particular day was fairly uneventful until we got into the Dummer Lake or the Brunswick area. As you well know, we were asked to record different things that we had observed. I informed the navigator, Freiland, that there was a flak burst out about 11 o'clock that knocked down a P-47 a few miles out to our left. Then I corrected myself to tell him that I was wrong and it looks more like there were two fighters in a mid air collision. One of them was silver colored. Later on I was to find out that it was true.

> Later that night, I met Captain Alvin Juchheim, the P-47 pilot — he was leader of the P-47 group. Juchheim had 17 aircraft to his credit and had or was on his third tour in England. He was senior officer in my room at Stalag Luft II while we were there from 6-6-44 to 1-29-45. He said a P-51 wingman ran into him on a cross over as 51's were taking over from the 47 group.

But first let me continue on with what we were doing that day. We assumed a bomb run somewhere around Brunswick, Germany and as you well know back in those days, anywhere from 30 to 50 miles from the target you just have to sit there and wait to come upon the target. It was obvious that there were fighters because we had been forewarned at the base and, of course, warned again as we entered this area. After the bomb run, we had some single engine fighters join us. A P-51 Group took over from a P-47 Group. They were flying in pretty close to us as they dropped their fuel tanks to go back with the first fighters coming thru. We were hit by three groups of German fighters flying at us in formation. The first group took us on our same level, the second group came in high and the third group came in low. We were pretty well torn up in the first pass of the enemy fighters. There must have been somewhere around 15 to 20 fighters in each group. Naturally, we were knocked out of formation because of the damage received. My navigator, Freiland, lost a right leg at the knee. I got Freiland out of the escape hatch after putting on his chute. I then hooked back to the oxygen and the intercom to see what was happening. At about that time a single ME 109 picked us up. I noticed he had a big white spinner since he almost put it in my compartment. He did a job on us. It wasn't too long before the airplane was unmanageable. Matthias gave us the bail-out order. I went out the nose hatch. We were gathered up by the Germans around the Magdeburg area. That night I was taken to an airfield almost in Magdeburg. The next day, the 8th Air Force evidently came back to that area because there was an air raid warning. They took us to the basement during the raid. There were about 60 of us that they kept in that area for a couple of days and then they moved us to Frankfurt, Germany. This was the location of the interrogation center for airmen which we had been warned about. We had been told about what to expect by our intelligence officers. I was there either three or four days in the normal interrogation as all airmen were. Then they took us to a nearby center a few miles away where they gave us clothing and whatever medical care we required. Up until that time there had not been any particular notice paid to most of us, so you can imagine what a hairy and nasty looking group of people we were. We were then taken on prison trains to a place in Poland which they called Sagan, Germany, where they had the internment camp Stalag Luft III. I arrived at Stalag Luft III on June 6, 1944, the day of the invasion of the continent. Of course, Stalag Luft III was an officers' camp for British and American airmen. There was a large group of fellows there. As we walked into the camp it was like a college reunion because we knew so many of the people (36 total) either from training or from other bases I served at. It happened to be that the particular Section that I had been assigned to, the senior officer, Colonel Darr H. Alkire, was the former commander of the 100th Bomb Group.

We stayed in Sagan until late January of 1945 when the

Russians started to advance toward our location. The weather was so bad, and the snow so deep, that they did not make too much progress in the inclement weather. We had felt that the Russians would take the base. About 1 or 2 o'clock in the morning on January 29, 1945, the Germans ran us out of the camp and put us on the road. We walked from Sagan, which is now 35 miles in Poland, to a place called Cotbush, Germany, which is in East Germany now. I measured it on the map and to the best of my calculations, it was somewhere in the vicinity of 70 to 80 miles. This march was done in terrible inclement weather. Most of us had a very hard time. We finally were put in boxcars at Cotbush and moved to Nuremberg, Germany. We arrived in Nuremberg on February 7, 1945. We were interned in an old Italian Officer's camp close to the rail yard. Nuremberg had not been disturbed too much except for the rail centers. The RAF bombed it a lot.

In late February, the 8th Air Force and the 15th Air Force came to Nuremberg and destroyed the city. The Germans took a lot of the prisoners into the community to help bury the dead. I was fortunate not to be one of that group that had to do that particular chore. The RAF came back five straight nights and did a real job on those folks.

We were moved from Nuremberg toward Munich on April 7, 1945. We walked an estimated 130 miles. It was across the Danube River, on back roads to a place called Moosburg, Germany, not far from Munich. We arrived at Moosburg on the 19th day of April. From the 7th to the 19th was not particularly bad. Of course, we knew the allied armies were right behind us. We were there a few days when Patton's Third Army over ran us on the 29th of April, 1945. After a few days while the area was secured by the military, they took us to a German airfield, Landshont, Germany where there were a lot of troop transports. They flew us into France and later brought us on home.

Jack E. Nosser in 1944.

Experiences of a *Cash and Carry* Crew Member

by *Jack E. Nosser*

Bombardier, 570th Squadron, Cash and Carry

IN April 1942, I took the tests for the Air Corps and was accepted for training as a bombardier. I then went on specialist courses at Santa Ana, Albuquerque and Las Vegas and eventually arrived at Framlingham, England, with the 570th Squadron in July 1943. Our B-17 was named *Cash and Carry* piloted by Lt. Robert McGuire.

At that time a combat crew in the 8th Air Force was lucky if it survived more than about eight or ten missions without something very drastic happening to them. Our crew had flown eleven missions, with myself one ahead at twelve having been on an extra raid with another crew, by 10th October 1943. On that day the target was Munster, an

180

important rail junction in western Germany, just north of the industrialized Ruhr Valley. "Happy Valley" we called it although there was nothing happy about going to that place!!

The mission went normally until our P-47 "Thunderbolt" escort left us shortly before the Initial Point (IP) due to their insufficient range. Just after passing the I.P. and turning to begin our bombing run to the target, things began to happen...rapidly. I saw the ship to our right take a flak hit. It appeared to me as though the whole left side of the cockpit had been blown away and the pilot was slumped over the lap of his co-pilot who was fighting the controls. Many years were to pass before I was to discover that the pilot was Paul Vance. He somehow survived and got home to Framlingham, badly injured.

It seemed as though the whole Luftwaffe was up to meet us. They had never previously managed to turn back an attack by the 8th Air Force but they seemed especially determined to do so that day. Targets all around the clock kept the gunners extremely busy. Tracers filled the air as streams of bullets curved away from our defensive formation. Our pilots had had it drilled into them that they had to hold those aircraft in the tightest possible formation, especially during the bomb run. More often than not we were practically in each others laps.

Then a flak shell tore through our Number One engine and almost immediately the supercharger on Number Two "ran away" forcing us out of formation. I'll never forget Capt. James Geary, the pilot of the lead B-17 *Pistol Packin' Mama*. His face was pressed against the plexiglas side window of his cockpit as he watched us slowly dropping back. The expression on his face, despite his oxygen mask, said it all.

We soon reached the rear of the 390th formation. The 100th Bomb Group below and to our left were being literally decimated by what seemed hundreds of German fighters. I was ordered to jettison our bombs and Lt.

McGuire and co-pilot Lt. Glen Oster banked our ship on one wing and dived steeply away. I was almost deafened by that screaming runaway supercharger. We finally levelled out and I thought at that time we could make it back to England . . . but no luck. Due to a complete loss of power of our remaining two engines, we crash landed. I could hear trees crashing down, shattered fences pinging like taut piano wires as we hurtled through them and, of course, the scraping and bouncing all over the rough ground which I thought would never end. Finally — complete silence as we came to a stop. As my inter-phone had ceased to function shortly after "bombs-away" I didn't know that five of our crew had bailed out on our way down. Our navigator, Lt. Drouhard, had been injured during the air battle and could not travel. We had to leave him beside the plane after making him as comfortable as possible with blankets.

We had no idea where we were and decided to split up. Lt. McGuire and the top turret gunner Sgt. Auger headed off in one direction whilst Lt. Oster and I took another route using our button compasses to keep going in one direction and so put as much distance between ourselves and our plane in the least possible time. We could hear distant shouts and the barks and spine-tingling howls of tracker dogs as the search for us got under way in earnest. It wasn't until then that we realized what a hunted animal must go through. Sheer terror isn't a pleasant feeling.

To cut a long story short we were arrested in a Dutch farm house the following night and on Tuesday morning, the 12th, we were turned over to the SS, in Arnhem, who interrogated us with a lot of unnecessary shouting and finger wagging. From there we were sent to Rotterdam prison and while crossing the prison yard early on the 14th of October we saw B-17s pass high overhead on their way to bomb Schweinfurt. From Rotterdam we were taken by train to Frankfurt for more subtle interrogation. While there we learned that Lt. McGuire and Sgt. Auger had been picked up when attempting to cross a bridge on the evening of the day we crash-landed. From Frankfurt we were taken, with the other survivors of the "Black Week" to our permanent prison camp, Stalag Luft III, at Sagan in Silesia

If it hadn't been for the Red Cross parcels we would have been in real trouble, both medically and food-wise. In the late Spring of 1944, about 80 Allied "Kriegies" tunnelled their way out in what later became known as "The Great Escape". We later learnt that about fifty of the escapees had been caught and executed by the Gestapo while "resisting arrest". The true facts were very different...

The camp radio was hidden in our barracks and the BBC broadcasts were a great boost to morale. I never did discover the exact whereabouts of this radio but neither did the Germans even though they ripped the place apart often enough in their efforts to locate it.

The Russian offensive from the East was getting closer and in late January 1945 we were marched out of Sagan for a bitterly cold and long walk through snow and sub-zero temperatures to Spremburg. The journey took us seven or eight days to complete. From Spremburg we travelled by rail to Moosburg in southern Germany. Rumors were rife here. Some said the SS were planning to take hostages to Switzerland so that they could negotiate better surrender terms. Glen Oster who had tried unsuccessfully to escape from Sagan, and consequently had spent many many days in the "Cooler" there, "Rod" Rodriguez, an absolutely fearless Mexican-American, and myself decided to make a break for it while on a working party in Augsburg. One of our closest calls, and there were several, came when we walked straight past an SS roadblock on a bridge while their attention was diverted when they questioned the occupants of a German staff car. We finally met up with an American armored column north of the River Danube a few days later. It had been quite an eventful two years with long periods of boring monotony in between. We'd made it and had luckily survived. A large number of very fine men hadn't been so fortunate.

First Meeting With the Germans

by Jack E. Nosser

I was a bombardier on one of the original crews in the 570th Bomb Squadron. Our B-17 was named *Cash and Carry* piloted by Lt. Robert McGuire.

We were shot down on the October 10, 1943 mission to Munster. This was the crew's eleventh mission. It was my twelfth since I had flown an extra mission with another crew.

Lt. Glen Oster, our co-pilot, and I were arrested by the Dutch Police two days later (October 12) and turned over to the SS in Arnhem. At the Headquarters Building in Arnhem, we were taken to a large office and pushed behind the counter that stretched across the room. A short time later, a German Corporal motioned us to take seats on opposite sides of the room. The Dutch Police were ordered out of the room by a German Military Policeman. In addition to the German Corporal the only other person left in the room was another enlisted man busily typing.

We waited patiently to see what was going to happen. While trying to anticipate what was going to happen next we watched while the Corporal straightened away objects in the room.

All at once from outside the door came the sound of a loud furor. There was the clicking of heels and yelling of "Heils" that seemed to go on for several minutes. I began expecting no less a person than Hitler to walk into the room. As I watched the doorway half in amazement and half in appre-hension, in walked a SS Colonel who was at least six foot six inches in height — a giant. The two German enlisted men came to a quivering attention with their eyes staring directly in front. Oster and I sat in our chairs and watched the proceedings with amazement as the Colonel walked, looking neither right or left, directly to a desk on the far side of the room. The Colonel seemed to fold in unusual places in order to seat himself behind the desk.

The Colonel called the Corporal to the desk and, as the Corporal stood at another quivering attention, the Colonel angrily and at great length chewed him out. When he was dismissed, the Corporal turned and trotted over to Oster.

"Do you men not know enough to stand when an Officer enters the room", he demanded in English.

Oster stared at the Corporal for a surprised second. He pulled himself straight up in the chair. "We are officers and we do not stand when other officers enter a room", he said haughtily.

As a dead precarious silence fell over the room, I felt a glow of pride at Oster's words. "That's telling them", I thought. My eyes were suddenly pulled toward the Colonel by the noise of the man unfolding from the desk. The Colonel bounded to Oster's chair. His face was bloodless and angry. The Colonel's eyes became wild and his mouth began slavering as he began ranting like a madman. As I watched and listened to the outburst of hysterical peevishness, my insides coiled violently. This sudden close perspective of the enemy I had been fighting from the distances of altitude, gave me some of the reasons for the war. This Nazi was a man without tolerance or reason; a bubbling mass of hate and terror. From the geyser that was his mouth poured molten cruelty and the live steam of fanaticism. He seemed to be unaware of his audience and became lost, like a pagan priest in a secret ritual, in the black depths of uncontrolled passion.

"This is the end", I thought sadly. "Another hour won't find us alive". I began wishing Oster had kept his mouth shut just once.

Finally like a spring driven toy that had been wound too

tightly and unwound with a broken governor, the Colonel ran down and stood panting and glaring around the room with the expression of a man finding himself lost in the wilderness. Oster sat stiff and straight studying the floor. The German soldiers were standing almost paralyzed, their eyes shifting rapidly to avoid a direct stare with the Colonel.

The silence of the room became deep and profound, which made the opening noise of the office door sound like an event of catastrophic consequence. Everyone watched with undivided fascination as two SS soldiers entered the room and snapped to rigid attention, their arms thrust rigidly out in the Nazi salute. "Heil Hitler", they cried out in unison to the Colonel.

"Heil Hitler", answered the Colonel fanatically and then he spoke rapidly in German pointing to the Americans.

The SS soldiers motioned us out of our chairs and through the opening of the counter. I hardly remember the walk to the street until the bright sunlight of the morning hurt our eyes. One of the Germans said something to me and I shook my head indicating I didn't understand. The German pulled up the flap on his holster and wrapped his hand around the grip of his luger. He glanced at me meaningfully. It was worth a thousand words.

"Watch out, Oster", I warned. "This bastard wants an excuse to shoot us".

"That Colonel wanted...". Oster began and stopped when the luger cleared the holster and was pointed at the end of Oster's nose.

The SS said something venomously in German. We were to remain silent!

It was a three block walk to the prison. The first solitary cell brought the soul searing realization of captivity and the knawing began its burning within me.

Loneliest and Happiest Point In One's Life

by Irving Lifson
Squadron Navigator, 568th Bomb Squadron

ABOUT three years ago, I was listening to a TV talk show. The subject was loneliness and the participants discussed the loneliest point of their lives. Had I been on the program, I would have had no trouble recalling the loneliest point in my life. It was December 11, 1943. I was in a parachute going down in the North Sea off the coast of Germany and watching the Eighth Air Force B17s going toward England.

At briefing, the morning of December 11, we learned the target was Emden, Germany, and Capt. Hiram Skogmo's crew would lead the 390th. The 390th was leading the 3rd Air Division and we would be the first plane over the target.

The make up of Skogmo's crew was altered slightly because of the lead position. It was as follows:

Capt. Hiram Skogmo, Pilot

Major Ralph Hansel, Co-Pilot (Group Operations Officer)

Capt. Irving Lifson, Squadron Navigator

Capt. Donald Warren, Group Navigator

1st Lt. Merle Cloud, Bombardier

2nd Lt. Whitney Poythress, Jr., Tail Gunner (Normally a Co-Pilot)

T/Sgt. Patrick Welch, Right Waist Gunner

S/Sgt. Ralph Sindeldecker, Top Turret Gunner

S/Sgt. Jack Fariss, Ball Turret Gunner

S/Sgt. Ernest Phillips, Left Waist Gunner

T/Sgt. Johnnie Adams, Radio Man

Before that day was over, all but three of the above were dead. Warren, Phillips, and Lifson (myself) survived and were taken prisoner. We spent the next 17 months in Prison Camps.

We were hit by a frontal attack of ME 110s just before the I.P. We were on fire and out of control in seconds. I followed Cloud and Warren out of the navigator's escape hatch. While going down in my chute a single engine fighter made two passes at me. It didn't fire at me but seemed like it was trying to collapse my chute. My other worry as I was drifting down was my religion. Although I purposely kept religion off my dog tags I was wondering what would happen if the Germans found out I was Jewish.

To my amazement and everlasting gratitude, with all the water below me, I landed on the Frisian Island of Norderney. The part of the island where I landed was sandy and barren. I looked around and saw two soldiers with rifles walking towards me. They were about 1/4 mile away. I learned later that they were German Marines of the 8th Marine Artillery Battalion. They frisked me and within seconds one of them had my wristwatch and the other my cigarette lighter. They let me keep my cigarettes. Then they made me tie my chute up into a ball with the lines. I was then ordered, by motions, to pick it up and the three of us headed for an observation tower about a mile away. At the tower, there was a third German marine. I passed around cigarettes to the three Germans and took one myself. The four of us were smoking when an armored car pulled up. Out of it came the smartest looking officer I'd ever seen. Boots, breeches, swagger stick — he had it all! The three Germans snuffed out and pocketed their cigarettes. The officer came up to us and struck my hand with the swagger stick. It sent my cigarette flying. In perfect English he then said, "Stand at attention. There's a German Officer here now." He then asked me for my rank. When I said "Captain," he struck me across the face with the swagger stick and said, "You're lying; you want to get to an Officer's Prison Camp." I zipped open my flying suit and showed him my Captain's bars. "We shall see," was his only comment.

I was then taken to a jail in the little town on the island. On the way we stopped at a beach area where they asked me to identify a body. It was Ralph Sindeldecker.

The next morning, I discovered Don Warren and a Sergeant from another Group were fellow inmates. With two guards, the three of us were taken by boat to the mainland still carrying our spilt chutes. We were taken by train to Oldenburg. At Oldenburg we went by streetcar to the Luftwaffe area headquarters. Along the way, on the train and street car, some civilians tried to be pleasant. They would invariably say, "For you the war is over," in English. Unfortunately, several times an ardent Nazi would come along and spit on us. Then the others (even those trying to be pleasant) would feel compelled to spit on us. We were beginning to know what it was to be a captive. We had lost our war.

We spent that night on a cement floor in the basement of the Luftwaffe headquarters in Oldenburg. We were awakened by kicks from a Luftwaffe pilot who knew

Warren and I were from the lead plane. He claimed he had shot us down. While saying all American equipment was shizen compared to German, he nevertheless relieved us of our leather A2 jackets.

The next morning we were off again by street car and train. We had two new guards. We stopped twice at railroad restaurants along the way. It must have been quite a sight, the three captives sitting at a table holding chutes, while the guards ate. We asked for food but they didn't bother to answer. Towards evening we got to the Frankfurt railroad station. There one of us asked if we could use the men's room. The guards then ran everyone out of the men's room and held the doors open while the three of us urinated. Meanwhile a crowd of approximately 100 people gathered outside the men's room and watched us. As we left the men's room I made the mistake of saying "I wonder if we should bow for our performance," as it caused the three of us to laugh. This seemed to infuriate the crowd. They apparently resented prisoners laughing. About 30 of them came at us and started to beat us up. The guards seemed stunned and tried to protect us but could do little till some Wehrmacht soldiers came to our rescue. Some one with a cane really clobbered me on my head and shoulder.

We were then taken to a nearby town called Oberussel. This was the interrogation center for the Luftwaffe. We were separated and put in solitary cells. They took our belts and shoelaces away. There was to be no suicides there. I was in there about four days before they took me out for interrogation. By this time I had a classic case of scabies all over my body. The interrogator gave me a cigarette (American) and told me my name, rank, and serial number was not sufficient in this war because many saboteurs were parachuting into Germany. He said I would have to identify myself by giving my Squadron, Group, altitude I was fly-ing, and MPI of target. When I refused he said that unless I properly identified myself I would have to stay in solitary a year or two. I still refused and then bared my chest to show

Stalag Luft I.

the rash from the lice and told him, "German officers don't get treated like this in American **POW** camps." The interrogator was very solicitious and said I would get medical attention. I never did. About five days later (you lose track of time because it is constantly dark) they took me out again and said they wanted to show me something. Then they startled me by showing me pictures of some of our 390th Group and Squadron officers wearing Indian head dress. Apparently they were **P.R.** shots taken at Great Falls, Montana, before the Group went overseas. They also asked me how "Pud" Good was? (Lt. Col. Robert Good, 568th C.O.) This tactic was, of course, to make you wonder why you were enduring lice and solitary confinement when they knew it all anyhow. I still refused to talk and was then sent to a former merchant marine ship's captain. The floor of his office was lined with the latest Air Force navigation equipment, including "G" boxes. His opening comment to me as I looked around the room was "Ach, you Americans are so careless," Nothing much happened there. He did all the talking.

The next day I was sent to Dulag Luft on the other side of Frankfurt. Dulag Luft was a staging area where they would fill up boxcars of POWs, and send them to a permanent camp. I ran into John Winant there. John was a 568th pilot shot down in October 1943.

I was at Dulag Luft one day when I was summoned to the German camp office. There I was told I would be in charge of the conduct of three boxcars of POWs. They then told me to sign a statement that there would be no escape attempts on the journey to the POW camp. If I signed they would then let us keep our shoes and socks. I told them that I had no authority to sign such a thing and refused. The German officer in charge then told me that if anyone got frost bite I would be responsible. I told him I refused to accept that statement and he would go down as committing an atrocity if frostbite occurred. They read me the riot act which I was to convey to the POWs. It was what was forbidden on the trip. They told me if a rule was broken, I would be court martialed and shot with the offender. I don't remember all the rules but here are most of them:

1. No singing of American National Anthem.
2. All German officers of equal or higher rank must be saluted.
3. No talking to German guards.
4. No talking to German civilians.
5. No talking to foreign workers (slave laborers.)

I was then given three can openers (one for each car) and told that if any were used for escape purposes or lost, I would be court martialed and shot. Each car was then given canned goods (American Red Cross origin) for the journey.

Our POW train obviously had no great priority, as we constantly found ourselves being sidetracked for other trains. Nevertheless, that night found us in the Berlin railroad marshalling yards. When the air raid sirens went off that night, the guards went to nearby air raid shelters and left us locked in the cars. It was, of course, the RAF and the

Prisoners at Stalag Luft I.

raid seemed to last forever. It was terrifying! Everyone was praying that we wouldn't be hit. I was praying that no one would lose a can opener.

The next morning we were on our way again and late that afternoon found us at Barth, Germany (about 25 miles northeast of Rostock.) When we disembarked we found ourselves ringed in by about 30 guards each with a leashed dog and machine pistol. I hurriedly collected my can openers and gave them to a German NCO standing with two officers. We walked through the town of Barth pulling the wounded on handcarts. The camp was about two miles from Barth and turned out to be Stalag Luft I. As we neared the camp, we could hear a chorus of voices yelling at us, "You'll be sorry."

Most of the officers of Stalag Luft I at that point were RAF. They ran the POW organization. Our three cars of POWs made the American population slightly larger than the RAF. It was then decided to have Americans take key positions. Because of this my responsibilities didn't end with the can openers. I found myself appointed a Squadron Commander and the American head of XYZ committee. XYZ was concerned with escape, security and espionage. I was referred to as "Big X." Any escape attempt by an American had to be coordinated through me. I had various committees to lean on for help. A certain percentage of cigarettes, for example, were appropriated for my trading committee. My traders spoke German and usually started out with innocuous trades with the guards, such as two cigarettes for a used toothbrush and one for an onion. After a while, the trader would then say, "All right, you S.O.B. We're going to turn you in unless…" Trading of course was verboten for the guards. Then the trading items became slightly more sensitive. Radio tubes, other radio parts, tools, passes, working papers, maps, time tables, etc. etc. were acquired. There was a committee of forgers, and another of people who could tailor anything to look like civilian clothes. There were Poles flying for the RAF who took empty toothpaste and shaving tubes, and melted them to make military insignia. There was even a couple of pick pockets in the event a German worker with tools decided to walk through the compound instead of around it. I even had RAF flyers who had flown captured German aircraft, give cockpit procedure lectures to potential escapees. We had a radio put together and broken down each night after the BBC news.

There were a few POWs that got out of the compound, but that would be only about 10% of the escape. Getting out of Germany was the big problem. In the five years Stalag Luft existed, there were two escapes back to Allied hands. Both were by RAF fliers before I got there. My business of escape picked up in the spring. In the winter, we huddled over our stoves trying to keep warm and my business dropped off.

Most of the time was dull and monotonous. Food was minimal and constantly on our minds. We were hungry a great deal of the time. A modest amount of athletic

Another view of Stalag Luft I.

equipment, musical instruments and books, would come in from various countries, Red Crosses or Salvation Armies. We had some very talented people who put on plays. Mail from home was infrequent and took months. My first letter from home was in transit a year. I gave up my XYZ position to a Lt. Col. after about eight months. In the fall of 1944, higher ranks started to appear. Lt. Cols., Cols., Wing Commanders, and Group Captains started to take over the key jobs. I stayed on as a Squadron Commander till the end.

It was January 1945 that the Germans stunned the camp by presenting two lists to Col. Einar Malmstrom, the Senior American prisoner. One list was "Jewish" and the other, "Probably Jewish." I was on the "probable" list. My fear from the time I bailed out finally came to pass. When the Germans were asked what the lists were for they replied, "They don't belong here. We're sending both groups to an all Jewish camp." At that point in time, we didn't know about the extermination camps, but we had a gut feeling that we were going to be killed. The camp we were supposed to go to must have been overrun by the Russians in Poland, because they kept postponing it, and on May 1, 1945, the Russians over-ran Stalag Luft I.

The Russians had liberated some Allied POWs in Hungary and Rumania, so SHAEF made a deal that for $5.00 per head the POWs would be put on the docks of Odessa on the Black Sea. The war had accelerated so fast that the deal was still in effect although our liberated camp was way up on the Baltic Coast. We learned all this when the Russians gave us two days to get ready and then we were to start walking to Odessa, approximately 1,000 miles away. Col. Hubert Zemke was then the Senior American prisoner. He protested that we were in no condition to walk that far. We had people interred three and four years and in terrible condition. It didn't move the Russians. Finally, news of our situation got back to SHAEF and they made arrangements with the Russians for us to be air lifted out. Before the Russians released us they fingerprinted and asked questions of each person. Name, rank, serial number, home address, parent's names, birthplace of parents, were some of the questions asked.

We were then taken by trucks to a nearby airfield where B17s flew us to France.

If I'm ever a participant on a TV talk show on The Happiest Point in One's Life, "Flying out of Germany," will win, hands down, for me.

Front:
C.L. Perry, Pilot; H.R.
Sproul, CP; C.E. Ryan,
N; B.W. Stubbs, B.
Back:
W. R. Shea, TTG; L.O.
Campbell, RO-G; L.J.
Perragallo, BTG; J.H.
Walker, WG; R.J.
Sinclair, WG; R.E. Hicks,
TG.

The Last Mission of B-17G
Angel-In-Di-Skies

by Charles E. Ryan

Navigator, 568th Squadron, Angel-In-Di-Skies

*A*NGEL-IN-DI-SKIES and her crew ran into calamity on (as it turned out) her last mission. It had begun (on August 2, 1944) as a "routine" bombing attack on a target in northern France. At perhaps the mid-point of the mission one of *Angel's* port engines malfunctioned and had to be shut down. Before long a second engine, also on the port side, malfunctioned and had to be shut down. To further aggravate the situation its propeller could not be feathered. Thus began *Angel's* long gradual descent toward a ditching in the North Sea, a few miles off the coast of Holland.

Luckily, the sea was calm and the ditching took place

197

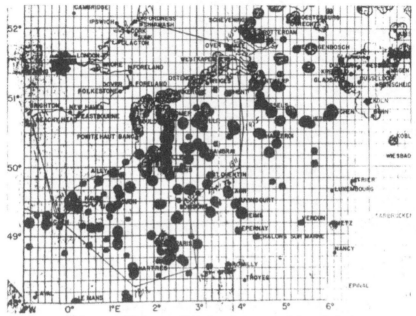

Flak map of 2 August 1944 showing route of the mission.

without serious incident, a real tribute to the piloting skills of Lt. Clay Perry and Lt. Harold Sproul. The entire crew then set what must surely have been a minimum-time record for abandoning the airplane and unstowing and boarding rubber rafts. Interestingly, the airplane did *not* sink immediately. It floated upright for several hours!

As you may recall, standard procedure after "ditching" a B-17 called for all crewmen to proceed to the radio compartment and to exit thru the overhead hatch. I did so but with one hand on each side of the hatch I managed to get only part way out (head and shoulders) when my strength gave out — the toll taken by my wound, I suspect. At that instant one of my crewmates (I wish I could remember who it was) grabbed me by the shoulder and jerked me out of the airplane. With the airplane rapidly filling with sea water you can appreciate my gratitude for that assist.

While we bobbed around on the North Sea all that fateful night we were accompanied for a time by — of all things — a seal! It stayed with us for perhaps twenty minutes or so. It wasn't one bit frightened of us and was probably curious. In any event, he probably became bored with us and left.

At one point during our night floating on the North Sea we drifted quite close to shore, right in front of a huge radar structure. Needless to say, we paddled hard to get away from there because it probably was manned, and the beach itself was probably mined. We did manage to get much further out to sea and in relatively less danger.

After the all-night bobbing in those rafts, the crew was rescued by a fishing boat. Unfortunately, the boat's "Captain" was a German soldier armed with a machine gun. *Angel's* crew thus began their period of captivity as Luftwaffe POWs.

At about this point I parted company with my crewmates to recuperate, in a hospital in Brugges, Belgium, from a wound received when *Angel* encountered ground-fire as she crossed the Dutch coast. After a couple of weeks, I, too, was sent to a POW camp, Stalag Luft III, near Sagan, Germany, 80 kilometers or so south of Berlin. I did not see any of my crewmates again until after my return to the "States."

In what probably was my last interrogation/processing while in Luftwaffe hands, my interrogator (German) remarked that I would probably be in position sooner than he would be to assure his sister, a resident of my hometown — Chicago — that he was alive and well. He asked me to call her upon my return, which I did a few months later but with mixed feelings I must say (he had been an enemy of my country, after all).

My experiences as a POW included (chronologically) my stint at Sagan until late in January 1945; a very long and unpleasant march in bitter cold weather (to move us beyond the reach of the approaching Russian army) followed by a long and very cramped train ride in "forty-and-eight" railroad cars to Nürnberg; and another long march several weeks later to Moosburg (north of Munich) where we were liberated, late in April 1945 by infantrymen of the American army. How good it was to see them!

A Disastrous Day
For The 390th

by Claude "Art" Carnahan

Ball Turret Gunner, 570th Squadron

I've heard 21 different versions of what happened to the 570th Squadron's formation on 9 September 44 from the 21 men who landed with me in Germany that day, and I am sure that there are many more, but here is mine:

I was the ball turret gunner on D. J. Harris' crew. Over the target, Dusseldorf, Hobbie's plane took a direct hit in the bomb bay and the bombs all blew in one terrific explosion.

Parts of his plane hit Gallagher's plane which caused it to also blow up. Other parts of Hobbie's plane took out our left outboard engine. We then got a direct hit from flak in our inboard engine. Part of that shell hit our radio operator, Curtis Anderson, in the left foot and then came over and hit

200

me in the right leg.

There were two planes just previous to this that blew up behind us. Our other inboard engine caught on fire and so we decided to "give it back to the Indians." We bailed out. Our intercom had been knocked out by the direct hit. We had to rely on sign language.

I learned when we landed that the co-pilot, Howard Ford, had received a broken leg in landing. Virgil Gordon, waist gunner, had landed on a house and crushed his ankle. A piece of the plane had hit the pilot in the face and his jacket had pieces of aluminum stuck in it.

Our crew all got out with the injuries listed. Bruno Lattic's crew also all got out. Of that crew, after landing, I met Lattic, P. Smith, gunner; Frank Brady, ball turret gunner; George Hines, top turret tunner; Homer King, tail gunner.

Others that I met were three from Gallagher's crew: Ed Kusek, Pittsburgh, Pa; Billy Ballard, Kansas; and the waist gunner from Kansas. A total of 21 men got out that I know of.

*An additional story about this mission, **Lamentations: Dusseldorf, September 9, 1944** is told on page 89*

Shot Down in Belgium

by *Wilbert H. Richarz*

Radio Operator-Gunner, 570th Squadron, Cocaine Bill

ON our 21st mission flying 097 *(Cocaine Bill)* we hit Frankfurt and picked up a lot of flak. We lost an engine and had considerable other damage and soon found ourselves on the deck. Our pilot was Jack Bouton, the co-pilot Tex Deffenbach, the navigator Bob Ennis, and I believe Art Krassen was the bombardier. Snake Myers was our top turret, Hap Halek the lower ball, Angelo Martin the waist gunner, Dixie Anderson the tail gunner, and I was the radio operator.

Jack called Bob and asked, "Where are we?" Bob answered, "My Gee Box doesn't work at this altitude (about 500 feet) so all I know is the general area and that we are

somewhere between Germany and Belgium." Jack went
down to the navigator position and together they figured
out about where we were. Jack called me and asked, "What
can you do to help find a place to land?" I quickly looked in
my "Flimsy" and found the nearest Belgium radio station
with a landing field and after challenging them in code with
the "challenge" of the day I called for a QDM (the course to
steer with zero wind to reach the station). The reply came
back loud and clear — five by five. Just to be sure I
challenged the operator again and he immediately came
back with the correct response. He gave us the course to steer
and I gave it to Jack. We were getting low on gas.

When we got close enough I switched to voice
transmission and received instructions to "come in right
over the church tower at 270 degrees and put her down right
away." Jack could hear this on the "call" position of the
interphone but couldn't talk over my Liaison Radio to the
other operator so he said to me, "I see the church tower but I
don't see the field (everything was covered with snow). Are
you sure we're not going into a German trap?" I answered
that I had already "challenged" the guy twice but that I
would challenge him again. When I did the other operator
said, "Look buddy, I know what you're thinking and I'll
answer your challenge one more time but I have you in sight
and you're in trouble so you had better come on in." Jack
and Tex then started the approach and came in low over the
church tower onto the snow. At touchdown all hell broke
loose — loud groans and cracks, bouncing up and down —
and some sliding. Finally we came to a full stop and with
snow piled up in front of us. All was quiet and we wondered
what would come next.

As we were getting out, a jeep came up, a staff sergeant
hollered out "How'd you like the landing?" It was then that
he told us that we had landed on a steel mat which had been
laid down for photo reconnaissance P-38s and that the mat
was frozen under the snow which accounted for the noise on
landing. He told us that we were in an area that had just

Flak over Paris, France.

been taken from the Germans and that there were no accommodations for us. He said that they (the Reconnaissance outfit) could probably get us picked up and taken back to England in a day or two. He took us to the village of Gosselies near Charleroi, picked up his beautiful Belgian girl friend, and after unsuccessfully asking several households in fluent French to put us up for the night (they all said that the Germans were coming back soon and they couldn't risk putting us up), he left us on the dark snow-covered narrow street.

There we were, still in our Bugs Bunny heated suits with our plug-in cords hanging out, and stranded. We wandered around a bit and finally found a bar. We had English pounds and I had studied the pointee-talkee cards well enough to know how to say such startling things in French as "Hello, how are you? I'm fine, thank you" and "Cognac." Thus armed I negotiated some hot lead Cognac and we got warm on the inside and glowed on the outside. Then we found the Hotel de Commerce where they also didn't want to put us up until we hauled out our trading material like one of those bars of green octagon shaped soap, gum, Hershey bars, and the clincher — cigarettes.

That night we were sitting in the "Lobby" listening to a real "smouldering boulder" of a staff sergeant who was off a cargo C-47. He had the carefully cultivated "fifty mission hat" and had his .45 slung low on his hip, and a mouth to go with it. He looked like a cross between "Sad Sack" and Johnny Ringo. He obviously considered us a captive audience so he regaled us with stories of "his" combat experiences. What an imagination he had! We were all wondering what he would do if he really got shot at when suddenly he was interrupted during one of his heroic epics by the sounds of a low flying aircraft and machine gun fire. We all rushed outside to find that an ME 109 had strafed the village on his way home. The villagers said the German pilots did it all the time if they had any ammo left. They said that the 109 had badly wounded an elderly woman who had been out in the street. We all went back inside and found that much to our relief our "combat veteran" was ashen faced — even a little green — and speechless. So much for self-made heroes.

The next day we were flown out and rejoined the air war. That week we learned that the Germans had indeed retaken the Charleroi area and the village in it.

Mission 243 — Derben, Germany

by Melvin L. Johnson
Navigator, 571st Squadron

OUR target for the January 14, 1945 mission was an oil dump near Derben, Germany. I was the navigator and the clear, sunny weather made that job easy, but it also was bad as it provided no cloud cover for our planes. We encountered some light flak at the coast, but everything went fairly well until noon. As we were approaching the IP about 100 FW190 and ME109 German fighters hit us. All eight aircraft remaining in the C Squadron and one from A Squadron were shot down.

We were shot down on the first pass. The 20mm shells were exploding in front of the plane and when they hit us we were really knocked around. The plane started spinning and Ross Hanneke called on the intercom, "Bail out! I can't hold her!" I was wearing my flak vest over my parachute harness so I pulled the quick release on the flak vest. The release worked, but the front half of the vest was hanging from my oxygen mask as I had clipped the oxygen hose to it. I pulled off the oxygen mask and grabbed for the chest chute pack laying by my feet. Instead of the carrying handle I got the rip cord handle and opened the chute in the plane! With no choice, I gathered the chute up and managed to snap it to the harness. Fred Getz, the bombardier, was near me, chute on and ready to bail out.

The next thing I remember I was on the snowcovered ground. I had a bloody nose, a contusion of my right knee, no gloves, no flying boots or heated inserts and most of the wires were pulled out of the right leg of my heated suit. There was airplane wreckage in the field about 1/4 mile from me, large chunks of aluminum but no definite part I could recognize. The German Home Guards, wearing arm bands and carrying shotguns, were approaching. I believe the plane had exploded and I had been knocked unconscious. The open parachute must have pulled me out of the nose section at some fairly low altitude, as I did not have frozen fingers or toes. The temperature was about minus 40 degrees Fahrenheit at the 29,000 ft. altitude where we encountered the fighters, and well below freezing at ground level. When hit we still had our bomb load and a large amount of gas. I know we were hit many times on their initial pass and I assume the German fighters continued the attack until something drastic happened. It's hard to believe no one else survived of our 10 man crew unless the plane had exploded.

The home guards ordered me to carry my parachute to a farm house near-by and sit on the parachute to await the military authorities. I had a "Mae West" life vest on and decided to see if the CO_2 cylinders worked. Only one side inflated but that scared the German Guards as they thought I was going to blow myself up. Later a German looked me over, took out his pocket knife, grabbed my wrist, then cut the cloth band on my wristwatch. It was about this point I found I still had my 45 automatic in the shoulder holster, and I didn't know what to do. I didn't speak German and the guards didn't speak English. When I tried to talk they indicated that I should just sit still and be quiet, that someone was going for an interpreter. The interpreter finally arrived and I stood up to tell him I still had my pistol. "Pistol" they all understood and it really upset them. The interpreter took the pistol and cut the holster harness to remove it, but it wouldn't pull off as the bottom was snapped around my belt. After several jerks I managed to have him allow me to open my coat and unsnap the holster. If they were trying to impress me with their sharp knives, it worked, but I expected them to shoot me anyway.

An hour or so later a German Air Force enlisted man came along on his bicycle. He had me walk to another farm house where he searched me and made a list of all my belongings. At this farm I met two other U.S. airmen. One had a bad leg wound while the other was uninjured. At dusk we were told to climb onto a horse drawn wagon which I believed to be loaded with parachutes, coats, and other items of Air Force issue. We rode for sometime and were told to unload the wagon. It was then I discovered the equipment on which we were riding was covering the bodies of eight or nine dead airmen. I didn't recognize any of the dead, but they must have been from our Group. The two of us lined the bodies up in the garage area and the guards then put us in separate jail cells and gave us ersatz coffee and black bread. I hadn't eaten since breakfast, and I was hungry, but just couldn't eat that hard, sour, black bread. The coffee was almost as bad. However, after a few days that black bread ranked almost at the angel food cake level!

The next day we were taken to Berlin by train and by doubledecker bus to the German Airport (probably Templehauf.) The wounded man was kept in the hospital there. I was given first aid and held in the air raid shelter area with the other flyer. The next day we were taken on a 17 hour passenger train trip to Frankfurt-on-the-Main for interrogation. There I was placed in solitary confinement in a small cell with one little, very high, barred window. We were not allowed to talk to anyone except the interrogator. Our cells had a "flag" arrangement to signal the guards that we had to use the toilet. They wouldn't talk to us and made sure no one else was in the toilet area when we were allowed its use. The food was very meager. The interrogator insisted that I was a spy because no one else had reported me as a crew member. They knew more about our base than I did! Even used our "secret and confidential" code number, 153, to identify the base. They knew most of the permanent personnel as well as all the Squadron Flight Leaders. After 10 days and several rounds with the interrogator they decided I didn't know much and shipped me out with about 200 other P.O.W.s being transferred to Luft 1 Camp at Barth.

We were loaded into boxcars and I thought we "had it made" with about 50 men in each car, but then the guards took over the center third of the car. We were so crowded that we had to take turns lying down. The trip was to take five days but on the fifth day we reached Berlin in time for the nightly air raid. The British did a fine job of bombing Berlin every night for the five nights we were there. When the air raid sirens sounded the guards would head for the shelter leaving us locked in the cars. It is very scary when bombs are exploding all around and you know you are in one of the target areas. We could see the parachute flares used by the Royal Air Force to mark targets for the following planes to drop their bombs. The marshalling yards suffered a great deal of damage but none of our boxcars were hit. Some of the prisoners developed fever. We had exhausted the food supply by the time we reached Berlin, so the authorities finally decided to forget Barth and take us to Stalag III A at Luckenwalde about 30 miles to the south. A day or two after arriving there we watched the 8th

AF hit Berlin. We were thankful to be out of Berlin but envious of those crews that would be back in England in a few hours.

A few hungry, cold, bed bug bitten months later we were liberated by the Russians but still confined to the camp. The Russians talked about taking us back through Russia to Odessa. The Germans strafed us a few times, so when we heard the Americans and Russians had linked up at the Elbe River, only fifty miles away, five of us decided to try to walk there. It took three days and was rather difficult but we all made it to the American Troops. Two months later I still had big blisters on my feet.

A few weeks later we were on a Victory ship, the Marine Dragon, headed for Boston and home. As mess officer on the trip back I managed to put on lots of weight. It's a wonder we didn't run out of food!

Fighters around the 390th formation.

Front:
M. Caldwell, TTG; L.D.
Lewis, RO-G; M. Ruta,
LWG; D. Helps,
Back:
E. Sechrist, Pilot;
J. Duncan, CP; C. Hessler,
N; G. Evancho, B.

Downed Airman and
The Maquis

by Mike Ruta
Gunner, 568th Squadron

I was shot down on 8 June 1944. Our assigned target was the German airport at Tours, France. The weather was very foul. After takeoff we could not see our wing tips at 50 feet. We had to climb to over 30,000 feet to break clear of the weather, upon doing so we were all alone. The pilot, Lt. Ed Sechrist, flew around for a time, all to no avail; the rest of the group was nowhere in sight.

We had exhausted much fuel in climbing to that altitude. At this point the pilot asked the navigator for a fix. The navigator, Lt. V. Turmenne (different navigator, not pictured above), reported our position, safe to let down. We saw a hole in the clouds. Ed the pilot let down to under the

211

solid cloud formation to 2,200 feet. Upon doing so we were directly over the huge German airfield in northern France. They had us. Upon breaking clear they opened up with everything they had. They hit our 2 left engines and the pilot could not feather the props. Also a fire was licking its way along the wing to the mostly empty fuel tanks (100 octane vapors).

The pilot opened the bomb bay doors and pushed the **ABANDON SHIP ALARM BUTTON.** Upon hearing the alarm I pulled the emergency release handle for the rear door. The right waist gunner, Henry Ford, Jr., jumped. I was in position to jump, but before doing so I glanced to my right and saw the tail gunner sitting down, feet dangling clear of his open hatch. I then jumped. I think that I assumed that the tail gunner, S/Sgt. David Helps, Golden, Colorado also jumped.

A short time after I jumped the Fort blew up! I have since learned that David Helps is listed as KIA.

I caught a piece of flak before clearing the Fort (left hand). I hit real hard upon landing, could not control my chute and was dragged along the ground. A sudden gust of wind flipped me backward on my head, back and right shoulder and I hit hard. I was bleeding from my hand, eyes and nose. I retained enough sense to realize I had to hide. I finally gathered my chute, started walking, came upon a path and followed it. It took me along and down the side of a crater. I spied a dark hole thru the vines, came upon a dugout section on the side of the crater and went in. I stayed inside for 4 days. I existed through the contents of the survival kits issued to the flight crews before each flight — concentrated malted milk tablets, benzedrine tablets, water purification tablets, plastic water bag, etc.

Meantime the German troops were looking for me. I could hear them overhead and occasionally caught sight of some of them, looking over the edge of the crater.

After 4 days of this I came out of my hole, back to the top, and started walking. I was disoriented and frankly at this point I think I was ready to turn myself in! It was at this point that I heard chopping in the near distance. I approached the sounds, observed 4 Frenchmen chopping down trees and then cutting them into short sections. I learned later that wood was converted into charcoal which in turn was used to feed a converter, mounted atop the cab of their vehicles, heating a small boiler, producing steam to propel their vehicles (at very slow speed).

I approached this group very cautiously my hand near my .45 caliber automatic. They in turn were not very trustful of me. Through the aid of the language card (issued before flight) I made my predicament known to them. They in turn took me over to the dense brush to hide and wait. I observed a member of the group separate himself and walk rapidly away. About 1 hour later I heard the sounds of an approaching horse and buggy. It stopped nearby, I came out, walked to him. He then questioned me thoroughly. He spoke English very well. After awhile I was told to lie on the buggy floor, covered with a blanket. We proceeded along a dirt road. Along the way I spied wheat and rye fields. Shortly after I saw a small town. As we approached the town I saw a sentry post. We stopped, the driver showed proper credentials, and we were allowed to pass. (The driver was the head Maquis leader of the entire area, Mr. Lucien Ravel.)

We approached the first iron gate, it swung open, we proceeded to the barn. I was told to climb to the hay loft. Shortly after they came for me, I went into the house where their doctor (I think) stitched my left hand and attended to my head, shoulder and back injuries. To lessen the pain I was given some of their local liquor (later learned it was called calvados, about 150 pr. aged in green walnut). They introduced me all around. I was embraced by all and made to feel welcome. I was fed lamb chops, white bread, some fruit and drank their home made apple cider. After all of this I felt no pain. The next morning I was given French clothing, false identity papers and work permit (photo was taken in nearby woods using green blanket as a backdrop). I was now an active member of their organization.

Some nights we went to nearby fields awaiting drops by the British. Parachuted canisters containing explosives, mills bombs, grenades, medical supplies, radios, spare parts, etc. All supplies were hurriedly gathered. We then took them to their dump, a large half tube-like structure completely underground (like London tubes). The entire outer perimeter was mined, only one member knew the safe path thru the mine field to the dump. Once inside we unpacked the canisters, distributed the supplies to predesignated shelves, assembled all arms (I was the arms expert), Enfields, shotguns, mausers, burp guns and armed the mills bombs, making them ready for use. Some nights we harassed the Germans by fouling up their communications. Every operation was well planned!

The town of Noyon (I stayed with a family located about 7 kilometers away) was part of the main escape route from the north. Also some of the main tracks from Paris to the west led thru this town, which also contained marshalling yards. The area was a prime target for the Forts. I was on the top dropping them before, now I was on the bottom, feeling the shock as the bombs exploded, and some of them were not on target. Meanwhile the P-51s, 47s and 38s were strafing every thing in sight. The Germans were in complete disorder. The site was total pandemonium.

The Maquis now gathered a group of about 20 of us. They had set up a camp where we stayed (cannot relate to time). Finally our area was taken over by a British armored column.

At this time I had developed a very serious case of bleeding hives. Very uncomfortable, messy, all due to fright, nervousness and stress. We finally came out of the woods in late September. We waited on the side of the road. The armored column came toward us, stopped. The commander questioned us, (there were British flyers in our group), was satisfied as to our authenticity, then fed us. Fortunately they had a doctor in the group and upon viewing my malady and

Late September, 1944 after rescue.

discomfort, took me to a nearby structure, had me strip and coated my body with some solution he had. Almost immediately I felt relief. Upon returning, the Sgt. in the first armored car grouped us together and took a photo. After this we split up in groups of 3 or 4 and hit the road to Paris.

My group passed thru the large town of Bouvais. It had just been liberated. The Maquis went around gathering all of the women that had collaborated with the Germans, shaved all of their hair, stripped them, painted swastikas on their heads and marched them down the main boulevard, jeering, spitting, and kicking them (outlet for their wounded pride, frustrations and deprivations).

After leaving Bouvais we were going down the hill on the road to Paris. I heard a vehicle coming down the road. I looked behind me, saw a U.S. Army recon. I managed to stop him (hollered at him in American) showed him my dog tags, was told to hop in the back. This recon was part of the Graves Registration outfit. They were bringing back 2 G.I.s picked off by German snipers.

This was how I reported back to active duty. I was taken under the direct care of G2 and S2, warned under threat of court martial I was not to divulge the background of the

At Cherbourg Air Strip after de-briefing and awaiting flight to England.

operations of the Maquis. I was isolated, given special privileges and ate in the officers mess. After they finished with me they trucked a group of us to an airstrip at Cherbourg for a flight back to London. In London we were again kept in isolation. Debriefed again, issued new uniforms, given a special pass, given most of my back pay, did the town (had much to make up for). I was the only American in London wearing a real Black French Beret.

It goes without saying that I was stopped many times by MPs questioning my uniform, but my special pass was equal to all occasions. I blew most of my money on London, wine, women and good food. I was then trained to Parham to collect my personal belongings. All I had left was my girl's picture and 2 sets of G.I. underwear. Everything else was gone.

Let us not lose sight of the main purpose of this missive. I and many others like me owe our lives to that organization known as the Maquis.

He Endured An 850 Mile Forced P.O.W. March

by George Zadzora

Radio Operator-Gunner, 568th Squadron

THIS was our 34th combat mission. If we completed this mission and one more then our tour of duty would be completed and we would be homeward bound — IF!

Our mission this morning January 14, 1945 took us over Germany flying a south-easterly heading toward Berlin. Our escort Mustangs were above us crisscrossing the formation, and watching over their "big brothers". The target was underground fuel storage tanks in the Berlin area.

We were about 10 or 15 minutes away from the I.P. I was in the radio room monitoring the code messages from the

217

station in England. I looked out the window and saw a P-51 flying about 150 feet below and going in the opposite direction to the flight of the bombers. I immediately signed "off watch" on the radio log, disconnected the oxygen and intercom, went to the right waist position, connected oxygen and intercom, then unhooked the gun from its stored position.

Over the intercom gunners were calling out the location and number of enemy fighters. An FW-190 flew past, then went into a loop with a P-47 on its tail. This is the first time that I saw a Thunderbolt fending off enemy fighters so I assumed that there were a lot of enemy fighters attacking. An ME-109 passed by very close, belly towards me and I let go a long burst from the 50 calibre. The other gunners were blasting away. An FW-190 passed by in the same manner as the 109 and I gave it a long burst. I looked momentarily inside the fuselage and saw there were long openings, about 2 feet in length. These were caused by machine gun and cannon fire from enemy fighters attacking from behind.

The next thing I experienced was a sensation that felt like about a dozen bee stings. I knew I was hit. The left waist gunner, Spence, went down but got up again, so I knew he had been hit. Over the intercom came the words, "Bail out, we're on fire."

Horan, the ball-turret gunner, got out of the ball and clipped on his chute as did Spence in the waist. My chute was in the radio room, so I had to go there to get it. As I turned and headed for the radio room, I could see flames and a grayish smoke in the radio room. I had no choice but to go and look for my chute.

As I went into the radio room, the smoke came in contact with my eyes, they began to burn. I inhaled a small amount of smoke and began to cough. The flames were about 3 feet from me. I got down on my hands and knees, eyes closed and began searching for the chute by feeling with my hands. At first, I couldn't find it so I began moving about on my knees and feeling for a bulge that would be the chute. It wasn't in the usual position where I kept it, but then I felt it with one hand, then both hands to be sure. I found the chute.

I got out of the radio room fast and to the rear exit door, clipping the chute to the harness as I went. I reached the exit door and without hesitation went out feet first.

Eight or ten seconds after leaving the ship, my right hand grabbed the chute ring and pulled — nothing happened. Pulled again — nothing happened. A few more tries and no results. Thoughts went through my mind — is something stuck? There seemed to be only one thing to do and that was to use both hands on the chute ring and pull hard. This was done and the chute opened at approximately 18,000 or 19,000 feet.

As I drifted down, 2 ME-109s came into view and circled clockwise around me. They descended at the same rate as my descent. After several circles they broke away and disappeared.

The ground was getting closer now and I was drifting toward a wooded area with several open spaces. By this time, I had a good idea of where the landing would take place: in a small clearing with a scattering of small trees.

As I hit the ground, I lost my balance and fell down. I then got up, unfastened the harness, rolled it and the chute into a compact roll and hid it in the nearby woods. It was now apparent that I could walk well. I felt a severe pain in my right arm. It now dawned on me that with a wounded right arm, I didn't have the strength to open the chute initially.

It was early afternoon, I checked the position of the sun, determined which direction was west and started walking. I found that by supporting the right arm in a position like that of being in a sling, the pain would lessen. Heading westward, I avoided small towns by walking around them, across fields and thru wooded areas staying off the roads until dusk. I came upon a haystack on the edge of a field and slept there the first night in enemy territory.

Surprisingly, I slept well that night and awoke just after dawn. Checking the position of the early sun, I headed in a westerly direction keeping off the roads to be less conspicuous. I was able to avoid people living in the area until late that morning. While crossing a small field, I was approached by 2 boys. One was about 15 years of age, the younger one about 10. I decided not to change direction or start to run but continued walking towards them until we met. The boys noticed my flight suit and asked me if I spoke German. I replied that I did not speak German in one of the few phrases I know of that language. Then I asked the older boy in the Slovak language if he understood what I said and to my astonishment, he replied in Slovak. We spoke for several minutes, then he invited me to go to his brother's home which I assumed to be a mile or two away.

As we three walked along, we were approached by a German soldier carrying a rifle. He was about 16 years of age and began conversing in German with the two youngsters I met some 10 minutes previously. The young soldier then indicated by pointing his finger in the direction that I was to walk and he followed me, and at no time did he provoke or abuse me. I still carried my right arm as though it was in a sling. It still pained me.

We entered a small town, walked past a number of houses, then the young guard indicated to me to walk through a gateway and to the front door of a house. This house was the Burgomeister's home.

The Burgomeister answered the door and he and the young soldier talked in German. Then I was asked to go inside the house by a hand sign along with the young soldier.

Inside the house, the Burgomeister dialed a number, presumably to notify the authorities that a prisoner was here in his home and to send a guard escort. He was on the phone for quite some time and it seemed to me that phone connections were difficult to make because of the time lapses between phone conversations and the number of times that he dialed.

The Burgomeister's wife was there and while her husband was phoning, she indicated to me to be seated at the kitchen table. This I did. She then placed before me, two slices of bread, butter, knife and a cup of black ersatz coffee, that had an acorn-like flavor.

While eating the buttered bread and coffee, she sat down at the table and spoke in German using only basic words and hand gestures rather than long sentences. I believe that she was saying that their son was in the service and that he was about my age.

Shortly afterwards, an army truck stopped in front of the house and two guards came inside while the driver remained in the truck. It was time to go.

As I approached the front door to leave, I turned around to the Burgomeister and his wife who were standing side-by-side, and said two of the very few German words that I knew — "Danke schon" — and departed with the two guards.

We climbed in the back of the truck with a canvas cover and sat on a bench seat facing backwards with myself in the middle and the guards on either side of me. The driver started the truck and we drove off into the night to a temporary cell at a military installation where I stayed that night.

The next morning I was escorted by two guards, taken on a train from Berlin to a camp about 30 or 40 miles south of that city.

After being searched, I was led to a cell that was barricaded with a stout piece of lumber about four feet long resting on steel brackets. Removal of this lumber permitted the door to the cell to be opened and in I went. The cell was about ten feet long by six feet wide with a very small window set high in the wall near the ceiling opposite the door. The only thing that I could see when I looked out the window was the sky.

There was a bed of rough lumber with a carpet on it about four feet long and two feet wide. These were the only items in the cell.

While in the cell, I received one bowl of watery soup in the evening that was delivered to my cell. I was permitted to the latrine three times a day — morning, noon and evening, each time accompanied by a guard. There was no reading material, no one to talk with so I spent my time with my thoughts.

I spent six days at this camp where I was interrogated then taken by train northward through Berlin and Stettin then eastward to a camp somewhere in the northwest or northern part of Poland in an isolated area.

I was taken into a small room and searched by a young English-speaking German. After being searched, he showed me, by pointing, a small wooden railing about 18 inches high and about 15 feet inside the wire enclosure. It was made of about 3/4 inch square wood stock having only a top rail and supported by vertical wooden stakes driven into the ground. He warned me that if I so much as touched that wood railing the guards have orders to shoot to kill.

I was assigned to a room in one of the barracks. This room was about 20 feet square having one door, one window and a single light bulb in the center of the ceiling. The double-decker bunks of rough lumber against each of the four walls provided sleeping facilities for 16 men. With my appearance that made 24 men occupying that room. Eight of us slept on the floor without the straw mattresses.

The first thing mentioned to me by the men with whom I was to share the room was that under no circumstances should I touch the wood railing because the guards have orders to shoot to kill. I was informed that a few of our guys didn't believe that warning, touched the railing and were shot dead by the guards in the tower.

That evening for our meal one of the fellows in our room was authorized to go to the central kitchen where the meal was prepared, usually soup with potatoes and whatever the G.I. cooks could find to add to the soup. It was brought to our room in a metal bucket and carefully ladled out so that each man would receive an equal portion. There was no meat in the soup but previously there had been. The meat came from occasional large dogs that ran loose in the compound, who were caught and added to the soup except for one tiny dog that was too small to qualify for the soup kettle so it became a pet.

Red Cross parcels were received from time to time that supplemented our evening meal of soup. Depending on the number of parcels determined the distribution to each individual. At times several G.I.'s divided a food parcel and each man kept his own food supply along with a ration of bread that was provided by our captors. For anyone to steal another man's food was considered a most serious matter.

Time was a commodity that we had in abundance. We kept occupied by walking around the compound, playing cards and checkers, reading, keeping diaries, playing softball during warm weather, hand washing the few items of clothing, writing a few letters and cards per month since that is all that was permitted, making pencil sketches on paper when it was available, preparing a snack during the day from our individual food supply, making items from the cans we received in our Red Cross parcels (such as hand-operated mixers for stirring coffee, tea and powdered milk), etc.

In early February, 1945, we were told at evening roll call to be prepared to move out the next morning. Nothing was said about our destination, just pack up and be ready. About a week before I had received some new G.I. clothing and a new pair of G.I. shoes.

Extra clothing was rolled up in a small bundle to be carried along with whatever food we had, plus the blankets that were rolled up and tied with rope or a strip of cloth in such a way as to carry it like a suitcase or over the shoulder like a set of golf clubs. Immediately after morning roll call the guards escorted us out the camp and we were on our way.

We could only assume that the Russians coming from the east were getting close to this internment camp and in all likelihood we would be marching west.

The weather was cold. After walking 4 or 5 days, it was

possible to determine the general direction in which we were going, using the sunrise and sunset as reference points. It was generally west.

About a day later, we crossed the Oder River, south of Stettin.

One week went by, then two weeks. Food was now more scarce. We began to search for anything edible along the road as we travelled westward. Sometimes a potato would be found by an alert pair of eyes, or perhaps a carrot or some other vegetable.

Whenever possible we were given shelter in a barn but some evenings we slept outdoors. Harry had three blankets and so did I. Three blankets were spread on the ground and the other three used to cover us. Sometimes the blankets would be spread on damp ground or damp grass since no dry places were available. Eventually the moisture would be soaked up by the blankets on which we slept which resulted in a soggy and uncomfortable night.

We walked almost every day but occasionally we would get a day's rest. When we did, a large part of the day was spent lying to conserve our energy for the next day's march.

During our march we crossed the Elbe river indicating that we were still going west. During the many weeks of the march, the weather varied — snow, rain, sleet, fog, sunshine — but generally cold and at times very cold. We usually travelled 15 to 25 miles per day and several times near 30 miles. Our bodies ached with fatigue and our stomachs pained for food, which was scarce causing loss of weight. We all developed short tempers. Morale was dropping even lower. Those unable to walk rode in horse-drawn wagons.

One clear morning, a few hours after sunrise, a loud noise shattered the calm air. It came from beyond a low ridge some 400 feet to our right. Moments later, a V-2 rocket appeared, accelerated rapidly and disappeared some 20 seconds later. We watched in awe while the guards, pointing fingers at the rocket, cheered loudly until it was out of sight.

We were all very fatigued from so much walking and so

little food. We were taken to a P.O.W. camp at Fallingbastel which was occupied by R.A.F. internees. This camp was located about 50 miles south of Hamburg and about 160 miles west of Berlin. The camp was crowded, tents were erected and we stayed there for about 3 or 4 days. The next day an R.A.F. internee came into our tent holding a piece of paper and asked that we gather around him while lookouts were stationed at each end of the tent to notify us in case German guards came near.

He then began to read from the paper in his hand. It was the latest war news from the B.B.C.

After hearing the news, I asked one of the P.O.W.s, a Canadian, how is the news obtained? He explained that when work parties were sent out to cut wood, a few of them drifted off to where a Lancaster bomber was downed and proceeded to bring in radio parts taken from that plane. They had to be careful not to be seen by the guards as they smuggled the parts into camp. In time enough parts had been gathered, a receiver assembled, tuned to the B.B.C. frequency and the news was then handwritten on paper and read to the prisoners at Fallingbastel.

After a short rest, we were then moved out of that camp. The march began again, this time eastward crossing the Elbe River and later the Oder River. This took us back into Poland not far from our original starting point.

Part of this trip we travelled by train. I have no positive way of knowing how far we travelled but I assume it was about 60 or 70 miles. The train would rumble along then stop for hours at a time.

We were jammed into the box cars and doors locked. During the night, it was pitch black inside; during the day only a small amount of light entered the box car and this was from small cracks around the door. Those who had food could eat; those who did not couldn't. No sanitation facilities were available, not even a bucket.

It was now about the end of March, 1945. Our march continued northward then westward from Poland for the second time. We again crossed the Oder River north of Stettin, followed the Baltic coast line, through the town of Swinemunde, then headed away from the Baltic Sea.

The days were getting longer and the weather became warmer. This was some consolation but we were still captives, hungry, weak, dirty and tired.

As we continued westward for the second time, ominous signs were evident. A flight of four Mustangs flew over at about 4,000 feet unchallenged. We went by an airfield of parked JU-88s none of which were operational; explosives were used to totally destroy the cockpits of these planes. A squadton of B-17s bombed a target several miles away at an altitude of about 4,000 or 5,000 feet with no enemy opposition.

With the Allies coming from the west and the Russians from the east, German controlled areas were considerably reduced and so were the distances that we walked each day. Now it was marches of only 5 to 8 miles each day.

Plodding along at a slow pace, we went past some buildings on a small rise of land that looked familiar. Suddenly the name came to my mind — Fallingbastel. This was the same camp where we rested some 6 weeks previously.

From the morning in early February, 1945, when we began our march, one name comes to mind immediately. The name is Dr. Pollack, an English doctor who with his medical assistants walked every mile of our trek. It was they who carried the medical supplies in addition to their possessions and administered to the wounded and sick during our entire journey.

One day after a tiring march, we stopped just outside of a small town to rest for the night. It was getting dark and we were almost totally exhausted. Dr. Pollack went to the nearby houses, knocked on doors and told the people that there were a lot of sick people in our group and requested that they bring hot water to us which they did. Buckets and buckets of hot water arrived enabling us to have a hot drink.

It was April 13, 1945. On this day, we walked through a

small town while some of the villagers watched as we passed. One of our guys named Gunzberg spoke German fluently and stopped momentarily to talk with a few of the local inhabitants. Moments later he joined us and gave us the news that he just received and that was that President Roosevelt died yesterday, April 12.

It was now late in April 1945. The outcome of the war was no longer in doubt. Our captors took us to a delousing station, divided us into groups of about 40 where we showered. Our clothing was placed in individual wire baskets and sent to a delouser. I looked at my body, arms and legs and couldn't believe how frail I was weighing about 75 pounds. I lost nearly 100 pounds during this ordeal of nearly three months. This was the second time that I was able to take a shower. The other shower was taken during the first visit to Fallingbastel.

I wore the same clothes, day and night, during this march from when it began in early February until May 2, 1945, when we were liberated by armored units of the British Second Army.

Recently I referred to maps of our march to determine the approximate distance that we travelled. After locating the names of familiar towns, I began measuring distances from point to point on a straight line basis; the distances that we walked would be greater since we walked on secondary roads with curves, hills and frequent changes of direction.

The first leg of our journey was from our camp in Poland westward to Fallingbastel, a distance of about 300 miles. From Fallingbastel, we travelled eastward some 250 miles back to Poland. Another 50 miles northward to the coast of the Baltic Sea. Westward again to Fallingbastel for approximately 275 miles and finally about 40 miles to the northeast near the town of Luneberg where we were liberated. This comes to about 915 miles less about 75 miles for the train ride which brings the total of approximately 840 miles point to point distance.

I assume that we walked a minimum of about 850 miles

and this distance was walked using a single pair of G.I. shoes.

The pilot of our B-17 was Paul Goodrich. He became the father of a baby boy while we were flying missions with the 568th Bomb Squadron. He sweated out each mission more so than some of us on his crew, because he looked forward to the day that he could be with his wife in the states and see their son for the first time. Paul was killed on our 34th mission.

Our tail gunner, Leonard Losch, was on his 35th mission. On one occasion, a crew whose tail gunner became ill, borrowed Lenny Losch for that one mission. This was the reason that Lenny had one more mission than the rest of the crew. Lenny was also killed on this same mission. Paul and Lenny were found in the wreckage of the plane.

Tribute to Zad

by Ralph Spence
Waist Gunner, 568th Bomb Squadron

HIS is about our radio man, George Zadzora. The day we went down 14th January '45 near Berlin. I was knocked unconscious. When I came to, Zad was shooting from the right waist gun and he really made a tune on it. I was facing the radio room, the bombay door was open and it looked like a furnace. I hit Zad on the leg and showed him the fire — our wings were on fire.

He said, "Get the parachute on." He grabbed me under the armpit and dragged me to the waist door and pulled the pin release. The door fell off and out I went with it.

He went back and got Jim Horan out of the ball turret. He was all shot up — his foot, knee and elbow. He put his parachute on him and dragged him to the door and pushed him out. By that time the smoke was so bad he had to crawl on hands and knees to find his own parachute and bail out.

I don't think there is any medal high enough to repay Zad for his guts and courage under fire. Jim nor I could never have made it to the door without him. "Thanks again, Zad!"

390th Formation approaches Emden, Germany, October 1944.

An Anoxic Ode to Code

by Wilbert H. Richarz

I sit in my radio chair,
As we fly through this rarified air,
And with the accompaniment of the clattering code,
My mind takes many a dreamy road.

I think mostly of the day,
When Uncle Sam will let me go my way;
When this war or wars is won,
And when my sentence on this clattering key is done.

My plans are definitely made,
And from my purpose I shall not be swayed,
For when that day of Victory comes,
And I march home to the roll of drums,
I'll march right down to Montgomery Ward,
And pick up my just and deserved reward.

And what, you may ask,
Could be reward enough for such a well-done task?
Why dammit — can't you read the writing on the wall?
A radio — with no insides in it at all.

(Framlingham England — 1944)

Potpourri

"YANKEE DOODLE DANDY"

James Cagney christens *Yankee Doodle Dandy* at the 390th.

Tom Jeffrey with James Cagney when he visited the 390th.

Almost An Unscheduled Mission

by Thomas S. Jeffrey
Air Executive, 390th Bomb Group

AFTER briefing the crews one morning, Col. Ed Wittan, 390th Commander, the Group Operations Officer and myself, the Air Executive, were in the control tower at Framlingham getting ready for the Group takeoff. It was dark as usual. It seemed like it was always night when we were getting ready for a combat mission.

The signal was given to start taxiing. The pilots were briefed to taxi in order of takeoff to the end of the runway. We would get about six planes on the runway initially in stagger formation. The remaining planes would be stretched out along the perimeter taxi strip.

Just before the time for takeoff, an engineering officer

232

came to the tower and told us the Group Leader wasn't on the runway. He was still back on the hardstand with a flat tail wheel tire. We realized immediately that we had a problem. Because of the radio blackout, we could not radio the No. 2 Wingman, who was the first on the runway, that he had to lead the formation up to assembly. Ed Wittan and I knew we had to get word to him. Ed said to me, "Take my staff car and ride around to the end of the runway and tell the pilot of the No. 2 airplane to take the group up to the assembly altitude of 18,000 feet.

So I jumped in the car and tore down the runway, pulled the car off the runway opposite the first airplane, left the lights on, left the engine running, and jumped in the back door of the airplane. I had on a flight suit without the rest of the gear. Well, you know what happened next. As I stepped in the airplane, the pilot pushed the throttles forward. Apparently, he was aware that the takeoff time had passed. I yelled trying to get the pilot to hold up. With four engines roaring no one could hear me. When I finally worked my way through the waist-gun compartment, the radio room, the bomb bay and up through the top turret, we were half way down the runway going about sixty miles per hour. It was too late to cut the engines since the next plane was due to start rolling in fifteen seconds. So I just stood between the seats. When we finally got the gear up and squared away, I reached over and tapped the pilot on the shoulder. He turned around and said, "What the hell are you doing here?" I said, "Man it's a long story, but let's keep on going until we can work out something."

We started to climb and at the same time circled around getting the other planes together. I realized that I was without a parachute or oxygen mask. I had on summer flying clothes. But — we were getting ready to go to Germany.

The only way to get me back down was to abort or bail out. Aborting was a very serious matter in our Group. In fact, anyone that aborted had to report immediately to my office, where I usually took the opportunity of "reaming" them out a small bit. Now if I was the cause of a plane to abort, you can see what a mess I would have on my hands. As for bailing out, I checked and quickly found out that we did not have an extra parachute. (As a side comment, can you imagine what Colonel Wittan would have said, if he had looked up and found his Air Executive floating down over the Base in a parachute.)

We continued to circle around the assembly point at 18,000 feet. I gulped on the emergency oxygen bottle. It was plenty cold with the light clothes I had on. Just before we were scheduled to leave the assembly point, the leader came up and pulled into the lead. We pulled off on his wing. Our hour of decision had come. We had to do something. But lo and behold, they cancelled the mission on account of weather over the target. I can't remember how many times I have thought, since that time, as to what would have been my decision.

We had a full load of bombs and a maximum load of fuel, so we had to circle for four more hours to get rid of the fuel before we could come back and land. We circled for it seemed like a half a day before landing. I got out of the airplane and went over to our quarters. I found Ed Wittan just getting up from taking a nap since he had been up at 2:00 AM for briefing. Ed said, "Jeff will you please tell me where in the hell have you been. Why did you leave my car on the end of the runway with the engine running and the lights on?" I looked at Ed and said, "Ed, you wouldn't believe me if I told you."

Tom Jeffrey was later appointed C.O. of the 100th Bomb Group. He stayed in the Air Force and retired as a Major General.

Crew of *Wild Children*

You Can't Believe
All Press Releases

by Bob Waltz

Pilot, 569th Squadron, **Wild Children**

ON our twentieth mission (Ludwigshafen, 7 Jan. 1944) numerous members of our crew were injured and temporarily taken off operations. I finished my first tour with a composite crew and/or as air commander for the group (riding with another crew). Following my 25th mission, the injured members of my original crew were returned to combat status. I, therefore, flew five additional missions so as to be able to be with them when they completed their tours. On that particular mission, to the Berlin complex, we again got the hell kicked out of us and we were all ready for a rest.

Upon our return to Station 153, from this Berlin mission,

I was immediately informed that I was being sent home (the good old U.S.A.) for R&R. Later that evening at the Officers' Club, the C.O. told me that I was leaving the next morning and that I should be home the following day. Hank Steinmetz, the Group Information officer, overheard all of this conversation and asked the C.O. if he could print the story. He got an 'oke' and thus begins my long tale of woe!

Because of the time element I had decided that I would not attempt to alert my wife, Ellen, who was living in Columbus, Ohio at the time, that I would be home within a day or two. The reader, by now, has probably gotten ahead of my story and assumed that I went back to the States by tramp steamer. Almost, but not quite—the troopship *George Washington* — and in a convoy! Thus, eleven days later, and with no commercial telecommunications possible, we arrived at the docks of New York. Within two hours I had obtained permission to go ashore and call my wife. I ran most of the way to a pay station only thinking about the great surprise that I was about to give my wife — informing her that I was in the States and only a few hours away from being with her! When she answered the phone I said, "Honey, I bet you can't guess who this is? Her immediate response was, "Where in the hell have you been?" I was not only shocked but also wildly confused; the accompanying newspaper article tells the story.

AKRON AIR HERO SETS RECORD IN LIGHTNING HOP HOME

Berlin, London, U.S.---In 3 Days!

Maj. Robert W. Waltz, one of Akron's fightingest air heroes, was due to arrive in New York today on his way home after making the fastest trip of the war between Berlin, London and the U.S.

Waltz, 23-year-old Flying Fortress pilot who has won the Air Medal and two oak leaf clusters, raided Berlin Tuesday, passed through London area Wednesday and expected to see Broadway today.

Officers of the Eighth air force based in England said Waltz' three-day jaunt between the world-famous cities was the first time for such a fast

AKRON AIR HERO SETS RECORD IN LIGHTNING HOP HOME

Berlin, London, U. S. --- In 3 Days!

Maj. Robert W. Waltz, one of Akron's fightingest air heroes, was due to arrive in New York today on his way home after making the fastest trip of the war between Berlin, London and the U. S.

Waltz, 23-year-old Flying Fortress pilot who has won the Air Medal and two oak leaf clusters, raided Berlin Tuesday, passed through London area Wednesday and expected to see Broadway today.

Officers of the Eighth air force based in England said Waltz' three-day jaunt between the world-famous cities was the first time for such a fast trip during the war.

The flying major is on his way to Akron to spend a 30-

day rest period before returning to the European theater for another tour of duty.

His wife, the former Ellen Snyder, lives at 218 Kenilworth dr., and his mother, Mrs. Celia F. Waltz, at 1708 Third st., Cuyahoga Falls.

As pilot of the Flying Fortress, "Wild Children," Waltz was captain of the 1943 all-American bomber team and by the first of this year had been credited with 24 missions over Europe.

On Jan. 16 of this year his plane was credited with destroying four Nazi fighters in one engagement. He has been recommended for the Distinguished Flying Cross.

The article as it appeared in the Akron newspaper.

trip during the war.

The flying major is on his way to Akron to spend a 30-day rest period before returning to the European theater for another tour of duty.

His wife, the former Ellen Snyder, lives at 218 Kenilworth, dr., and his mother, Mrs. Celia F. Waltz, at 1708 Third st., Cuyahoga Falls.

As pilot of the Flying Fortress, "Wild Children," Waltz was captain of the 1943 all-American bomber team and by the first of this year had been credited with 24 missions over Europe.

On Jan. 16 of this year his plane was credited with destroying four

390th planes leave smoke rising from Marienberg target.

Nazi fighters in one engagement. He has been recommended for the Distinguished Flying Cross.

Subsequent to the printing of the news article several newscasters and press services contacted my wife to determine what had happened to me. Someone or some news agency had picked the word "Lightning" out of the news article and thought I was flying a P-38 from East to West and would be landing at Idylwild Airport. When I didn't show they couldn't get a thing out of the War Department, since of course they had no knowledge of such a flight. For the next eleven days Ellen worked every possible source, including the Red Cross, in an attempt to find out where I was or what had happened to me.

Over these past thirty seven years I had grown quite comfortable about my participation and activities during WWII. During these latter four years, in the friendship of my old comrades at our reunions, I have found great interest and enjoyment in many of our reminiscence conversations. As the Reunion Chairman for our Tucson affair my wife and I have been very active and in close contact with many who planned on attending the affair. Recently she stunned me with the remark "Perhaps we'll get the true story out of you, or one of your 'friends' at the next Reunion."

Robert W. Waltz.

Crew of *Gloria Ann.*

Combat Diary Excerpts

by *Albert L. Buehler*

Bombardier, 569th Squadron, Gloria Ann

WE flew *Gloria Ann,* CC-E for Easy, and joined the Group and 569th Squadron in November, 1943, replacing the Becker crew which went down off Norway. I was the bombardier.

When we were ready to go overseas our first thrill was discovering that we were going over on the *Queen Mary* without any naval escort — the theory being that she could outrun any submarine. Real doubt arose one night when the Captain took violent evasive action, laid her over in a 45 degree bank and threw us all out of bed! My duty was to inspect troop quarters seven decks below the water line. When I learned that should we be hit by a torpedo, all lower

239

decks would be immediately sealed off, regardless of how many men might be trapped, since the ship was more valuable than the troops — I never went below again!

« « « » » »

After landing at Greenock, we arrived at Stone, a replacement depot. I have two vivid memories of that place. One, it was a sea of mud and we ate from a field kitchen. Nevertheless, the C.O. insisted Class A uniforms be worn (with galoshes) and everybody dipped his mess kit into the wash and rinse water barrels, etc. Also, while awaiting assignment to a Group, most of us ran wildly over the countryside trying to find something to shoot with our new 45s. That came to a sudden halt when a farmer, carrying a huge shotgun came over a hill saying, "I say, are you rabbiting?" We quickly learned we had encroached on his source of scarce food!

« « « » » »

My sixth mission was to Paris on New Year's Eve. Flak was intense and a burst hit me in the chest. Fortunately, I was wearing a flak vest but was cut in the neck by shrapnel and wound up flat on my back. Then I had to battle Dee Marsh, our navigator, who had his foot on my chest and was determined to render first aid although I really was okay. We had our moments — the next time out we had a fire in the nose section and tore up most of the flooring in extinguishing it.

« « « » » »

There was fire of a different nature on a bomb run at Wilhelmshaven in February. I had a sudden, sharp pain in my hip and was sure I'd been shot. Then I saw the smoke — the electric lead to my heated flight suit had burned out and scorched my skin after burning completely through my other clothing.

« « « » » »

At Brunswick on 11 January 1944, we had some fierce fighter attacks but no casualties. However, we almost became a statistic when twenty minutes after leaving the

Old 010.

target, a new crew flying in the high Squadron salvoed its load on us. All but one bomb fell between our right wing and tail section. That one hit us and left a huge hole in the wing plus knocking off the flap. Nothing vital was hit and upon landing, Major Price's ordnance people found the bomb fuse inside the wing.

« « « » » »

About the last week of January, I lost my cadet class ring. One week later, Bernie Strait discovered it was my ring he had been wearing and returned it to me on 3 February. Bernie was shot down the next day.

« « « » » »

Our No. 876 was scrapped after Johnnie Flottorp took it to Berlin and we then acquired a new unpainted B-17, No. 010. Since it was one of the first ships without paint, we felt naked and seemed to be an exceptional target as we flew to Brunswick on 23 March 1944. But it must have been a good airplane because later, while stationed in Colorado Springs, I was happy to see *Close Crop,* E for Easy dropping food to the starving Dutch pictured in the local newspaper of 9 May

1945.

« « « » » »

Going home after completing our tour became a problem for our co-pilot, Harley Beem and me. We had been sent to Debach, a new B-24 base, as flight control officers. There was no radio in the tower and when the first B-24 arrived and crashed, we jeeped all over trying to find someone who would authorize our return to the States, but with no luck. Then one night in our own Club, a visitor heard us bemoaning our fate and he just happened to be the right guy. Soon we were on our way.

Outstanding memories of that trip by convoy:

1. We were in mid-Atlantic on D Day and rumor had the ships returning to England and we'd fly another tour!

2. The Navy dropped depth charges constantly. Were we to be torpedoed at this stage of the game?

3. Many Anzio veterans and numerous pregnant WACs were aboard my transport. The soldiers had lived too long on G.I. rations and couldn't take the rich Navy fare, breaking out in boils and facial sores. They had to resume a Spartan diet but I don't know how the girls solved their problems!

Dick Perry greets
French prisoners entering
this 390th plane.

A Memorable Mission
After VE Day

by Richard H. Perry

Pilot & Operations Officer, 570th Bomb Squadron

AFTER the hostilities in Europe ceased in May 1945, there was an important and memorable activity in which many of us with the 390th participated. This was the transporting of former French Prisoners of War back to France.

I was assigned with a mini-crew and on the day of our "mission" the weather was perfect. We flew at a reasonable altitude on our briefed path across some varied and beautiful countries to Linz, Austria. This trip was surely a much different kind of mission than those I had experienced over the past 20 months — no oxygen, flak, enemy fighters, high altitude or formation flying. We were able to enjoy a

French prisoners waiting to board planes to return to France.

view of the country side.

As we approached the airstrip at Linz, Austria, we could see miles of fields, with fences, that resembled the stockyards in the midwest of the U.S. As we came closer, however, we were able to see that these enclosures did not include cattle, but rather people. These former prisoners of the Germans had been accumulated from numerous prison camps and grouped at Linz for transportation back to France.

After we landed and were directed to a parking location, off the runway with a great many other B-17s, we found 30 weary French soldiers formed in two lines behind our aircraft. They were being directed by a group of MP's. There were many groups already formed stretched along the parking area waiting for additional aircraft to arrive.

The group assigned to my aircraft were very sober. Some tried to smile but most of them stared wild-eyed and moved only on orders. I surely could feel for them. Some of them had been under very harsh treatment as prisoners for about five years. Their clothes were dirty and ragged. I assumed some were wearing things they had on when taken prisoner. They reacted to orders like well-trained animals.

The ex-prisoners were loaded on our aircraft. There were no seats, but we had laid some tarpaulins on the floor of the aircraft for them to sit on. Boards had been laid in the bomb bay. About ten men sat on these boards.

The trip back to France was uneventful. I let it be known that after takeoff, the Frenchmen could come up to the cockpit, one or two at a time, to look at the aircraft. Many hesitated to leave their assigned positions. A few, as time went on, got sufficient courage to come to the cockpit to visit us. By that time, they were starting to smile more.

After we landed at an airfield south of Paris, the ex-prisoners disembarked. Some kneeled down and kissed the ground. Others could not realize that they were back in their homeland. They seemed to be in a daze; still suffering from the prison camp experience.

Before taking off, I shook hands with the former prisoners. I can assure you that I had tears in my eyes. It was a great sight to see these people free after five horrible years under German control. This one event left me with a feeling that our war effort had been worth it.

Prisoners at Linz, Austria, airfield await their repatriation.

Presents For The Reich
Other Than Bombs

by William Carr
Navigator, 570th Squadron

DURING my twenty-five combat missions with the 390th Bomb Group, we were called on several times to drop propaganda information over German controlled territory. We also delivered our bombs on assigned targets.

On September 25, 1944, we dropped the following leaflet on Ludwigshafen:

One side seems to be directed at the great number of Polish workers in the Ludwigshafen area. The other side is in German.

Robotnicy

Ta wiadomość jest skierowana do robotników polskich
w zachodnich i północno-zachodnich Niemczech

. Załamanie się armii niemieckich na froncie zachodnim oznacza,
że wkrótce pewne części Niemiec staną się terenami walk. W związku
z tym Naczelny Dowódca Sił Sprzymierzonych poleca wszystkim
robotnikom cudzoziemcom znajdującym się na obszarach działań
wojennych co następuje:

1. Nie porwólcie ustępującym Niemcom na wciągnięcie Was głębiej
w obszar Rzeszy. Z chwilą zbliżania się Wojsk Sprzymierzonych
korzystajcie z każdej nadarzającej się sposobności by ukryć się
poza miastem i tam oczekujcie ich nadejścia.

2. Korzystajcie z każdej sposobności aby zebrać informacje, które
przedstawiać mogą wartość dla Sprzymierzonych — przedewszystkiem o poruszaniu się oddziałów niemieckich, ich przynależności i o położeniu pól minowych. Zwracajcie baczną uwagę na zachowywanie się Niemców i bądźcie gotowi dostarczyć dowodów okrucieństw niemieckich, których będziecie świadkami.

3. Jeżeli nie możecie ukryć się poza miastem, zróbcie wszystko co
w waszej mocy by zapobiec zniszczeniu komunikacji i urządzeń
przemysłowych. Starajcie się by dostały się one w ręce Sprzymierzonych w jak najlepszym stanie. Chrońcie przed zniszczeniem przedewszystkiem składy paliwa, oleju, i smarów. Wszystkie te
ważne rzeczy będą wkrótce potrzebne wojskom sprzymierzonym.

4. Z chwilą nadejścia sił alianckich spełniajcie dokładnie polecenia
wydane Wam przez alianckie władze wojskowe.

WG7P

ALLIIERTES OBERKOMMANDO

(Supreme Headquarters, Allied Expeditionary Force)

Der umseitige Aufruf des Alliierten Oberkommandos in polnischer Sprache richtet sich an die polnischen Arbeiter in den westlichen und nordwestlichen Teilen des Reiches. Er gibt den ausländischen Arbeitern Anweisungen über ihr Verhalten in dem Augenblick, in dem diese Teile des Reiches zum Kriegsgebiet werden.

Der Kampf der ausländischen Arbeiter richtet sich nicht gegen die deutschen Arbeiter. Er wird geführt im gemeinsamen Interesse aller Arbeiter, die entschlossen sind, das Ende des Krieges zu beschleunigen.

Hier ist eine wortgetreue Übersetzung des umseitigen Textes:

Der Zusammenbruch der deutschen Armeen im Westen bedeutet, dass Teile des Reiches bald zur Kampfzone werden. Angesichts dieser Tatsache erlässt der Oberste Befehlshaber der Alliierten Streitkräfte folgende Anweisungen an die ausländischen Arbeiter in den Kampfzonen:

1) Lasst Euch von den fliehenden Deutschen nicht tiefer in das Reichsinnere treiben! Während die alliierten Armeen sich dem Gebiete nähern, in dem Ihr arbeitet, ergreift die erste Gelegenheit, auch Land zu flüchten, um dort die Ankunft der alliierten Streitkräfte zu erwarten!

2) Nutzt jede Möglichkeit, um Informationen zu sammeln, die für die alliierten Armeen wertvoll sind; vor allem Informationen betreffend die Bewegung deutscher Truppenteile, die Identität deutscher Wehrmachts-Einheiten und die Position deutscher Minenfelder. Ferner: beobachtet auch genaueste das Benehmen von Deutschen und bereitet Euch vor, über jedwede Grausamkeit, dere i Zeuge Ihr gewesen seid, Bericht zu erstatten!

3) Wenn Ihr nicht in der Lage seid, aufs Land zu flüchten, so tut alles, was in Eurer Macht steht, um die Zerstörung von Verbindungslinien und Industrieanlagen zu verhindern. Sorgt dafür, soweit es Euch möglich ist, dass sie in guter Verfassung sind, wenn sie den Alliierten in die Hände fallen! Vor allem: schützt Treibstofflager vor der Vernichtung und Feindeshand! Alle diese Lager und Einrichtungen werden in Kurz von den alliierten Armeen gebraucht werden.

4) Sowie die alliierten Truppen Euch erreichen, befolgt aufs genaueste die Anweisungen, die Euch von den alliierten Militärbehörden gegeben werden!

Two days later, on September 27, 1944, additional leaflets were dropped over Mainz:

An die deutsche Frau!

Deutschland selbst wird nun zum Kriegsschauplatz. Von jetzt an wird jede Bombe und jede Granate auf deutschem Boden explodieren. Deutsches Blut wird deutsche Erde tränken. Städte, Dörfer und Felder werden in Rauch und Flammen aufgehen. So wollen es Hitler und seine Partei-Fanatiker.

Willst Du den Krieg im Lande?

Frage den heimkehrenden deutschen Soldaten,
ob persönlicher Opfermut und Heldentum die anglo-amerikanische Kriegsmaschine zum Stehen bringen können.

Frage den heimkehrenden deutschen Soldaten,
ob er für deutsche Frauen und Kinder die gleiche Loyalität will, das der Zivilbevölkerung der Normandie, Italiens und Russlands.

Frage den heimkehrenden deutschen Soldaten,
ob er will, dass sein Heimatort so aussieht, wie die zerschossenen Dörfer und Städte der Normandie, Italiens und Russlands.

Die Treue des deutschen Soldaten gehört nicht der verkrochenen Partei, sondern Dir, deutsche Frau, Deinen Kindern und der Heimat. Und Du kannst den deutschen Soldaten, Deine Kinder und die Heimat vor einer Vernichtung bewahren, wenn Du forderst:

SCHLUSS!

WG9

Deutsche Frau, Du hast das Wort!

Das ist das sechste Kriegsjahr. Der deutsche Soldat ist zurückgekehrt. Er hat Unmenschliches erduldet auf den Schlachtfeldern Russlands, den Wüsten Afrikas, unter dem Trommelfeuer der Alliierten in Italien und dem Bombenhagel an der Westfront. Aufs neue, auf Heimatboden, soll er nun den Kampf gegen die ungeheure Übermacht der anglo-amerikanischen Kriegsmaschine aufnehmen. Ohne genügend Panzer und Luftwaffe. Du, deutsche Frau, hast die Macht, unendliches Leid, Schrecken und Tod zu verhüten. Sage dem heimgekehrten deutschen Soldaten:

● Dass Du diesen sinnlosen, letzten Widerstand nicht willst.

● Dass Du nicht willst, dass Deine Städte und Dörfer in Grund und Boden geschossen werden.

● Dass Du genug hast von der SS und der Partei, die die Zerstörung der Heimat befahlen, nur um sich selber noch ein paar Tage länger im Sattel zu halten.

● Dass darum Soldatentreue ausschließlich dem Volke gehört.

● Dass dieses Volk verlangt:

Schluss mit dem Krieg!

Weg mit den Kriegsverlängerern!

Sofortfriede und Wiederaufbau Deutschlands!

This leaflet was aimed at German women urging them to do what they can to end the war.

At about the same time in 1944, we dropped sheets of meat ration coupons. Here is a copy of some of these coupons:

The original coupons were blue. It was expected that the people finding these coupons, would use them and in turn disrupt the German ration program.

I have never heard how effective these propaganda efforts were but they added a little intrigue to our bombing missions.

"Hap" Howell

Stories From "Hap"

by Roger P. "Hap" Howell

Assistant Group Operations Officer, 390th Bomb Group

THERE are three missions that stand out in my mind more than others:

« « « » » »

The shuttle mission to Russia when we dropped supplies, medicine and munitions, by parachute to General Bor in the Warsaw Ghetto. As I recall, we went in at 18,000 ft. and 109's hit us on the 10 minute bomb run. As I recall, the Russians were holed up east of the Vistula River purposely waiting for the Germans to annihilate the Poles. When we dropped at Warsaw, the Germans got their flak going and I always said that the Russians were shooting at us too.

249

Unfortunately, the Poles only got about a third of the drop — the Germans got the rest. Then at Poltava, we had to put a gunner on the B-17 as the Russians were stealing everything they could get their hands on.

« « « » » »

The food drop to the Dutch. We went in at 500 ft., with an exact land-fall set by the Germans. If we missed it they would fire on us — and oh boy, at that altitude! But we made it and I'll never know where the Dutch got all of those little American Flags! They were waving them like mad, those poor starving people, and along with the bed after bed of Tulips, it was a most impressive sight!

« « « » » »

The last mission, Number 301 to Oranienburg, north of Berlin. We figured it might be the last and I was glad to be on it at the end.

« « « » » »

Here are three stories that have a humorous twist:

My brother Pete, a P-51 pilot had arrived in the ETO and had been assigned to the 357th Fighter Group stationed at Leiston, only 8 miles from the 390th. The first evening he arrived at Leiston a JU87 came over and pumped his mess hall with his machine guns and then came over our Base and dropped his bomb load. He phoned and asked me, "What the hell is going on?" I could think of only one thing to say, and that was, "Welcome to the ETO!"

« « « » » »

One night there was a party at the Club. One of the 570th pilots, who had been on oxygen for 5 or 6 hours on a mission, and was exhausted, proceeded to get "bombed" and passed-out cold. We carried him out to the front of the Club and laid him over the hood of a Jeep. I got my horn and played "Taps" for our departed buddy. In the middle of our "service" the owner of the jeep came out and asked, "What was going on?" The owner of the jeep happened to be Lt. Col. George W. Von Arb, the Air Exec!

THE EPILOGUE of the story is this: The 570th pilot got through his missions OK along with George and myself. We are now members of our Association and when the three of us get together at reunions we have many a laugh about this 40 years later!

« « «   » » »

I was coming home from the Club one very dark night with a pretty good load. They announced over the Tanoy that there was a German bomber in the area so I took cover immediately. It had rained very hard and there was a ditch alongside the road — so I hit the ditch! And who did I land on top of, and was almost drowning but Major McCaffrey, our Personnel Officer. We got to laughing so hard that we really had problems getting out of the ditch when the "all clear" came through!

Officer's Club bar.

Carl (Andy) Anderson

Reflections of a Ball Turret Gunner

by Carl (Andy) Anderson
Ball Turret Gunner, 568th Bomb Squadron

WHEN I volunteered for Aerial Gunnery, I was sent to school at Las Vegas and assigned to train in the ball turret. It was very apparent when one looked at a bomber crew who the ball turret gunner was. The turret was not made to accommodate a six foot, 200 pound man. I weighed a mere 130 pounds and stood five foot five inches tall — a perfect fit!!

Our gunnery training took place at Indian Springs, which later became the atomic test site. I remember the target tow ships' pilots complaining about the turret gunners zeroing in on their plane then following back to pick up the tow targets. It was difficult to find the target

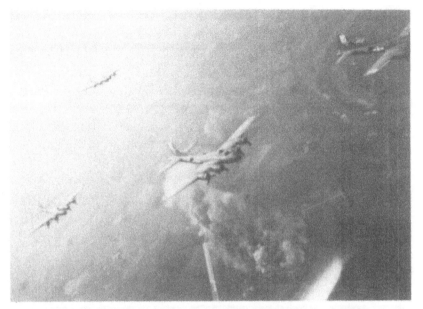

Heading for the Rally Point after bombing Marienburg, Germany.

alone in our computing sight.

I was intrigued with the turret from the beginning. I was never affected by the close quarters, and I never had a feeling of claustrophobia. Some of the combat missions we flew required a rather long stay in the turret. A lot of the time was spent lying on my back with both legs extended forward alongside of the guns. There wasn't room to change my position appreciably. It was a welcome relief when we reached a safe point on the trip home when I could finally leave the turret and stretch.

The ball turret was a lonely place at times and one learned early on that you had to lay off that extra cup of coffee before take-off. The relief tube consisted of a chamois lined funnel and a plastic tube that drained to the outside under the seat. The problem only started when you did. With the freezing temperatures at high altitude, it didn't take long to freeze in the plastic tube and then the funnel started filling up. Guess what next — you've literally got your hands full.

Our radio operator devised a means to get a cigarette lit

while up at altitude. He used the transmitter and his pencil, dragging an arc off the antenna while inhaling a mouth full of oxygen and punching the transmitter key. He blew the oxygen through the cigarette which flared like a torch. Probably not the safest means of relieving a "cigarette fit", but it got the job done. The lit cigarette was passed through the bomb bay to the others forward that smoked. Unfortunately the air currents were such that I inherited the smells that originated from inside the airplane. The first time I smelled a cigarette at 25,000 feet, I thought I had flipped. Finally Ken admitted that he had lit up. After that I would be in my turret hanging under the belly of the ship, with the radio room door closed, and would say over the interphone, "Hey Ken, put that cigarette out." He used to say, "How do you know I'm smoking?" There were other smells that were quite pungent that came my way occasionally.

I always said that the ball turret gunner had the best seat in the house — unlimited visibility 360 degrees around and 90 degrees down. I could scan the whole country-side ahead, around and behind. Occasionally I could see the flashes from the German flak batteries on the ground and announce to the crew to get ready for the bright orange flashes and black puffs of smoke that would soon arrive.

Back:
R. DeWalt, C. Pecorella,
G. Dadario, D. Quinn,
A. Oleksiok, W. Warren,
E. Schmidt, O. Steele.
Front:
A. Cummings, R. Sterr, P.
P. Geiselman, C. Baker,
B. Sorensen, R. Malfitano,
J. Curtis.

I'll Be Around — Sterr Crew

by Earl Schmidt, Jr.

Co-Pilot, 570th Bomb Squadron, **I'll Be Around**

STERR'S Crew was part of the first replacement cycle to join the original 390th team as they completed their combat tours. They flew the famed B-17 "Miss Carry" on their early missions, moved into element lead, and when selected for Squadron and Group Leadership were given a new ship which they named *I'll Be Around* in mid-March 1944.

The crew participated in "Big Week," The First Berlin Missions, Second Regensburg, Poznan, and Brux raids and saw heavy air to air combat action losing all but 2 of the composite Squadron planes in the second German formation rocket attack experienced by the Eighth AF.

The gunners racked up the highest fighter "bag" in the theater during the months they were in combat. Six of the plane's eight gun positions had scored at least one "probable" with seven "confirmed." The left waist gunner had a "confirmed" 18 inch tip of the left tail surface, and the radioman got all upper antennas every time he tried.

I'll Be Around was kept in operation-ready condition by the efforts of a small but hard working ground crew headed by the 570th Squadron's senior Crew Chief Arthanasis "Pop" Cummings. The entire crew finished combat just prior to "D-Day" and completed varied post-operational assignments on base and elsewhere in the ETO before returning Stateside.

The crew has been active in recent 390th annual reunions. On March 13, 1982, five of the original crew members were on hand at Davis Monthan AFB, Arizona for the dedication of B17NR231892 — *I'll Be Around*. After the dedication, the World War II heavy bomber joined the other historical United States Air Force aircraft at the air museum.

So *I'll Be Around* from now on.

Stories From the
Liberty Belle Crew

by Albert M. Bell

Pilot, *570th Squadron,* Liberty Belle

IT had been a routine mission up to and including take-off. We climbed up through a very thick overcast
and assembled "on-top". We had been assigned the first
Model G (B-17) on the field, and to our dismay, the chin
turret picked up so much ice climbing up through the
overcast that the chin turret guns were frozen and inoperative. Shortly after we got over enemy territory, an enemy
aircraft (ME-210) lobbed a rocket into the formation and it
knocked out our number 3 engine, took out most of the
plexiglas nose and knocked our oxygen system out in the
ball turret. The radio operator noted the strange action in
the ball turret and had the waist gunner check it out. The

257

ball was rolled up manually, the ball turret operator removed, and plugged into an emergency oxygen bottle. This meant that both the ball turret and the chin turret were inoperative. By using emergency power, we were able to stay in formation and drop our bombs on the target. When the plexiglas nose was blown off, the concussion knocked the bombardier back with such force he broke the back of his chair, and although he did not get a scratch, he had eleven holes in his flying suit from the fragments of the rocket. A short time after the bomb run, we were hit with a burst of flak which took out the rest of our oxygen system. The pilot, co-pilot and navigator were given emergency bottles of oxygen and the rest of the crew were without oxygen for the rest of the trip. All personnel sat still and by a minimum amount of exertion, were able to remain conscious or semi-conscious until we let down to a lower altitude over the channel. We had elected to stay with the formation as long as we could rather than drop down to a lower altitude as enemy fighters were in the area and were picking off stragglers.

Other than the ball turret operator having a bad headache, the only other human casualty was the navigator who froze his feet. When the plexiglas nose was blown off, there was a direct air blast on the navigator's feet and both of his feet were frozen. He was unaware of this fact until some time after we were on the ground. This was the last mission that he flew with us as he was hospitalized and subsequently sent back to the States. All the way home, our airspeed indicated 175 which was about 20 MPH above normal airspeed. Since we were drawing emergency power, we were using more gas than normal, to stay in formation. As we were coming over England, our number 2 engine quit, due to no gas. Since we were letting down we were still able to stay in formation. We decided not to transfer any fuel in order to start up our number 2 engine since we were so close to home. We peeled off on the first pass over the field and landed. While taxiing to our hardstand our number 4 engine quit. When we stopped, all of the gas gauges indicated "empty". The crew chief took a stick to measure the gas left in the tanks, but was unable to show any gas in any of the tanks.

« « « » » »

During one of our missions, the co-pilot was making a routine oxygen check. The tail gunner did not check in. After several unsuccessful attempts to contact him via interphone, the waist gunner went back to the tail section to investigate. The tail gunner said he had heard himself being paged, but he did not answer the oxygen check because he was busy praying.

When the mission was over, the pilot told the tail gunner to get down on his knees and pray. He said he should pray until he had accumulated such a surplus of prayers that he would never again have to neglect his "crew responsibilities" by praying when he should be manning his guns. The pilot told the rest of the crew that he did believe in prayer, but that they should get all of their praying done before the aircraft left the ground. Anyone caught praying when airborne would be kicked off the crew. In other words, you will knock down a lot more enemy aircraft by shooting at them than praying at them.

« « « » » »

As was the custom on most crews, the enlisted men brought their letters over to the officer's barracks in order to get them censored. One day our tail gunner brought over a letter for the pilot to censor. The letter began, "Dear Ma, we are scheduled to go on a mission tomorrow and I have a feeling that this will be it. Have Father - - - - (Priest) burn a candle and say a prayer for me, etc. . . ." The pilot went over to the tail gunner's barracks and said, "I don't know what your mother ever did for you to hate her enough to write a letter like this to her. She no doubt cries every day in fear of just such a thing as you have suggested. I don't think you want to pull such a dirty trick on your mother as you are doing with this letter." The tail gunner thanked the pilot for making him realize what a stupid thing he had almost done and said he would rewrite the letter. After a short period, the tail gunner returned and handed the pilot another letter to censor. The letter began, "Dear Sis, We are scheduled to go on a mission tomorrow and I have a feeling that this will be it. Have Father - - - - burn a candle and say a prayer for me, etc." The pilot took the letter and told the tail gunner to come back after the mission tomorrow and he would have the letter censored. The next day after the mission, the pilot gave the letter back to the tail gunner and suggested that he not send it since his predictions had been proven incorrect. To the best of my knowledge, the letter was never sent.

B-17 at its hardstand.

Do B-17s Back Up?

by Marshall B. Shore
Group Navigator, 390th Bomb Group

MOST of the original commanders and air staff for the 390th Bomb Group came from the 34th Bomb Group at Blythe, California. In January of 1943, while flying with Captain Joseph K. Gemmill, who was to become the Squadron Commander of the 570th Squadron in March, we were checking out a new crew. It was about 11 PM, a night training mission. We were to fly a three ship formation at night. The B-17s were to take off one after the other. While running up our engines at the end of the taxi strip prior to taking the runway for take-off, our airplane was run into from the rear by a new crew on their first mission without an instructor. Joe had all four engines revved up and the noise was loud as usual. The only thing we felt was a crunch and a slight lurching of our aircraft. There was some cursing over the interphone and Joe shut down our engines. He opened the left cockpit window and looked out at a very angry First Lieutenant looking up at him who then shouted up to Joe, "Why in hell did you back into me"?

Search Light Training at Orlando

by Marshall B. Shore

SHORTLY after activation of the 390th Bomb Group in February of 1943, the advanced Air Echelon was sent TDY for a month of Tactical Bombardment training at Orlando Army Air Base, Florida. This month of training during March brought us face-to-face with the modern tactics being used in England by the 8th Air Force fighting units. Our instructors were combat experienced including one Royal Air Force officer who was a veteran of many night missions over enemy territory. Naturally he was rather expert in evasion of enemy search lights. Well, they had a battery of three triangulated search lights set up over Orlando or very nearby. One night I happened to be flying with Colonel Wittan as pilot and we were doing maneuvers to evade these three white beams of strong light pointed up at us. The RAF instructor was standing behind the pilot encouraging him to be more violent in getting out of the light. Being an old fighter pilot with experience in the First Fighter Squadron in Iceland, Col. Wittan was pretty good at racking that B-17 around. He didn't fly it like a bomber that night. I spent as much time against the ceiling in the nose of the B-17 as I did on my navigator's seat. There was a full moon out. After being in the bright light for a few minutes on one maneuver, we managed to get out of the rays. When they turned the lights off, one of the large lamps glowed for several minutes. It looked like the moon. Col. Wittan was partially blinded by the bright beam of light and leveled out basing his position and altitude on the ground light instead of the moon. For a few moments, we were headed straight for the ground. When he pulled us out, the air speed meter was pegged at the top. A damned exciting ride.

Formation over Germany, Fall 1943.

Emerson Smith
Won't Forget B-24 Pilot

by Emerson A. Smith

570th Bomb Squadron

EMERSON A. Smith has never forgotten the World War II day in 1944 when he was the sergeant in charge of loading explosives on an aging B-24 Liberator bomber at a secret site in England.

He's also never forgotten the name of the plane's pilot, although it was years before he mentioned the name aloud — even to Mrs. Smith.

In the terrible years of war, he was a ground crew member of the 570th Squadron of the 390th Bomb Group, 8th Air Force. His assignment? Loading and fusing the bombs from 100-pounders to 2,000 pound blockbusters, which the crews of the 390th's B-17's unloaded on targets deep in Hitler's

Germany.

One time he was put on detached service at Fersfield. There he loaded war-weary B-17s (considered unsafe for flying). Pilots took them up, then bailed out after other planes took the drone plane under radio control. The drone then was guided to the target and crashed on it.

It was while Smith was at Fersfield that he loaded hundreds of explosives, secured by light steel cable, on a B-24 to be flown by a Navy pilot who had volunteered for a hazardous mission.

He learned later that the pilot was killed. And he also learned that the mission was cloaked in tight security and he was ordered not to talk about it.

It was several years later, when he was back on his war-interrupted job, that he saw a story in a nationally circulated magazine about the flier's death. It wasn't until then that he believed himself free of the fetters of security, and told Mrs. Smith that he was one of the last to see Joseph P. Kennedy, Jr. alive.

The oldest brother of the man who was to become President of the United States, Kennedy was posthumously awarded the Navy Cross and the Air Medal, decorations of valor for the missions he flew.

Kennedy and a fellow officer who was expert in radio control projects, were killed at 6:20 PM Saturday, August 12, 1944.

In a collection of essays written in 1945 and named "As We Remember Joe," John F. Kennedy wrote that his brother, who arrived in England in September 1943, had flown so many missions that he twice was offered the opportunity to go home, the last time in July 1944. It was about then that his brother learned of a new and special assignment for which volunteers had been requested, John Kennedy wrote. He added:

At the time of his death, he had probably completed more missions in heavy bombers than any other pilot of his rank in the Navy, and therefore was pre-eminently qualified (for this mission), as he told a friend in August. He considered the odds at fifty-fifty, and Joe never asked for any better odds than that.

Rose Kennedy, mother of the eight Kennedy children, wrote in her book published in 1974 that there were several accounts of her son's death. But probably the most accurate, she said in "Times to Remember," was the one written in 1948, "Tenth Anniversary Report, Harvard College Class," by a friend of her son.

That account said, in part:

Joe (and the fellow officer)... was to take a 'drone' Liberator bomber loaded with 21,170 pounds of high explosives into the air and stay with it until two 'mother' planes had achieved complete radio control... then they were to bail out over England; the 'drone' under the control of the 'mother' planes, was to proceed on the mission which was to culminate in a crash-dive on the target, a V-2 rocket launching site on the continent.

The airplane... was in flight with routine checking of the radio controls proceeding satisfactorily, when... two explosions blasted the 'drone' resulting in the death of the two pilots. No final conclusions as to the cause of the explosions has ever been reached.

A POSTSCRIPT to that account came in November 1972 when a British policeman, whose hobby was searching for the wreckage of World War II aircraft, found the remains of Kennedy's Liberator near the village of Saxmundham, about 25 miles north of Ipswich.

Emerson still remembers Joe Kennedy's final remark to him after they had loaded the B-24, "Here is a pound note, go buy some beer for yourself and the others."

CLUBMOBILE DEPARTMENT SECOND ANNIVERSARY.   OCTOBER 22nd - 28th, 1944.

A Potpourri of Memories

by *Wilbert H. Richarz*

Radio Operator-Gunner, 570th Squadron, Cocaine Bill

MEMORABLE BITS OF G.I. WIT

AT Scott Field, Illinois, during a course in Radio School we were subject to rigid discipline, severe military courtesy regulations, and all the rest of the many little mannerisms of the "regime militaire." One day we were standing a "muster" roll call and the officer in charge was fulfilling the duties of his post admirably as he called out the names on the roll call. As he went down the list he seemed to gain inertia toward becoming even more demandingly military as he progressed. "Jones," "Jameson," "Johnson," he shouted and to each name called came the prompt "here, sir" in an equally military tone of voice. Then, since there seemed to be some unnecessary

267

conversation among the ranks, the officer cried out "at ease" — without changing his tone of voice. A prompt "here, sir" came from one of the back ranks — with no change in tone of voice and in a truly military manner.

« « « » » »

In England, in a small village named Framlingham, we had just come from a dance at the Anglo-American Club and were standing in the small village square awaiting the return of our truck so we could return to the base. In the center of the square a small group of well saturated G.I.'s were giving their all in loud braying voices. In that quiet little village of narrow winding streets I imagine every sleep-groggy villager was soundly cursing those enthusiastic though untrained voices as they gave their version of "Down in the Valley." Perhaps, though, they may have smiled, if they could make out the words of those unquenchable characters, for those words went something like this: "Write me a letter, send it by mail, send it in care of the Framlingham Jail."

« « « » » »

On another night — in the same village and in the same place with the same serenaders — a British Lorrie (truck) was negotiating a backing up and turning around process — with the able assistance of the British soldier in the back end who kept calling out in a typical "Suffolk" accent "ohky mite bahk her up a bit." One of the ever present wits among the "mild and bitter" brigade mocked him in a vain attempt to imitate the difficult accent. Without a second's hesitation the "back seat driver" corrected himself and though still in the clipped "Suffolk" accent he called out "ohky youse guys git 'er back will youse." This he said with no change of voice and no sarcasm whatever. What more could you ask in the way of Anglo-American cooperation?

« « « » » »

There had been considerable pressure from the higher-ups to keep the turret gunners in their turrets throughout the whole time of every mission instead of them getting out for a stretch when they became cramped. Jack, our pilot, was never one to try to "command" the boys to do anything, but being a very conscientious guy he couldn't help but check up on the boys from time to time to see if they were keeping the turrets moving. Needless to say, a ship with turrets standing still was easy game for fighters who would pick out these ships to attack because of their reduced fire power. One particular day Jack called back to Hap and said, "Hap, are you down there in the ball?" Hap, sounding severely hurt at such an implication, leaned over and pushed the mike button on the waist gun and said, "Yes sir, I'm down there." Incidentally, Hap never talked himself out of that one!

BARBARA

The first time I saw her was at the Christmas party and from that moment on I knew I had found the very essence of my idealic longings. A shy little thing with eyes as blue as a summer sky — her hair dark against the fairness of her face. She stood there in the open doorway as might a fairy queen about to brighten our day with her coming. I stood there enraptured — unable to speak or move, yet feeling myself drawn to her as if by some magnetic power. She stepped slowly into the room and with dignity and a certain shy poise made her way unerringly to where I stood. The soft appeal in her eyes gave me courage and without a word I took her warm little hand in mine.

The events of that day are still a bit hazy to me, but I remember Barbara — for that was her name — as vividly as this morning's sunrise — her beauty, her slow shy smile, her words so softly spoken bring to me a memory ever treasured. We spoke, but little, and that in hushed, almost reverent tones as if afraid we would break the spell with one harsh

word; but even in silence we seemed in harmony as the
strings of a beautifully tuned violin. With closed eyes I can
remember her still as she sat so close to me her hand in mine,
the warmth of her breath upon my cheek, the fragrance of
her all about me. The memory of Barbara, the adoring,
almost imploring look of her eyes so clear and blue will
always haunt me.

Time, the inevitable, brings me to the end of my story, for
it was time that parted Barbara and me. It was at the close of
the Christmas party that we parted, each with a lingering,
backward glance and the hope that we would meet again
very soon. I left her with those with whom she had come and
waved goodbye to her as she rode away — waved goodbye to
Barbara — a tiny English girl of five who came to the
Christmas party we gave for the children of the
neighboring village.

—England, 1944

THE ROAD BACK

There seems to be a collective opinion among the current
edition of the "troops" that the Army is much like God in
some respects, because it works in such mysterious ways!
With this bit of sagacious deduction I heartily agree, and
I'm sure that I may speak as well in this respect for the other
8 thousand, 9 hundred and 99 "troops" that I may consider
as my fellow travelers on this ocean-going tub.

Way back when, in the days when we were considered
"replacements," our trip from the States to England was a
matter of 13 hours traveling time. The trip, however,
through the courtesy of our benevolently beaming Uncle
Sam, was negotiated in our trusty B-17 — otherwise known
as the big gas bird — and not in this lumbering Leviathan
which is plainly nothing more than a not-so-sea-worthy
cattle boat going under the very complimentary name of
"Ile de France." Its traveling time to the States has been
roughly computed as being somewhere between 7 days and
17 days — in good weather.

I have a sort of vague remembrance of the morning that our train finally came to a screeching halt in Glasgow, Scotland. I say vague remembrance because, after all, it was still an ungodly early hour — six o'clock I believe it was — and I was rather pre-occupied at the time with the task of rearranging my vertebrae into some semblance of their intended positions. Some high-ranking tech.-sgt. had already formed us into our travel groups when I came to comparative consciousness, and some officer was asking me if I had the travel orders and records for Group Ten. I mumbled I did and started digging. It being the duty of the man who was entrusted with the orders to call the roll of his group and form them in a column of twos, I was duly amazed to find that I not only had the orders, but that I was the only enlisted man in the group — a group which boasted a Lt. Colonel, three Captains, and 15 or 16 Lt.'s. Well, I called the roll and I must admit that watching those officers answer their name and fall in at my bidding was something I wouldn't want to forget if I could. Thus flushed with my success I took my place in the group — at the end of the line!

We were marched directly from the train station onto the ferry boat via a narrow gang-plank — at least that was the intention — I think most of us stumbled, staggered, and fell up that gang-plank. At the top of the gang-plank our high-ranking tech.-sgt. was engaged in some sort of important looking procedure — exactly what I wasn't aware of until I heard him say, "Heads up, Sergeant," and saw from under the brim of my steel helmet that he was holding out a ticket for me to take. So there I was, with an early morning outlook on life in general, on one arm a very heavy ominous-looking B-4 bag that looked like a pregnant booby trap due to explode any second, my mussette bag, rain coat, overcoat, and two army blankets on the other arm — all this topped off by the crowning glory of that oversized steel helmet that looks like something entirely different just upside down — which prevented me from seeing any higher than the end of my nose — and he says to me, "Heads up, Sergeant."!

Our first view of "Gourock" harbor was the kind even a sleep-walker would remember. The harbor was well filled with boats — I hear the Navy calls them "ships" — and our ferry boat, which I have since learned is called a "tender," seemed to be looking for the one that was the farthest out. All of the ships looked alike to me and when we finally pulled alongside of "our" ship I was unimpressed — still am for that matter! We entered the "Ile de France" through a sort of a door in the side of the ship and thus began my "life at sea." I took one last backward glance at the hills of Scotland before I entered the ship and that was the last land I was to see for quite some time.

To say that I am glad I didn't join the Navy would be just about the biggest hunk of understatement since Adam told Eve that he loved no other woman but her. However, being a sailor may have its compensations, though I'm sure I haven't unearthed them as yet. A description of this trip could very easily be called "Life in a London Subway," for that is the next worst form of habitation I can think of just off-hand. I used to think that those blitz refugees who slept in those three-high metal bunks along the side of the subway tunnels in London had reached a new low — what with trains rushing by within ten feet of them, people crowding, pushing and carrying on conversations, and all in complete disregard of those stoic sleepers. Now, however, I can see that in time you can tolerate practically anything.

Our quarters for this cruise are called compartments. It seems that a ship has several decks starting from A deck on top down to D deck and E deck on the bottom. We — the troops — are quartered on D and E decks. Our compartment consists of bunks — period! These bunks are in three-high tiers, 12 to a section, and a three-foot clearance between the sections. The bunk itself is a frugal looking thing made of pipe and a piece of rope-held canvas for a mattress. There are clothes, B-4 bags, and countless other items hanging from the ceiling, lying in the aisles, and just in the way — all of which reproduces a scene reminiscent of a fire sale in a pawn shop. The highlight of our hectic day is when the "Wheels" from A deck come down to inspect our fair abode with emphasis on cleanliness and neatness.

Narrow corridors that always have slanting floors, crowded washrooms where it seems the water always has just been shut off, deck scenes of railings decorated by the sight of rear-ends and elbows, some people sick and some wishing they were — just to break the monotony; Canadians, English, Americans; infantry, Navy, Merchant Marine, Air Force, Nurse Corps, Wacs, and some few civilians. This is the ever-present, never changing picture of this trip. If it weren't for the rumors the monotony would be worse than it is — unbearable!

The latest rumor which is fast gaining in impetus and popularity is that we will dock tomorrow morning in New York Harbor at pier 87. This is considered a good rumor mostly because tomorrow is Tuesday and docking tomorrow would mean that the trip only took a mere 7 days. I think it is a malicious exaggeration myself, but nonetheless it is a beautiful thought.

Of course, a rumor such as this always brings forth the best in the way of eloquence among the sages of our compartment. The washroom — by virtue of its lovely atmosphere I suppose — seems to be the place where they wax most eloquent, so every time I want to know the latest plans that are being made for the commodore I hold my nose and sally forth into the aforementioned rendezvous of the latrine-o-gram specialists.

This morning I made such a trek and while I tried manfully to wash the dirt from between my whiskers — both of them — I heard two guys giving the boys a pre-docking briefing. One guy said that as soon as he spotted the Statue of Liberty he was going to tell her "Put down that torch honey, I'm home now." The other guy came out with this one. "I heard," he said, "that we are all going to sit on our B-4 bags along Broadway and the civilians are going to parade for us." "Yeah," said the first one, "well, I heard that we are the first troops to dock in New York since the war ended and that they are going to have a big parade for us — boy, they'll treat us like Kings." Yes, I suppose it is true that wherever there is a soldier there is a rumor and wherever there is a rumor there is hope.

So here we are, doing the same things that our fathers were doing 27 years ago — probably on the same boat, too! Complaining and griping about everything, especially this boat, this ramshakle resurrection of Noah's Ark, this repulsive refugee from the ship-wrecker's union, this object of our insults and our wrath, but lest you take me wrong, let me say that we love this old boat — for you see, it's taking us home!

(Somewhere in the Atlantic, '45)

Wallace H. Phillips

Purple Heart Mission

by *Wallace H. Phillips*

Flight Engineer-Gunner, 568th Squadron

THE CQ plodded wearily down the row of Nissen huts at 1 o'clock on the morning of 22 April 1944. His job: to awaken the combat crews who were scheduled to fly the big B-17s from this East Anglia base in England. Their mission: to continue the effort to destroy Germany's ability to carry on the war. He opened the door of each hut and called out the name of the pilots who would fly today's mission.

Bang — the door of my quarters popped open — "Everly, Tuck, Nielson, Shaver, Parke" that was enough. Parke was my pilot — we were scheduled for a mission against some unknown enemy target today. The CQ continued,

275

"Breakfast at 2:30, briefing at 3:30," then departed, to continue down the line to rouse the other crews in the Squadron who would fly today.

I hadn't been asleep — it was too cold and I was too tense — it seemed so long since I had enjoyed a good rest. I thought of the trips to London which were a real Godsend to a weary GI — a good warm bath, a bottle of black market Scotch for $20.00, and a bed with a full sized mattress instead of these little three-piece biscuit mattresses which seemed to be stuffed with cold rocks. What I wouldn't give to be able to sleep now instead of going out where I might be shot. I thought, "I really should get up and get started but I can afford a couple of minutes more rest." My thoughts returned to London and the female companions who seemed to be able to relax me completely and take my mind off of the war. We would stroll down the blacked-out streets, pop into a restaurant for a meal, perhaps take in a show, then into a nice warm pub for a drink or two, and perhaps a dance; then home at last, either to her place or to my hotel. Fighting a war wasn't so bad after all, but there was a hell of a lot of work in between those trips to London.

"Well", I told myself, "I can't lay here and daydream any longer — I've got to get the rest of the crew up and get started — lets face it, in just a few hours we will be a nice fat target for the best flak gunners and some of the best fighter pilots in the ETO."

I dressed hurriedly, OD's pulled over the Long Johns I slept in, then the heavy, fleece lined leather jacket and pants. The other boys on the crew, Vince from San Francisco, Joe from Brooklyn, Johnny from South Carolina, Nick from Chicago, and Bill from West Virginia were grumbling as they dressed. "Oh, what I would give for two more hours sleep." "I got a notion to go on sick call and see if I can get some rest." "Damn this war, I didn't work this hard back in the coal mines."

We went out into the icy English weather and piled into the truck which would take us about a mile to the chow hall.

I hoped that a cup of coffee would perk me up. We were all wondering what kind of mission was scheduled — a D.P. (deep penetration) — or a milk run. Sometimes our buddies on the ground crew would give us a clue by telling how much fuel was loaded. A full load of fuel, including the Tokyo tanks, on the B-17 was 2,800 gallons and that meant a long haul, at least 10 hours. This meant less bomb load, but since we would be over enemy territory a long time, there was a much better chance that we would be shot down.

I walked in the door of the combat mess and got a pleasant surprise. That good looking Red Cross girl was serving the salty bacon and powdered eggs. "Even that sweet smile doesn't make this lousy chow tast any better," Vince growled. "Let's go ahead and eat and get to the briefing and see where we're headed," I threw in my two bits worth. We all drank some powdered coffee and tried to eat the eggs but it was too early in the morning for such a meal to stay in our queasy stomachs.

We sat in the briefing room, smoking and talking, all of us wondering whether this would be a real bad one or a milk run. My stomach tightened as I remembered our last mission — it was just a short one to one of the V-1 buzz bomb installations near La Glaciere, France. Lt. Mann, who opened his window and snapped a picture of our plane as we were lined up on the runway, flying on our wing tip got a direct hit in his bomb-bay during the bomb run. He was there one minute, about 40 feet away from us and then all we could see was a huge ball of fire — no parachutes came out of that mess. That was the first time in my life I had been completely scared — not frightened — plain scared, and I realized this was a serious business we were mixed up in — somebody could be killed mighty easy.

"Ten hut," the Operations Officer strode briskly down the aisle, followed closely by our Group Commander, Colonel Wittan.

"At ease gentlemen, our mission today is to ..." the screen covering the large map of Europe on the wall of the briefing

room was pulled back and a gasp came from the group —
the string marking our route led right into the heart of the
Ruhr, "Happy Valley" where the flak came up so heavy you
could almost walk on it. This was also near the Luftwaffe
fighter bases around Doomer Lake ". . . the rail marshalling
yard at Hamm, Germany. This is the greatest traffic center
in Western Germany, and if we do a good job today it will be
a big help in the effort to neutralize the German war
machine. The RAF bombed the area last night but results
were not very good. If you men are up to your usual
performance on today's mission we shouldn't have to go
back there for a long time."

The Colonel left and we were briefed by the Weather
Officer who predicted good visibility over the target and the
Intelligence Officer who gave us the latest on the number of
flak guns defending Hamm and the estimated number of
fighters that could harass us, and the Operations Officer
who gave the usual advice on good, tight formation flying
for effective bombing results and protection against
fighters, also the fighter escort scheduled for us.

We changed into our electrically heated flying suits, left
our personal belongings in lockers in the briefing area,
picked up our escape kits which held maps printed on nylon
handkerchiefs, money of the countries we would fly over,
malt tablets and benzedrine. We also checked the little kits
attached to our parachute harness which held a first aid kit,
including syrettes of morphine. Then we headed for the
hardstand where our B-17 was parked.

Our first job was to mount the 50 calibre guns and I had to
pre-flight the plane. The navigator, Lt. Durkee, and the
bombardier, Lt. Kilkelly came out next and mounted their
guns and started to prepare for the flight. "It looks like it
could be a rough one today, thats in real Injun Country,"
Kilkelly remarked. "Man, I sure hope our escort makes its
schedule. Its mighty rough having Spitfires escort us across
the Channel and then having ME-109s and FW-190s escort
us to the target and back," I grumbled. Our pilot, Lt. Bob

Parke, and Copilot, Lt. Bill Gower, drove up in a jeep and told us the schedule. "We start engines at 0350, taxi at 0400 and take off at 0415. We assemble over Felix Stowe and leave the English Coast at 0530. Keep a sharp look out for fighters all the way," Lt. Parke announced. We climbed aboard and waited for the flare that would signal the time to start engines. Finally it came, a long green streak across the night sky. I could hear the roar of the powerful engines before the light from the flare died away. The next flare, the signal to start taxiing, came and the long trip started when the pilot gunned the engines and we left the hardstand and headed for the end of the runway. My squadron was the second to take off so we had to be ready as soon as the first squadron departed. We watched the first squadron of those beautiful B-17s as they lumbered down the runway and, finally were airborne.

Our turn came at last and we lined up on the end of the runway, brakes set and engines at full power. The old bird quivered and shook and then, as the brakes were released, it shot forward, gathering speed as we went down the runway. From my position between the pilot and copilot I called off the airspeed to the pilot, "60, 65, 70, 75, 80, 85, 90, 95, 100, 105," and at about 110 miles per hour we broke loose from the ground. "Wheels up," the pilot called and already we were over Framlingham Castle. I looked down and, as always when we passed over the old castle, thought of King Arthur and King Richard, and other English heroes of the past who had lived and loved in a castle like this one.

We watched for flares from other aircraft and finally found our unit in the crowded sky. Lt. Parke slipped into formation as if he had been born to fly this big bird. We climbed and contacted the various checkpoints, and, at the exact time scheduled, in group formation, headed out over the channel. After we cleared all land areas and checked for ships below, the pilot told us to check our guns. All guns were firing OK and we settled down for the long haul to the target. The crew checked in, one at a time. "Oxygen OK, everything's fine."

Nick, the radio operator, was supposed to stay tuned in on the command channel but he had a habit of tuning in on AFN and then would tell us, over the interphone, to switch over and hear some good music. We were over the Continent now, flying straight into the rising sun. The farms below gave a checkerboard appearance to the ground — it had a homey look, the same as the farms in Oklahoma and Kansas looked from the air, and then, to top it all off, as I switched to AFN I heard "Oh, What A Beautiful Morning." It was hard to realize that we were over enemy territory and could be attacked at any time. I thought, "We mustn't relax for it would be real easy for enemy fighters to appear out of the sun and, for some unknown reason, we don't have our promised escort."

The navigator cut in on interphone, "The IP is only twenty minutes away. Two squadrons of FW-190s are reported near us."

"Keep a sharp lookout and be ready to shoot if they show up," from the pilot.

After what seemed an eternity we could see the huge black bursts of smoke ahead at our level. "Those flak gunners have our correct course and altitude and we've got to fly right through that mess," I said over the interphone. "We can do it, you just watch out for fighters," from Lt. Gower, the copilot. The pilots pulled in to an even tighter formation and the bomb-bay doors were opened. The bombardier watched for the first bomb to drop from the lead plane and released our bombs on time. "Bombs away," he shouted as the plane gave a slight lurch upward. "Bomb-bay all clear, close the doors," I told the pilot. The bomb doors closed and the pilot told the crew, "Let's go home — watch real close for fighters. What does the target look like, Johnny?" "I see a lot of smoke and it seems to be right in the middle of the target area," Johnny, the tail gunner, reported. We pulled out of the flak area — what a blessed relief to have only a few holes from those 88s — and then,

"Fighters at 9 o'clock low," from the left waist gunner. "Fighters at 12 o'clock high," from the copilot. "They're coming in, pick your targets and make your shots count," the copilot would direct the fire in addition to his other duties.

I felt real hot suddenly, didn't really need all the heavy clothing to keep warm, and, as I looked forward I saw about 40 FW 190s closing fast. Their wings appeared to be on fire as all of their guns were firing at our formation. The bursting 20mm shells looked like pretty little rosebuds in the air and I sure hoped none of them came too close to us.

I heard a terrific noise and felt a sharp pain in my back as I was knocked down. I saw my right boot already filling with blood and thought, "I've had it now, but at least I can catch up on some rest if I get back to England."

The crew checked in to the copilot and I found I was the only one hit. The oxygen system was knocked out so the emergency bottles were passed to the front for the pilot and copilot to use. Nick gave me a shot of morphine to dull the pain and pulled my pants off so the extreme cold would slow down the bleeding. I was beginning to relax when it seemed like a million guns went off at once and holes appeared in the side of the radio compartment where I was laying. There was a thud and it seemed that the plane stopped in mid-air, then we struggled on. A German fighter had rammed into our left wing tip — he went down but we kept going — headed for home.

"We are alone but I'm going to pull in below a formation ahead for protection in case the fighters come back," the pilot told us. "I know you need oxygen but we have none and I can't drop down lower for it would be too easy for fighters to pick us off if we are alone, so exert yourselves as little as possible."

I kept asking, "How far are we from the channel?" I got the same answer for hours, "Only about 10 minutes away," from the navigator. He told me later that, due to headwinds and one engine out, our ground speed was the slowest he had ever experienced.

Eventually, we did cross the channel and since we were shot up real bad and had wounded aboard, we fired flares as we approached the field to alert the fire fighters and medical personnel. We stopped as soon as possible and let the Flight Surgeon come aboard. He had a thermos jug of coffee and a bottle of Scotch. I took the Scotch — you can get coffee anytime but Uncle Sam doesn't pass out good whiskey except to his combat crews. I got a tetanus shot to go along with the Scotch and a blanket to wrap up in and was taken off the plane and put in an ambulance. At the base dispensary I was given a pajama top and some blankets before getting into an ambulance for the trip to the hospital. The Flight Surgeon stayed in the back of the ambulance with me and I found it necessary to have a swig of that good Scotch quite often. I kept feeling drowsy before we got to the hospital and my last thought before going to sleep was, "At last I'm going to get some rest."

Commanders and Histories

Headquarters complex of the 390th

Edgar M. Wittan

Edgar M. Wittan, 1910-1944

by Joseph A. Moller
Commander, 390th Bomb Group

No anthology of the 390th Bomb Group would be complete without acknowledging the debt the Group owes to the man who was its first commander — who activated it, trained it, took it overseas, commanded it during its first eight months of combat and who, until he was killed on 13 September 1944, maintained a strong and abiding interest in the Group's activities and its welfare.

A few days after Colonel Wittan was assigned to command the 13th Combat Wing, he sent for me. I had been flying with the 95th Bomb Group, first as a GI pilot with a pick-up crew, and later as an air leader. The mere fact that he just didn't have me assigned to the 13th Wing, which he could well have done, indicated his consideration for those under his command. When I reported to him I found he wanted to know how I would feel about becoming part of the 13th Wing staff and whether I thought I could become an enthusiastic member of his team.

The function of the 13th Wing, which consisted of the 95th, the 100th and 390th Groups, was not to deal with any administrative problems, but confined its work to all of those things affecting the combat operations of the three groups making up the 13th Wing. During our discussion it developed that all of the top personnel except Colonel Wittan were no longer combat operational having finished their combat tours. That meant that he was the only available combat leader in the 13th Wing and he welcomed another qualified air leader and wanted me to be, except on specific occasions, the 13th Wing Combat Air Leader.

I believe that in the first fifteen minutes of that interview, Ed Wittan and I had a meeting of the minds — though the meeting lasted for an hour or two. I welcomed the Wing assignment.

As he had dealt with me, so had he dealt with all those who came under his command. He was thoughtful, considerate and understanding. However, if the occasion demanded, he could be stern and could deal forthrightly with any situation which arose.

In the very few days he was there, Colonel Wittan had created a tightly knit group of some six officers together with the necessary airmen to feed, house and do necessary chores for the Wing War Room. The staff reflected the respect and admiration we all felt for the "boss." He knew his job and he helped us with ours. In addition, at least several times a week, Ed found time for quite lengthy sessions with me during which we would discuss every aspect of the air war as we were fighting it. I was privileged to have these opportunities to learn how his sharp mind worked. I dare say, he was also checking on me when he assigned me to take command of the 390th Group. Unlike my assignment to Wing from the 95th, he had my orders cut and given to me shortly after he left for an afternoon and evening of meetings at 3rd Division Headquarters. This gave me no opportunity to talk it over with him, and he knew I needed none.

Having set the groundwork, so to speak, as to why I feel particularly qualified to write about Ed Wittan as a man, as an airman and as a commander, I shall start with a few statistics.

Edgar M. Wittan was born on the 26 November 1910, the son of Mr. & Mrs. David Wittan, in Baltimore, Maryland. He graduated from Staunton Military Academy in 1928, and took his B.S. Degree at the University of Pittsburg. He was commissioned in the Air Corps Reserve 4 June 1932, and immediately entered flying training, completing primary and advanced at Kelly and Randolph Fields, Texas. He won his wings in early 1933.

After some five years in the Reserve, he returned to service as a Major 1 October 1938. He served with the Neutrality Patrol off the Florida coast. After Pearl Harbor he joined the first AAF tactical unit to set up operations in Newfoundland where he won his senior pilot's wings in 1942, and was promoted to Lieutenant Colonel.

In February, 1943, he was assigned to activate, command and train the 390th Bombardment Group (H) which he took overseas and into combat until 17 April 1944, when he was selected to command the 13th Bombardment Wing.

At times he would attend mission briefings for each group in the 13th Wing. On 12 September 1944, he came down to the 390th fairly early in the evening just as the orders for the mission on the next day began to come into the War Room. Ed and I talked in the War Room for some time and when time came for breakfast, we had breakfast together.

While sitting and listening to the briefing, I quietly asked him if he wanted to say a few words. Strangely, I thought, he declined, so when I spoke during my portion of the briefing,

I simply introduced him, which he graciously acknow-
ledged.

I had decided to monitor the mission during the assembly
over England and to coast-out so I had had a B-17 set up to
take off with the mission.

After briefing, he took me to the hardstand where my
airplane was. Again we talked until about time to start
engines, when he stepped to his car to drive, I thought, back
to Wing Headquarters.

Note that we had both been up all night, which was not
too unusual.

I took off with the mission and watched the boys getting
into Group formation which was being led by Lt. Col.
William (Bill) Jones. I followed the bomber stream to just
beyond the coast-out point.

Flying above, and somewhat to the east of the 390th as it
departed the south coast of England at Beachy Head, I saw a
P-47 somewhat above and to the west of the bomber stream.
The P-47 turned back about the shoreline of the channel. I
followed to about mid-channel and then returned to base.
After but a few minutes in my office, I went to my quarters
and slept until just before the mission returned. After de-
briefing, I received a call from Colonel Bill Veal (later Major
General) asking whether Colonel Wittan was still at the
390th. I told Bill that Ed had left when the mission took off,
but that I had seen a P-47 at coast-out and thought it was the
13th Wing P-47, a war-weary which was used for
monitoring formations since it had no fighter group markings. Bill got busy, found that Ed had taken off in the Wing
P-47 and had not returned. Bill and I talked several times.
We both hoped Ed had landed on some other base and
would check in before long.

I should judge it was about midnight when Bill again
called and told me there was a report that a P-47 had crashed
and the pilot was killed either in Wales, or near Wales. I
checked weather which had been deteriorating and found
that portion of England and Wales was zero zero.

Bill called a little later and said it was Ed's P-47 and that Ed had been killed. It was on 13th September 1944 that he died while flying and checking his three groups as they left England to attack their assigned target.

He was buried in Cambridge Cemetery — an American cemetery — on 15 September 1944, with Major General Earl Partridge (later General), the 13th Wing Staff and myself in attendance.

Those who served with Colonel Wittan will always remember him as an outstanding leader on the ground and in the air. His insistence on tight formation flying not only gave a closely knit bomb pattern on the target, but provided a maximum of fire power against enemy fighters.

No one will ever know how many lives and planes came home because of his wise and careful leadership. We were all better combat people for having served with him and under his command. He will always be remembered as a warm and understanding friend.

Control tower at Station 153 where Col. Wittan waited out so many missions.

Frederick W. Ott

Frederick W. Ott

by Robert W. Waltz
Group Operations Officer, 390th Bomb Group

IN mid May of 1944 the 390th Bomb Group was fortunate to fall under the Command of an individual who had already had an extensive and diversified military career. Col. Frederick W. Ott came to the organization with a background in both military and commercial aviation, schooling in communications and armament, and practical experience in administering military personnel.

Frederick Ott was born in Western Pennsylvania, raised in Cleveland, Ohio and attended the University of Michigan. He entered flying school at Brooks Field, Texas and graduated from Advanced Flying School, Kelly Field, Texas, in September, 1923. In early 1925 Fred went on the inactive roster and became a commercial pilot, but returned to active duty by August of 1927.

Prior to WWII Lt. Ott served with the 94th Pursuit Squadron and the 19th Bomb Group. He saw duty in San Diego, March Field, Chanute Field, Ft. Monmouth, France Field Canal Zone, and Randolph Field, Texas.

Colonel Ott came to the 390th Bomb Group, replacing Colonel Wittan, following a tour of duty as Air Inspector of the 8th Bomber Command. Having previously inspected the 390th, Col. Ott was well versed in the capabilities, past performances, and any shortcomings that we may have had prior to his assumption of Command. His outstanding abilities in the field of logistics were of great value during the period of the Russian shuttle missions. His planning and guidance were responsible for the manner in which the aircrews were accommodated and supported while operating away from the home station. He remained with the 390th until early September, 1944.

Colonel Ott's eventful military career continued following World War II, with a great deal of it being in the inspection functional area. His detailed understanding of logistics was employed again, by the Army Air Corps, during Operations Crossroad. He served as Chief of the Logistics Section for the first Atom Bomb Test.

Following a tour as Chief of the Air Mission in El Salvador Colonel Ott retired in 1958 and is currently a resident of Florida. Colonel Ott's background knowledge, his ability to properly employ that knowledge, and his understanding and consideration of his assigned personnel were most significant contributions to the 390th Bomb Group and to the successful Air Campaign over Europe.

Joseph A. Moller

By Example

by Robert W. Waltz
Group Operations Officer, 390th Bomb Group

THERE are many qualities and characteristics which a good combat leader must possess: A certain amount of raw guts, knowledge and understanding of mission objectives, display of confidence, professional ability, and an oral capability of communications. In addition to these, an outstanding combat leader must also possess commitment, appreciation and the respect of his men. He must disregard self-interest and well-being. He must have the ability to outperform his assigned personnel, and have the faculty of "hanging in there" when the pressure is really on. Joseph A. Moller is the one individual whom I have encountered in my sixty plus years, who has

Joe Moller at helm of racing yacht.

all of these distinguishing qualities — and all of them to an outstanding degree.

I think that those of us who came in contact with Colonel Moller the week in which he assumed Command of the 390th Bomb Group knew we were to have the great pleasure of serving with a truly great gentleman and an extremely able combat leader. Over the forty years which I have had the good fortune to remain in contact with Colonel Joe, my original beliefs and initial opinions of him have grown stronger on each encounter.

Perhaps his greatest attribute in getting us to work with him was his ability to make us realize that each of us was important to him as an individual — and that we were individuals he had chosen as personal friends.

Shortly after he came to the Group (I was the Group Operations Officer at the time and a Major), during a discussion in his office, he addressed me as "Sir". I was some years his junior and was startled by his use of the title. I made some rather bogy remark concerning his use of the term to a junior member of his staff. "Dutch," he said, "It didn't cost me one cent to say it, and perhaps it made you feel better and a little more at ease, didn't it?'' You bet it did. Within weeks of his arrival at the 390th, because of his friendly mannerisms and our great respect for him, we began to refer to him as "Uncle Joe." A name that we continue to use to this very day.

Joe was born, the second child of Vennette, who graduated from Wellesley College, and Carl N. Moller, an Episcopalian minister, in St. Louis, Mo. The family moved shortly thereafter to La Crosse, Wisconsin, where Joe and his older sister spent the next twelve years. Later the Mollers moved to New York City when his father was given a Church there.

As he grew up, he participated in the usual sports, worked a paper route earning enough money to buy a one way ticket to Montana, where he found work on a large cattle ranch, first as chore boy and later as a full ranch hand on a ranch near Hobson.

Joseph Moller started his illustrious aviation career early in life. He soloed in one hour and twenty minutes — and having flown with him many times, I'm sure he probably started instrument work in one hour and thirty minutes — a real professional pilot. One summer he barnstormed, receiving fifteen percent of each ten dollar ride fee with which he maintained himself and the plane. He pushed his luck a little, won eighteen hundred dollars in a crap game, gave up barnstorming and entered Sibley College of Engineering, Cornell University, where he worked his way through school, graduating as a Mechanical Engineer. During his last year in college, he became a building construction superintendent of one of the larger hotel buildings in New York City at that time.

Joe then moved into research and sales operations with the Pure Oil Company. Through his efforts, Pure was the first of the petroleum companies to have their own mechanical laboratory which, under his guidance, made several significant contributions, in conjunction with similar laboratories operated by the automotive companies, in the field of fuels and lubricants over some of which he acquired certain rights. There was no commercial one hundred octane gasoline. However, some was made in certain laboratories for research purposes. Wright Field technicians were experimenting with it at that time. Joe remembers tying down a drum of hundred octane gasoline behind his pilot's seat in his airplane and delivering it to the Wright Field boys on more than one occasion.

In addition to his research and development work, he found time in conjunction with a partner in each venture, to own an airplane and a sail-plane (soaring plane) and he also sailed and raced a series of fine sail yachts. He and his crew, placed or won some twenty-four of the last thirty races he entered.

Among the earlier aircraft that "Uncle Joe" owned or flew were: A JN-4, with both the OX-5 and the Hispano engines, the early four place Waco, the open cockpit two-place Waco (for acrobatics), the two-place, low-wing Ryan, the early and the later gull-wing Stinson, a Howard, a stagger-wing Beechcraft, a Cessna 165, and, of course, a two-place Schweitzer soaring plane.

As seemed to be usual with the earlier pilots, he had the customary problems with weather, engine failure and too small gas tanks. For example, he recalls one evening in the Spring of 1940, he was caught in a non-forecast freezing precipitation with all the commercial airports closed due to low ceilings in the Chicago-Ft. Wayne-South Bend area. Closed or not, he broke out of the low clouds headed for the runway, finalizing his approach and landing with nearly full throttle because of the ice load he was carrying. He ran out of fuel as he attempted to taxi.

Major Moller, a Reserve Officer, came on duty in early 1942. After his initial assignment as A-4 of the Troop Carrier Command under Colonel (later Major General) Fred Borum, he transferred to the Martin B-26 program at McDill Field under Brig. General (later Major General)

James E. Parker, with full intentions of flying the B-26 type aircraft in combat in the European theater. He earned his "Unlimited B-26 Pilot's certificate" in 1943.

However, there is a complete story (almost book length) as to how "Uncle Joe" managed a combat assignment with the 95th Bomb Group, where Lt. Col. Dave McKnight checked him out as a B-17 first pilot. Recently Dave McKnight told Ian Hawkins, one of our English friends, that Colonel Joe Moller was the best pilot he had ever checked out in a B-17.

One evening, after he had flown a practice formation mission, he remarked to Dave McKnight, who by then had become a good friend, that he was being told to fly almost too close to his element leader. He still remembers Dave's answer; "When you see the bandits coming in, you will fly in closer than you flew today." Somewhat later in combat, Joe said he found how right Dave was since "he was flying much closer and glad to be there."

Colonel Moller flew as a line-type pilot from his second mission through his thirteenth mission, flying nearly every position in the formation, which enabled him not only to learn the techniques of formation flying in various slots, but also to evaluate the role of formation leader as it affected the formation itself.

While still flying with the 95th, Joe flew in various leadership slots up to and including Group Leader, and even more importantly, as Wing Leader. In his next eighteen missions from Horeham, he led the 95th Group nine times, the 13th Wing six times, the Third Division twice, and the Eighth Air Force once.

As Commander of the 390th, "Uncle Joe" led our Group on three missions, the 13th Wing on six missions, the Third Division on six, and the Eighth Air Force on three missions. Of course, on all of these missions our Group was the Lead Group. In all, Col. Moller flew 49 missions (he flew others as a G.I. Pilot) and led more heavy bombers in combat than any other senior officer. On the occasion during which the

Chicagoan Leads 3,000 Plane Attack

LONDON, Nov. 16.—(AP)—More than 3,000 heavy bombers sparked a great new allied aerial offensive that opened today, with American and RAF planes hitting Germany's West Wall in close support of ground troops rolling into a big Winter campaign.

British Lancasters, 1,150 strong, attacked the heavily fortified towns of Duren, Julich and Heinsberg, flying in tight formations. About 250 Mustangs and Spitfires escorted the RAF bombers.

An armada of 1,200 Flying Fortresses and Lib-erators started a raging inferno 15 miles long be-tween Duren and Eschweiler, east and north of Aachen, pouring 36,000 fragmentation bombs into German positions in front of American armies hammering on the front door to Berlin. The bomb-ers were escorted by 450 Mustangs and Thunder-bolts.

Col. Joseph A. Moller, of 132 De Wint road, Winnetka, Ill., who led the show, said:

"It was the big parade five miles above Europe."

"As we made the horseshoe turn and started back we saw wing after wing of heavies coming as far as the eye could see."

Ninth Air Force medium bombers ripped into Siegfried Line installations along the western front, and RAF Typhoons raked roads and rail-way lines in Holland with cannon and machine-gun fire.

Railway yards at Munich were left battered and burning by 600 15th Air Force heavy bombers escorted from Italy by 300 fighters.

German air force pilots failed to come up and battle, even though the weather was suitable for dog-fighting. Flak, too, was described as meager by Eighth Air Force crews.

Fighters strafed enemy troops and ground in-stallations near Duren and Frankfort, but still the Nazi planes kept on the ground.

Nearly 3,000 tons of fragment bombs were laid across ammunition and gasoline supply dumps.

Continued on Page 7, Column 5.

IKE'S ALL OUT DRIVE
6 ARMIES ATTACK

Led Reich air blitz

Col. Joseph A. Moller, 132 De Wint rd., Winnetka, was leader of big parade of 1,000 heavy bombers over Germany's West Wall to speed up Allied aerial offensive lashing Reich's winter campaign on Western Front.

491,249
Daily Average Net
Paid Circulation in
OCTOBER

Herald CHICAGO American

**DIAMOND
EDITION**

THURSDAY—NOVEMBER 16—1944

The Chicago Herald-American heralds story of raid led by Col. Moller on front page.

bombers of the 8th Air Force, the 9th Air Force and the RAF were combined into one gigantic task force, Colonel Moller was the combat leader for this entire task force.

In addition to his quality performance as combat leader, Colonel Moller applied lessons learned and observed. For instance, by analysis, he noted that crews with less than seven or eight missions suffered the greatest loss ratios during the deeper penetrations. Thus he had us schedule those crews for more shallow efforts until their experience factor was increased. Not only did this operational directive improve our bombing accuracy (best in the 8th) but resulted in the 390th having the lowest losses per mission flown/ bombs dropped.

At one time I asked "Uncle Joe" what effect the recogni-tion of our great respect for him had upon him as an indivi-dual. His response was, "It made me mighty humble, perhaps generating greater caution on my part."

It has been my very great fortune to have known "Uncle Joe," to have served under him and to have worked with him, and now to share the memories of the men and the activities of the 390th, the 13th Wing, the 3rd Division, and the 8th Air Force during those memorable days.

His love of the 390th people was very pronounced to me during the war when I overheard a telephone conversation between Colonel Moller and the Commanding Officer of the Third Air Division. It was evident that the General had just informed Joe that he intended to move Joe up as the 13th Combat Wing Commander. Joe said, "I want to stay here and fight with the men of this outfit (the 390th)." In my opinion "Uncle Joe's" determination to remain with his men probably cost him his star.

His magnificent contributions made deep and lasting impressions on all of his assigned personnel. His willingness, his professional abilities, and his dedication demonstrated his outstanding leadership. Throughout his life he has given freely of his time, energy and talents to the Country he loves so dearly. He has done it quietly, but effectively — By Example.

George Von Arb

All The Way With George

by Robert Waltz
Operations Officer, 390th Bomb Group

GEORGE Von Arb took the 571st Bomb Squadron to England, as Commander, and brought the 390th Bomb Group home, as Commander. An outstanding leader, an understanding commander, and a fine, polished individual. George was with the 390th when it was first activated, in February, 1943. He was immediately selected as the Commander of the 571st. The brilliant history and heritage of the Squadron is traceable, to a large degree, to the care, training and guidance that George Von Arb provided in the early days of the organization.

Colonel Von Arb's military career dates back to the days that preceded the War Years. By the time he was assigned to the 34th Bomb Group, at Geiger Field, in Oct., 1942, he had

298

acquired 1794 flying hours in B-18s, B24s and B-17s. His excellent training, experience, accumulated flying hours and outstanding professional abilities served the United States Air Force well for many years — until his retirement in 1965. Even after that George continued to provide his talents towards the security of the United States; he worked with the Goddard Space Flight Test Center (NASA) in Greenbelt, Maryland until 1980. Forty years of unselfish service to the people of this great country!

As the Commander of 571st Bomb Squadron and as the Air Executive (Deputy Commander) of the 390th Bombardment Group Colonel Von Arb lead the Squadron, the Group, or the 13th Combat Wing on 38 missions. Some of these lead missions were to Regensburg, Stuttgart, Bremen, Paris, Berlin, Romania, and Munich. While none of the combat missions, in the 390th, were a "piece of cake", it is evident that George was never hesitant to take the deeper penetrations.

As an insight into Colonel Von Arb's tremendous span of technical and professional abilities, during his military assignments: (1) he interrogated Japanese prisoners of war, collecting special items of information; (2) he supervised the maintenance, and tender loving care, of war time fly-away kits in support of Strategic Air Command deployed strategic bombers; (3) he was commander of one of the larger SAC bases; (4) he activated, trained and commanded a Titan II missile wing, and (5) in 1960 he graduated, with distinction from the Joint Chiefs of Staff Industrial College of the Armed Forces.

Testimony of Colonel Von Arb's dedication, commitment and valor is the fact that he was eligible to rotate to the United States, and receive an excellent assignment, months before he returned the 390th to Souix Falls, South Dakota. He elected to remain with the organization and personnel with whom he had commenced his combat tour. He was there from the first to the last combat mission. All The Way With George!

The History of the 390th

by John Quinn

THE roots of the 390th go back to the 40th Bomb Group in Puerto Rico and Guatemala and the 6th Bomb Group in Panama before World War II. At that time these Bomb Groups were engaged in training of combat crews while flying B-18s and B-18As.

In January of 1942 the B-18s were phased out with the receipt of B-17Es. Six planes from Ecuador and six from Guatemala were dispatched daily on parallel tracks to the Galapagos Islands to protect the Panama Canal. Crews flew 200 hours per month and accumulated a total of 1,500 to 2,000 hours of flying time as well as being cross-trained in all phases of a strategic bombing mission.

In October of 1942 at Geiger Field, Spokane, Washington the 34th Bomb Group became the parent group of the 390th. Personnel from the 40th, the 6th, and other organizations formed the cadre force of the 391st Bomb Squadron. Weather conditions prevented the achievement of minimal training requirements. Therefore, operations were moved to Ephrata, Washington on 25 November 1942. However, similar conditions were encountered there and on 8 December 1942 the Squadron was moved to Blythe, California.

On the morning of 16 February 1943 at one end of the Group Headquarters building the teletype began its clacking sound. When it stopped the Communications Clerk tore the message off, glanced at it, walked down the corridor, knocked on a door, entered and handed the message to the Commander of the 34th Bomb Group, Lt. Col. Irvine "Bo" Rendle. As the Colonel read the message a slow smile broke across his face. The message was from Headquarters 2nd air Force; Subject: Organization of Bombardment for March 1943. It was a directive to activate the 390th Bomb Group (Heavy).

Tom Jeffrey, the Commander of the 391st Bomb Squadron of the 34th Bomb Group, remembers that day when Col. Rendle came to his office and said, "Jeff, I have secret information that no one knows about. The next Bomb Group that we turn out from here is going to be called the 390th and I'm going to be the C.O. I wonder if you would consider going along as Deputy Group Commander?"

Tom remembers saying, "Man that's great!"

Then Col. Rendle said, "Since we will be going together, would you put together the best Squadron that you can?" Tom was sure that "Bo" went to the other Squadrons and said the same thing.

Joe Gimmell recalls the day that "Bo" Rendle called Bob Good, George Von Arb, Larry Gilbert and himself into his office and asked if all four of them would accept assignments as Squadron Commanders. Without hesitation they all accepted. The new assignments enabled them to select the finest personnel from each Squadron to form the cadre.

Joe also remembers that, "A short time later Col. Rendle summoned us to his office and informed us that he would not be going with us, since he was being reassigned as the Commander of a B-24 Group." Col. Ed Wittan was designated as the Commander of the 390th Bomb Group. "Col. Rendle then asked us if we would consider going with him to his new B-24 Command. After careful consideration Bob Good, George Von Arb and myself decided to stay with the 390th. Larry Gilbert elected to go with 'Bo'. Upon his arrival Col Wittan selected Bob Tuttle to replace Gilbert."

On 23 February 1943 Special Order Number 54 (HQ) AAB Blythe, California arrived transferring Major Thomas S. Jeffrey, Jr., Deputy Group C.O., 40 officers and 83 enlisted men of the 34th Bomb Group (H) to the 390th BG (H), Geiger Field, Spokane, Washington with temporary duty orders for the School of Applied Tactics, Orlando, Florida.

After thirty days of special training at Orlando, the cadre arrived at Geiger Field where other crews and ground people were assembled. After about a month of training as a Group, the cadre was deployed in Squadrons (568, 569, 570, and 571) to Great Falls, Glasgow, Cutbank and Lewistown, Montana for additional training.

By 29 June of 1943, the Group had grown to a complement of 375 officers and enlisted men. On that date, the Group was ordered to proceed to Grenier Field, Manchester, New Hampshire for training exercises (Special Order 180). On 9 July the Group was directed to Presque Isle, Maine subsequent to movement overseas. Upon arriving on the other side of the Atlantic most crews were processed at either Stone or Valley, Wales, enroute to Station 153, Framlingham, England. The Air Echelon arrived at Framlingham on 17 July 1943. The Ground Echelon arrived on the 28th.

The 390th flew its first mission on 12 August 1943. Col.

Frederick W. Ott succeeded Col. Wittan as Commander on 15 May 1944 and remained in that post until 6 September 1944 when he was succeeded by Col. Joseph A. Moller. Col. Moller commanded the Group through its last and 301st mission to Oranienburg, Germany on 20 April 1945 and continued in command until 21 May 1945. At that time Lt. Col. George Von Arb assumed command and subsequently returned the Group to Sioux Falls, South Dakota. The Air Echelon arrived in the Continental United States on 4 July 1945 and the Ground Echelon arrived on the 11th of August. The 390th Bomb Group was inactivated on 28 August 1945.

The 390th received the Presidential Unit Citation for the Schweinfurt mission on 14 October 1943. The Group also shared in the Presidential Unit Citation awarded to the 3rd Bomb Division for the part it played in the mission to Regensburg on 17 August 1943. In addition, the Group established a record for enemy aircraft destroyed by any one Group on any one mission by destroying sixty-two at Munster on 10 October 1943. On this same mission the crew of *Cabin In The Sky*, a 571st Squadron aircraft, shot down eleven enemy aircraft. In total, the 390th destroyed 377 enemy aircraft and recorded fifty-seven probables and seventy-seven damaged. And, they were never turned back by the enemy.

John Clark, George Von Arb, and Irv Lifson

390th Bomb Group Heritage

by John J. Clark

Squadron Navigator, 571st Squadron

FIRST of all I would like to set the scene... It starts in the desert in a swinging little town called Blythe, California — two stores, a gas station, a post office — you were through the town going 20 mph in three seconds — nothing but sand, cactus and wind for as far as one could see. For excitement you chased the tumble-weed — whoopee! This is where the 34th Bomb Group was stationed and where the 390th was born.

To start with I guess I must say that fate, whatever that is, must play an important part in our lives as I think the 34th Bomb Group, which was originally an observation group, had the greatest bunch of men in it that I have ever known and it carried right through to the 390th. There was not a lot of men but each was a pro. Everyone just seemed to fit together and worked like a well oiled machine. I think that the opposite also happens — all the screwups land together. This was not the case in the 390th.

Getting back to the wind and sand at Blythe, I would like to relate a story about Louis (Lucky) Dolan, our Squadron Operations Officer. Dolan and I were room-mates. Being the lower rank, it was my job to keep our room in the barracks neat and orderly. Lucky would drive me crazy saying I was a lousy housekeeper. No matter how hard I tried, the damn sand would blow through the smallest cracks and in the morning there would be little piles of sand all over the place that had drifted in during the night. One night after "Lucky" was asleep, I filled his G.I. shoes with sand. You should have seen the look on his face when he tried to put on his shoes the next morning. It was something I'll never forget. But he really never forgot about this incident also. Every once in awhile when we were in England, he would call me "Sandy Sam the Cleaning Man".

Another story that comes to mind — it was again in Blythe — it involved Col. Wittan, the C.O., Col. Jeffrey, our Deputy C.O., and myself. We were standing on the edge of the runway by the Squadron Area when the newly formed group was coming back from a practice bombing and gunnery mission in formation. Col. Wittan turned to Jeff and remarked about the formation — Jeff looked at Col. Wittan and said, "Colonel, that's not a formation, that's a casual gathering." Wittan turned to Jeff, grunted and walked away. That grunt made the original 390th fly the best formation in the E.T.O.

A personal note — Colonel Wittan was the only man I ever knew that could chew your a-- out without saying a word. He gave you a look that was unforgetable when he was dissatisfied.

Another story that I remember occurred again at Blythe. We had a gunnery range near by that had targets on the ground for the gunners to practice on. One afternoon a cow wandered onto the range while gunnery practice was in full swing. A half hour later the cow walked off the range unharmed. We could never figure if we had the best or worst gunners in the Air Corps. But as it turned out we had the best. Somewhere in California is an old, old cow to prove it.

I always thought the Air Corps was very smart putting an air base at Blythe. After a short stay there you were ready for anything — even combat. George Von Arb, the newly designated 571st Bomb Squadron Commander, said to me one day in February 1943, "Johnny, are you ready to go to combat?" I replied, "George, let's get out of here." That's how I became the original 571st Squadron Navigator.

The closeness of other Square J members is heart warming.